MIDWESTERN
GOTHIC
SUMMER 2014
ISSUE 14

Midwestern Gothic Issue 14 (Summer 2014)

To learn more about us and our mission, or for more information on our submissions policy, please visit our website or email us at MWGothic@gmail.com.

Subscriptions: 1 year (4 issues) - $40 (print) / $10 (digital)

www.midwestgothic.com

ISSN: 2159-8827
ISBN: 978-1500233198
Cover photo copyright © Tara Reeves

MIDWESTERN GOTHIC

FICTION EDITORS
Jeff Pfaller
Robert James Russell

POETRY EDITOR
Christina Olson

COPY EDITORS
J. Joseph Kane
C.J. Opperthauser
Andrea Uptmor

INTERNS
Lauren Crawford
Jon Michael Darga
Cammie Finch
Kelly Nhan
Katie Marenghi

COVER IMAGE
Tara Reeves

BOOK DESIGN
Jeff Pfaller

CONTENTS

THE DAY OF NEW THINGS
JESSIE ANN FOLEY

The summer her father was sentenced to 150 years in federal prison, Sandy Boy-chuck got a job prepping cold salads at Europa Deli. Her co-workers were the two sisters of the owner; middle-aged matrons with lumpy bodies and tired, brittle hair who clucked at her when she didn't wipe down the cutting board properly and otherwise ignored her. She had to hide her long ponytail under a hair net and stuff sausage into casings with a big metal machine, and if she tried to sneak a look at her cell phone while the matrons' backs were turned, her fingers smeared the screen with a patina of grease that made her face break out whenever she had to make a phone call.

"This has to be the world's worst summer job," Kenzie remarked one after-noon when she stopped by the deli to visit Sandy on the way home from her camp-counseling gig. "Not only can you not work on your tan, it *smells* in here." She looked up at the fat brown links of sausage coiled from the ceiling and wrinkled her little nose.

"Don't forget," Sandy said, lowering her voice and channeling her finest East-ern European accent, which she'd been honing all summer, "no mobile phones when I'm on zee clock!"

"Ugh," Kenzie said, squatting down to get a better look at the trays of salads and meats behind the counter. "Hey, at least you won't be tempted to get fat on any of the disgusting food here. What *is* that? Blood?"

"It's borscht. Beet soup."

"*Sick.*"

Kenzie held out her phone and took a picture of the tub of borscht. Sandy had tasted it earlier that morning, and liked it, but she certainly wasn't going to admit that now. Seeing it through Kenzie's eyes, it *did* look like blood, and it bobbed with bald-peeled vegetables like dead white fingers. Later, when she was sitting in an overturned box in the alley, eating a ham sandwich on her lunch break, Sandy would see Kenzie's picture on her Instagram feed with the caption:

Beet soup/murder scene at Europa Deli #worstjobever

Kenzie could be harsh, but given the way the summer was going, she was exactly the kind of friend Sandy needed. From Kenzie's perspective, there was nothing in life so awful that it couldn't be cured by an EDM show, some illicit substances, and the hot moving tongue of a new boy. Like Ava Gardner or Mia Farrow or John Travolta before her, Kenzie was one of those people whose personality and physical appearance was a perfect reflection of the times in which she lived. Her Lebanese mother and her Cuban father had pooled their genetics to create a beauty of dark, cervine grace: the future face of an Apple ad. And perhaps it was partially because she was so beautiful that Kenzie was totally lacking in nostalgia. People, ideas, clothes, art, music, love: according to Kenzie, all of it was up for transformation, none of it lasted, all of it was replaceable. Even her own name— "Kenzie"—was a pop trend; in ten years it would be ridiculous, and she would be embarrassed to write it on job applications. But that was ten years from now, and ten years was longer than it had ever been.

"I'm getting bored with your depression," Kenzie declared now, putting her hands on the counter and strumming the glass with her two-toned nails. "I know you've been through a lot lately. *However*, that does not give you the right to spend all summer feeling sorry for yourself." Her eyes moved past Sandy, to the back room, where the two matrons were leaning over mounds of floured dough in their dusty aprons, their foreheads creased, their kneading arms hairy and power-ful. "Jesus Christ, what *year* is it in here?"

"I'm not depressed," Sandy said.

"Of course you are," Kenzie said. "But luckily for you, I have the cure."

She reached into the back pocket of her denim shorts and slapped two tickets on the counter.

"DizzyVision. They're these new DJs, from Brazil or something."

Sandy pulled off her hairnet and examined the tickets.

"I know it's not the white dad music that you normally listen to," Kenzie con-tinued, "but if you don't come for the music, come for the boys. Come for the tequila that I plan on stealing from my parents' basement. Just *come*, okay?"

"*Okay*," Sandy sighed. She forced a smile. "Hey—do you think Darry will be there?"

Kenzie leaned over and banged her head theatrically on the glass counter. The two matrons looked up from their kneading.

"You're hopeless. Be ready by seven."

*   *   *

When Sandy's shift ended, she went home, put on her bikini, dragged her lounge chair across the pool deck and positioned it in the path of the late afternoon sun. Lifting up her sunglasses, she examined a white arm. Maybe Kenzie was confusing actual depression with just *looking* depressed. It was already August, and Sandy was still as pale as a Goth. Last summer, when her dad was still a good man and Darry still loved her, Sandy had a beautiful golden tan, acquired on the days she spent babysitting the neighbor kids at the beach. Well, those days of part-time work for five bucks an hour weren't going to cut it anymore. She couldn't help it that she had to pay her own cell phone bill now, plus pitch in for groceries and gas and, for the last two months, the electric bill. She flipped on her stomach and began scrolling through her various social media accounts and hoping, while knowing it was hopeless, to be fed some digital scrap of Darry's life.

Darry had been raised Buddhist, or Transcendentalist, or, as Sandy's dad had put it, in the Church of Our Lady of Liberal Mumbo-Jumbo. His family didn't give gifts at Christmas or on birthdays, and they had a compost heap in their backyard. They even had a chicken coop out by their alley, and in the warmer months they sold the eggs at the Logan Square farmer's market. Darry's parents didn't allow him to have any social media presence: he didn't even own a cell phone. So when he had stopped talking to Sandy at the end of last summer, his absence from her life was immediate and total. She had never experienced anything like it: it almost felt like he had died, and she'd mourned him as intensely as if he had.

"Hey, Sandy Girl." Sandy looked up from her phone. Her mother, dressed in an old tank top and pleated khaki shorts, stepped onto the deck and slid the glass door behind her. She was holding a Solo cup, and from the smell of it, it contained a beverage strong enough to remove nail polish. "Mind if I join you?"

Sandy patted the empty chaise lounge to her left.

"Be my guest."

Sandy's mom scooted the chair to the edge of the deck and stuck her feet into the water.

"How are we, kiddo?" This had become her mother's question of the summer. Maybe she thought that using the first person plural made the question less annoying or intrusive, or maybe it was her way of reminding Sandy that they were in this together. *You* lost a father, *I* lost a husband, and now we are broke and humiliated. How are we doing with all that, kiddo?

"Look what I found when I was cleaning the bathroom today." Her mom reached into the pocket of her khaki shorts and pulled out a golf tee. She held it in the sun between her thumb and middle finger. "I guess he won't be leaving these lying around anymore."

"Guess not."

Her mother took the tee and tossed it into the pool with a soft splash.

"Why'd you do that, Ma? It's gonna get stuck in the filter now."

Her mother shrugged and leaned back in her chair. She took a sip of her paint-thinner cosmopolitan.

"Who cares? It's all going to be repo'd anyway."

In Lisa Boychuck's mind, the sentencing of her husband had dismantled several generations of their family's American Dream; in the space of a year, the Boychuck family had been cast off the middle-class mountain—their boat slip in Belmont Harbor, their three-bedroom colonial with its above-ground pool and cedar deck and real bamboo tiki bar—and now they were thrown back into the penurious state of their Serbian ancestors, those sad Stockyard denizens who signed predatory leases and lived in apartments with worm-infested carpets and communal bathrooms.

In Chicago, the name Boychuck was the new Capone, the new Dillinger, but without the cache: Sandy's father did not have the softening distance of history to romanticize him. In a city of warring baseball teams, machine politics, and systemic segregation, hating Sergeant Stephen Boychuck was the one thing that everyone could agree on. The poor hated him because his Shakespearean-scale corruption had put guns on their streets that killed their children, and because he embodied their long-held belief that the police were simply another kind of street gang, but with legal weapons and shorter haircuts. The yuppies hated him because he was the exact kind of burly white meathead from which they tried to distance themselves. And his fellow cops hated him most of all, because he'd sold the names and addresses of his fellow tac officers to his gang member friends and used the profits to buy a speed boat, a boat he had christened the S.S. Sandy Girl, a boat in which Sandy had caught her first walleye up in Door County the summer she turned twelve. Maybe it was because the city was so full of hatred for her father that there was none left for Sandy, who had sat in that courtroom and heard him found guilty of charge after charge—racketeering, drug conspiracy, forgery, battery, bribery, attempted murder—and still loved him in her uncomplicated way.

*   *   *

On the Addison bus, Kenzie dug into her purse and produced a large Gatorade bottle filled with a murky green substance.

"Whoa," Sandy said, sniffing the concoction. "Who made this for you—my mom?"

"Shut up and drink—I am hereby banning you from making any references to your crumbling family for the rest of tonight. We're having *fun*." She reached out and brushed back a curl from Sandy's forehead. "Besides, your hair looks amazing. What'd you do to it?"

"Spray-gelled and air-dried," Sandy said shaking her long mane, finally free of its hair net, so that it soughed around her bare shoulders. "Just like you told me."

"Gorgeous," Kenzie said. "You're finally learning to work your curls. And look at those *legs* of yours. I mean, they're disgustingly white, but with thighs like those, you almost don't even *need* a tan."

Outside the Metro, they were barely past the police horses—Sandy hiding behind her sunglasses and hoping that none of the officers would recognize her—when Kenzie stopped short.

"Oh my God," she said, grabbing Sandy by the arm. "That's *Michael*."

"Which one is he again?"

"That's the guy who started following me on Twitter after he met me at that party at the forest preserve for Sami's birthday," she said. "And he's been, like, professing his love for me to everybody at Payton ever since."

Michael was standing in line, smoking a cigarette and laughing loudly with a few of his friends. He was just the kind of obnoxious boy-toy sort Kenzie went for: he had a baby face partially obscured by a flat-brimmed hat, fake diamond earrings in both ears, and wrists weighted down with neon bracelets. His flip-flops were plastered with a Ralph Lauren logo, the kind of shoes you buy at Marshall's when you don't have a ton of money but you want people to think you do.

"If he's so madly in love with you," Sandy said, shading her eyes and looking down the block to where the line ended, "why don't you see if he'll let us cut the line?"

"I was *just* thinking that." Kenzie pulled down her tank top to expose the rim of her paisley-patterned bra and flounced in the boys' direction, leading with her breasts, which were as round and pink as the Krakus hams on display in the window of Europa Deli.

"Hey, Twitter Stalker," she said, brushing her hand against his bare arm. "Trade you some tequila for a cig?"

Kenzie was such a child of the digital age that even her spoken words were like text messages: the tone was impossible to interpret. Michael didn't seem to even notice that she'd just insulted him. The two girls shuffled into the line behind him and his two friends.

"These are my buddies, Jordan and Aidan," Michael said, handing Kenzie a cigarette and trying with all his might not to stare at her impressively cleaved chest. "This is Kenzie Hernandez and—uh—sorry, what's your name?" He looked at Sandy.

"This is Sandy Boychuck," Kenzie said, before Sandy could warn her not to reveal her last name. Jordan and Aidan, who wore flat-brimmed hats just like Michael's, looked up from their phones. One of them, with reddish hair that was almost iridescent in the setting sun, squinted at her.

"Wait, Boychuck like the cop guy?"

Sandy said nothing, but straightened up her shoulders and stared at the boy evenly. It was the hard-assed look of a cop's daughter, daring him to continue his line of questioning. He didn't, but his finger trembled over his phone screen. She could see that he was just waiting for her to walk away so that he could tweet it out into the all-seeing world:

Holy shit hanging out with Boychuck's daughter yes
THAT Boychuck #150years

Inside the DizzyVision show was like being at a high school dance, except with better music and more drugs. No one there was old enough to buy a beer in the bar area, but everyone had arrived either already drunk or rolling. A relentless light and fog show intensified the effect of the tequila-Gatorade mixture, and Sandy caught the white of Kenzie's eye, the flash of Michael's fake diamond earring, before losing them to the anonymous thumping crowd. The two Brazilian

DJs stood in the middle of the stage, crouched over their turntables like monks huddled in prayer. The beats they produced were so deafening that it was hard for Sandy to think or breathe or move. She hadn't eaten anything since the ham sandwich on her lunch break, and the tequila sloshed in her empty stomach. She stumbled up the stairs, chased by the *whoomp* of the music and the jagged motion of the lights, and found the women's bathroom just in time to spray a toilet seat and part of the toilet paper holder with a green jet of puke. Her body purged of the spiked Gatorade, Sandy felt better immediately. She wiped her mouth at the mirror, feigning innocence when a girl in a turquoise wig walked into the bathroom and proclaimed, "Um, someone just effing *vommed* in here." Sandy fluffed her hair, folded a stick of gum into her mouth, and walked out of the bathroom and straight into Darry's chest.

He wore the same pair of shorts he'd worn all last summer and a plain white t-shirt delicately sweat-stained around the armpits. Sunglasses were perched at the peak of his perfect, smooth forehead.

"Sandy. Hey."

"Hi, Darry." She began tossing her hair and chomping on her gum as if possessed by a tic. Her palms felt cold and sweaty.

"I didn't think you were into this kind of music."

"I'm not," she said quickly. "I'm here with Kenzie."

"Oh." He looked disappointed. "I thought maybe you were having another Day of New Things."

She guffawed, an ungracious, tough-sounding laugh that she immediately regretted.

"What, you don't remember our Day of New Things?" He smiled at her, his eyes golden and Sphinx-like.

"Of course I do." Sandy crossed her arms tightly. She could feel her bra strap slipping down her shoulder.

Last summer, on the Day of New Things, she and Darry had spent the day riding around the city on their bikes in search of totally new experiences. First, they went to the Museum of Contemporary Art and walked through an exhibit room full of stuffed animals laid out on embalming tables. Then, they rented surfboards and tried, unsuccessfully, to catch a wave at Ohio Street Beach. After that, they tried *canh chua* at a Vietnamese restaurant in Uptown. When a fish head bobbed to the surface of the broth, Sandy had stifled a scream, while Darry, in the spirit of the day, had deftly plucked out the eyeball with his chopsticks and eaten it. They played bags with a pair of old men in the alley behind D'Amato's Bakery, bought star fruit from a little Ecuadorian grocer in Albany Park, and ate it with sticky fingers on the swings of a children's playground. Later, when the moon came out, they rode back up to the far northwest side, abandoned their bikes at the entrance of the forest preserve, and together, in the soft grass cooled by the shade of the trees, Darry had gently peeled off Sandy's sweaty shorts and unrolled the condom and they'd engaged in the final New Thing of that day, a thing that felt as odd and sweet as the juicy yellow flesh of the star fruit.

The next day, her father was arrested. Soon afterward, Darry vanished from Sandy's life. It made sense, of course: a guy whose parents sold organic eggs at the Logan Square farmer's market was not going to fall in love with the daughter of the most corrupt cop in Chicago history. But still, it would've been nice to have a boyfriend around to be there for her during the trial, which lasted for the entirety of Sandy's junior year. When her dad was finally found guilty, reporters had actually camped out on their front lawn, like in a movie, and Sandy's uncle Jimbo had tried to run them over with his riding mower. This made things even worse, because someone recorded the incident and posted it on YouTube, where it racked up 200,000 hits in one weekend. Sandy had punished herself, compulsively, bleakly, by reading all the user comments.

*   *   *

As she and Darry stood there contemplating each other in the corridor outside the bathroom, a pretty Puerto Rican girl in a yellow romper and gold hoop earring came up the stairs.

"There you are!" She slunk under Darry's arm, rubbing her lip-gloss into place.

"Sandy," Darry said, still smiling in that dreamy way that had pulled her in last summer and was now pulling her in again, "this is my girlfriend, Maritza."

*   *   *

Back inside the concert, Sandy didn't even attempt to locate Kenzie in the sea of dancing, tripping teenagers. She slumped against the back wall, taking solace in her phone. She opened Twitter and searched #DizzyVision. The first thing that came up on her feed was the blurry picture of a curly-haired girl in a pink neon bra and white tank top and it was only when she read the tweet that she realized who it was:

> #boychuk daughter at #dizzyvision show, kinda hot
> but did she buy her ticket with daddys drug money?

She put her phone in the back pocket of her shorts and slipped out the heavy front doors and into the gauntlet of cigarette smokers who were convened outside the Metro's entrance. A block away, a night game was on at Wrigley Field, and the collective roar and sigh of the crowd sounded almost like the tide of an ocean. As Sandy walked toward the bus stop she began to imagine she was in Klamath, California, where her family had vacationed last summer, shortly before her father's arrest. One morning, she and her dad had gone whale watching along the promenade behind their hotel. Together they had leaned over the fence at the top of the cliff, and suddenly her dad cried out, pointing to a black speck out on the water,

"I see one! I see one!" As Sandy craned her neck to look, a Yurok Indian who was fishing with his kid nearby laughed.

"That's just a big ol' rock!" he said, and handed them his binoculars.

"I could've *sworn* that was a whale!" Her father squinted through the binoculars at the waves that crashed against a black boulder. "Hey—is there any other wildlife we might see around here?"

The man said that if they heard dogs howling at night it was probably because a cougar or a bear was lurking around, and Sandy's dad told him about the time when a cougar—"a fucking *mountain lion*—thing weighed almost 200 pounds!"—wandered down from the Dakotas and ended up strolling down the middle of Hoyne Avenue in the 19th district "like it owned the place", and how the cops hadn't known what to do with it, "so we just shot the fuckin' thing. Gangbangers, we can handle. Drug dealers, child molesters, murderers—no problem. But a cougar?" he had laughed. "We shot first and asked questions later."

The Yurok had shaken his head.

"No wonder you can't tell the difference between a whale and a rock," he'd said, and turned back to the water.

*   *   *

On the last day of their trip, they spent the afternoon sightseeing down the 101 from Klamath to Fortuna, stopping for dinner at a microbrewery in McKinleyville. On the drive back to the hotel, as her dad sang along to the Tom Petty song on the radio and her mom fiddled with the GPS, Sandy sat in the back seat looking out the window at the gray Pacific. Her phone was in her lap, but only out of habit: she hadn't had reception in days, which wasn't as annoying as she thought it would be. The sky was spreading in gradations of twilight and the ocean was calm and shimmering when Sandy saw the puff of vapor about a half mile out from shore. Then, a spinning dark shape rose from the water, turning like a screw, and the gray whale breached into the purpling sky. By the time Sandy had fumbled for her phone to take its picture, the whale was gone, leaving no proof of itself but the rocking waves. She opened her mouth to tell her parents what she had just seen, but then her mom started talking about how fresh the avocado in her Cobb salad was and her dad said the waitress kind of reminded him of that actress with all the DUIs, and by the time Sandy had a chance to say something, she had convinced herself that maybe all she'd seen was just another boulder.

*   *   *

Now, the morning after the DizzyVision show, as she stood in the backroom of the Europa Deli, peeling the shells off hard-boiled eggs for an order of potato salad, Sandy was suddenly angry with herself. Why had she been so quick to believe in Darry's Day of New Things, and just as quick to dismiss the things of her own experience? Seeing the breaching whale wasn't like eating a star fruit or going to an art exhibit or even opening your legs to a boy for the first time. It was something raw and artless and entirely unforeseen, and because it had happened without the calming distance of someone else's newsfeed, without the filtering pixels of the Internet, Sandy had been barely able to stand it.

She began chopping the peeled eggs into pieces and mixing them into a bowl of mayonnaise. Her phone buzzed in her back pocket, and it continued to buzz off and on all morning, churning with texts and tweets and photos and messages and status updates and the whispers and shouts of the whole digital world, clamoring for her attention. But Sandy was happy to be standing alone in the back room of Europa Deli, shredding pork for a batch of *nalesniki*, because it made her fingers greasy, and she could not look.

THE SKULL HOUSE
JOHN COUNTS

Lillie Korpela collected skulls.

She disappeared deep into the federal forest behind her family's old dairy farm in northern Michigan's Bear County during all seasons for sixty years, trudging through knee-high snow in the winter to find the remains of animals that had starved to death. In the summer, the waxy green woods were a hot riot of mosquitoes and flies. She would brave the heat and bugs to find deer, raccoon, and porcupine carcasses decomposing and rank in the steamy swamps and drag them back to the farmhouse to clean, a process Lillie had learned when she was 18 and checked out a book on osteology from the Sampo branch of the library.

It required ammonia, bleach, peroxide, a sharp paring knife, forceps, dissecting scissors, a paint brush and rubber gloves. Her dad gave her permission to take over a back shed used for storing farm equipment they didn't use anymore. Over the years, the dairy farm was becoming non-operational and the family subsisted on selling off parcels. Lillie turned the shed into a laboratory for skeleton preparation, including digging a fire pit outside its doors and obtaining a large cast iron pot for boiling.

She immersed herself in it, repeating the process with possums, raccoons, minks and beavers–anything she could find.

Lillie would remove the outer skin and fur of the skull until just the red meaty flesh was showing. Then she would put the skull in cold soda water and let it soak for a bit before putting in on the fire and bringing it to a bubbling boil for about a half hour. She learned that larger skulls of deer took longer than the small skull of a squirrel. When the flesh on the back of the head started to fall away from the bone, the skull had been boiled sufficiently.

She would run water into the pot to gradually cool it, otherwise the skulls would crack. It was a lot like boiling eggs. Lillie would then take out the skull and use the paring knife to scrap off the remaining bits of flesh. It was at this point she also ripped out the eyes and threw them into the fire where they would hiss. The ligaments holding the jaw were cut and the two pieces were separated and rejoined with twine.

Lillie then had to remove the brain with the large forceps through the foramen magnum, the very large hole at the back of the skull. She sometimes had to fill the skull with water and vigorously shake it for the brain to come loose. The skull would then have to soak in solutions before being set in the sunshine to finish bleaching.

Lillie Korpela repeated this process thousands of times, beginning when she was a teenager during World War II. The fear, death, and sadness is what drove her into the woods where she had spent so much time with the two brothers who were lost overseas. By the 1960s, Lillie had acquired thousands of skulls that crowded the shelves of all the outbuildings on the old dairy farm. When both of her parents died, leaving her alone on the property, Lillie constructed a house out of them.

The Skull House wasn't very big, only about 600 square feet, built in the style of a rustic pioneer cabin. On the exterior walls, for every layer of brick there was a layer of skulls embedded in concrete. The wooden roof had standard shingles to keep out the weather, but on top of them, Lillie created rows of skulls. When it rained, the water gushed through the eyelets and mouths of the various creatures as it ran off the roof.

There was a small porch with railings adorned with even more. Two bear skulls stood on top of their posts—places of honor. Inside there was a large hearth big enough for her cast iron pot to boil off the flesh. There was a giant sink linked to the water pipes of the main house for cleaning off the animals. There was also a small well-ventilated room with an exhaust fan for the chemicals. It was everything Lillie had wanted while preparing skulls in the makeshift sheds of her youth.

The town of Sampo and others in Bear County were initially bewildered when the tarps and scaffolding were removed and the Skull House unveiled. Cars would slow to a crawl and housewives would gape aghast out the window while their husbands ducked down to get a quick glance from behind the wheel. Children pointed and laughed. While some could never accept such a monstrosity—one local minister called The Skull House a "demon-influenced blight on the wholesome, healthy populace of Bear County"—public tide soon changed in Lillie's favor. People were curious. Lillie started charging admission and giving tours and demonstrations.

She ran the house by herself for years, making a modest income. There was a spike in business when it was featured in the *Guinness Book of World Records* in the 1970s. She soon started getting more requests from books, magazines and television shows. *Ripley's Believe It Or Not* came and filmed a segment. In the 1980s, a crew from Hollywood arrived and used it as a location in a horror film Lillie never watched—she preferred classic cinema, her other passion in life.

By the 1990s, the few people in Sampo who had shunned her were dead. The Skull House had become an institution, featured in state and national travel guides. There was even a sign on U.S. 31 a few miles out of town that read: "Come see the World Famous Skull House."

Lillie still forged on in the woods collecting skulls she used to further adorn the house, though not as often as she got older. She only got out a few times a year now, but collecting and cleaning skulls was so comforting and soothing it had become mechanical and necessary to living.

One morning in early winter, the slim and strong 85-year-old woman once again crossed the land between the farmhouse and outbuildings to the edge of the property and walked into the woods. She moved steadily but slowly, wearing a fleece-lined red woolen coat she bought at a shop in Bear River a few years back. Her long hair the color of corn silk was mashed inside a black fleece winter hat that wrapped warmly around her ears and fastened under her chin with a Velcro strap. She walked toward Swanson Creek, which fed into Bear River.

Lillie carried a burlap sack, three finely sharpened knives of varying sizes for any skinning that needed to be done in the field, the walking stick she had carved from a handsome oak branch and a hacksaw for any beheadings. In a small backpack, she carried a first-aid kit, flashlight, compass, tarp, rope, matches, a few cans of beans and a blanket. She'd hauled the emergency backpack around for years and had never needed any of the items inside.

She moved through the cold forest, the sky white and deep with potential snow, which would have been the first of the season. Fallen leaves crunched under her footfalls. This time of year, there were always deer carcasses from careless hunters who injured the animals with a bullet or arrow, but never tracked them. She'd found many deer with arrows poking out of their sides down by the creek. Now she scanned the ground and saw nothing but stumps, leaves, branches, and tree limbs. She smelled the air for rot, but found none.

Lillie's knees began to ache from arthritis, but she continued on, relying more on the walking stick. The pain in her knees had become so bad that she hadn't been out collecting during October or November, which she usually avoided during the thick of deer hunting season anyway. This walk might be the last chance her knees would allow her to get out before the full force of winter came. Lillie planned a short trip down to the creek and wanted to be home before 3 p.m., when one of her favorite movies, Alfred Hitchcock's *Rear Window*, was scheduled to be on television. She'd seen the movie about as many times as she walked this same path in the woods, but also never tired of it.

As she approached Swanson Hill, a flash of black high up on the incline caught her eye. The thought that it might be a dead bear came in an instant. It was a bear skull she held most sacred. When she was little, her grandfather, an immigrant straight from Finland, told her that when a bear died it went back to the stars and was reincarnated and returned to walk the earth once more. In the days of the Indians, Lillie knew bear were plentiful in the area. She had heard all the stories as a child, how the woods teemed with them until a mad 400-pound beast devoured the famed French Jesuit minister Father Gabriel Pierre LaFlur alongside the mighty river and many of the animals were hunted with a vengeance by the arriving white men. She knew about the lumbermen who followed and clear-cut much of the timber until the land was worthless and abandoned to the government whose only recourse was to turn it into a huge federal forest and let the trees grow again. She imagined bear running out of the woods and then back in again. When she was young and started collecting skulls, she'd stumble across a dead bear at least once a year during her daily treks. As more retirees and tourists flocked north to set up permanent homes, continued development of the land in the area made the creatures scarce. Lillie was lucky to find a bear carcass every five or six years.

It had been even longer, probably about a decade, when she saw that flash of black on Swanson Hill. Even though she had avoided the hill in as many years because it was too dangerous, Lillie began laboriously scaling it. She had to make sure.

Lillie had to stop and rest when she wasn't even a third of the way up. She shimmied out of her pack and set in on the ground, happy to be relieved of its weight. The black patch wasn't visible from where she sat down in the leaves next to some saplings. Lillie clutched her sore knees to her chest and massaged them. Maybe Karen was right; Lillie was far too old to be hiking in the woods by herself, even if she knew the forest better than most people knew their own backyards.

Karen was technically Lillie's employee at The Skull House, but had in fact become something of her caretaker. She was 30 and had grown up in Sampo like Lillie, but hadn't wanted to go either of the two routes a girl from town went these days: get pregnant at 16 and live off government aid or go to college and never return. Karen started hanging out at The Skull House when she was in high school, back when she wore all black clothes and gobbed on layers of black make-up. Lillie was frightened of the young girl, who was a hundred pounds overweight and had a silver metal chain going from a piercing in her nose to one in her ear. Lillie told her if she took the earrings out, she could have a job taking admission money at the tourist attraction. Despite her shocking look, the girl was very shy and sweet. Karen removed the piercings and thrived in the job. She had worked for Lillie in some capacity for almost 15 years now. It wasn't long before Lillie was walking Karen through the woods and teaching her how to collect and clean the skulls.

Karen quickly lost a lot of weight from hiking so much. She learned bookkeeping and other skills related to running the small business. Even though the girl remained living with her parents, who ran a motel at the edge of the village, she became something of a daughter to Lillie, who had already stipulated in her will that Karen would inherit The Skull House when Lillie died.

In the last few years, Karen had become very hesitant about letting Lillie go out into the woods alone.

"Just let me know and I'll go out with you," she would say. "You should not be out there by yourself."

Lillie loved the girl, but didn't need anyone telling her what to do, even if it did make sense to her now as she sat on the slope of the hill rubbing her knees. The first few flakes of snow shook down from the sky. Lillie could either continue up the hill toward what she hoped was a dead bear and take its head, or she could turn around and go home and turn on a movie and call Karen to bring over dinner. She didn't ponder it long. Lillie hoisted the pack up on her back and started trudging up the hill towards the black patch that again became visible, convinced more than ever that it was a dead bear.

She didn't take more than five steps when both knees buckled and Lillie fell backwards. There were no trees to reach out and grab for balance. Everything was awhirl and spinning. Her head hit the ground hard and she began tumbling down the hill. She was worried one of the knives in the scabbards on her waist would jostle loose and stab her in the side or that the hacksaw lashed to the pack would cut her, but neither happened. Lillie came to a rest at the base of the hill. The pain in her right side was immediate and shocking. Unable to move, she took stock. She felt the hot rush of blood on her head. The pain became more intense on her right side where she had likely broken her hip. She didn't cry. She lay on her back and stared at the whiteness of the sky and the flakes rocking gently down toward her.

*   *   *

Lillie knew very well she could die at the bottom of Swanson Hill with a broken hip and possibly a concussion if she didn't move. She slipped out of her pack and slithered painfully away from it so she could unzip it. The first-aid kit contained some painkillers she'd been prescribed for the arthritis. She swallowed three of them dry and continued rummaging through the bag. Her side continued to burn with electric pain. The matches and an emergency fuel stick were in a large Ziploc bag. Lillie also pulled out the tarp and blanket. Then she realized she couldn't stand up and walk to find a proper place to try and set up camp, so she returned everything to the pack and zipped it back up.

She lay on her back for ten minutes staring at the white sky until the painkillers kicked in and dulled the scream on her right side. It didn't feel like she was shattering each time she moved.

There was a large pine stump amid several medium-sized trees that had fallen to the ground about twenty excruciating yards away. If she could somehow crawl to them, Lillie could fashion a makeshift tent with the tarp over the fallen trees and use the branches to start a fire. If she was to survive the night, she had to have heat and some sort of shelter from the snow, which steadily swooped down from overhead.

Lillie rolled onto her stomach and gripped her pack. She used her arms to pull herself painfully across the forest floor toward the stump. She grunted through the pain and had to rest for a moment when she was about halfway there, but then continued dragging herself through the leaves and twigs until she arrived. Her breathing was deep. After resting, she once again unzipped the pack and took out the matches and fire stick. There were plenty of dead branches to burn within reaching distance. She snapped some apart and cleared a spot where she piled the branches on top of the fire stick, which she quickly lit with a match. A small fire began crackling.

The tarp was draped over the stump and weighted down with branches and dirt. She crawled down to the loose end and weighted that end down with more branches and her pack. In one last burst of energy and pain, she crawled under the tarp with her blanket, a can of beans and the remaining painkillers. It was only afternoon, but she was ready for the night. Lillie adjusted herself until she was as comfortable as possible. After the rush of activity, she settled into the natural rhythm of the woods and the crackling fire. The snowflakes tapped the blue tarp overhead. The fire shot up curls of black and grey smoke. If she didn't move, she was quite comfortable.

Lillie didn't know whether she wanted to be found or not.

*   *   *

Dusk came early and brought more snow, frenzied and swarming like bugs in the sky outside her tarp. She continued feeding branches to the fire while an inch of snow accumulated around her. The more it snowed, the more insulated and warm she would be.

She opened the can of beans and ate a third of it, drinking them straight from the can. Just a little bit of them satisfied her hunger. She didn't think about what was going to happen to her. She was just happy to be warm and have the beans.

It was soon pitch black and the woods became wrapped in mystery. Even Lillie didn't know them any longer. The sounds changed. Lillie was more alert than before now. She knew opening the can of beans and not finishing them was a bad idea. It would attract animals. So she took one more sip even though she wasn't hungry and threw the can as far away from her as possible without jarring her hip.

It was a stupid idea. The can only made it ten feet. Now she really couldn't sleep. She waited for a visit from critters as the clouds moved on and the snow was replaced by stars in the sky. In the moonlight, Lillie saw a raccoon waddle in and find the can. She had encountered numerous coons in the past, but never while she was completely incapacitated under a tarp.

Lillie could hear the raccoon ravenously eating the beans and saw the glint of the can in the moonlight. But then another coon came up and a screeching fight commenced. This is what she was afraid of, that the animals would fight and end up on top of her and she wouldn't be able to defend herself. She gripped a large flashlight in one hand and a walking stick in the other as the animals clawed and screamed at each other a few feet away. The coons eventually settled their dispute when there were no more beans. One of them took the can and the ground around Lillie was peaceful again. Still, she clutched the flash light and walking stick.

*   *   *

Dawn broke cold and painful. The woods creaked into frozen positions it seemed the trees would maintain all winter. Lillie came to full consciousness not from a deep sleep, but from a haze of restless pain and light slumber. It was a raw morning in every way. The fire was down to embers. Lillie didn't know if she had the strength to stoke it back to life.

She swallowed two more painkillers, her last, and lay under the tarp not knowing what she should do next. Her leg hurt too bad to even move just a little. The crawling around she did the day before wasn't going to happen again. She did not panic, however.

Lillie had never been afraid of dying. She welcomed it in every living moment, conscious of it with every breath. Long ago she decided she needed to love death just as much as she loved life. Otherwise, she felt she would just go crazy. She knew it was one of the reasons she surrounded herself with skulls. Lillie didn't believe in an afterlife but didn't disbelieve. It wasn't knowledge human beings needed to have, apparently. She accepted that.

She revisited these thoughts. She also thought about the way the muscles wrapped the bones in her father's neck as she could see it from the backseat of their old Ford. She thought about the clean sweaty smell of her brothers Alex and Waino when they returned from the woods. She thought about her mother's laugh, which was rarely heard but high-pitched and startling and made everyone else in her family also laugh.

Then she heard rustling from afar and thought maybe critters were returning to look for more beans until she heard Karen's voice.

"Lillie? Is that you? Oh my God."

Lillie looked over and saw the young woman approaching with a Bear County sheriff's deputy who was pulling the radio microphone from his shoulder, pressing a button and mumbling something into it.

Karen ran to Lillie and knelt down next to the tarp.

"I was so worried," she said frantically. "Are you OK? Please tell me you're OK?"

"There's a bear at the top of the hill," Lillie said. "Go see if it's a bear."

"That's not important right now," Karen said. "Can you move?"

"I think I broke my hip."

"Ambulance is on the way," the deputy said.

*   *   *

It took another hour and a half to get Lillie out of the woods. The paramedics who arrived had no choice but to park their ambulance at the Skull House and walk a stretcher out to Swanson Hill, where Karen knelt down and comforted Lillie, who remained under the blankets.

The pain screamed loudly in her side when they lifted her on the stretcher, but then one of the paramedics, a young woman wearing a ball cap, primed her arm for an I.V. with a cotton swab and alcohol and stuck it in.

"You'll be feeling better soon," the young woman said.

The other paramedic was a young man wearing the same type of ball cap. They got on either side of the stretcher and began walking Lillie out of the forest. Karen and the deputy followed alongside.

Lillie looked up at the sky and the gnarled tree limbs bent and twisted every which way as she bobbed up and down and up and down on the stretcher. So this is what it's like to be dragged out of the woods, she thought.

*   *   *

They took her to the hospital where a doctor confirmed she had broken her hip. Lille was pumped full of narcotics and bland food. They turned on the television. Karen said she would check in the next day and left. Lillie fell asleep. It was all pleasant enough until the fever set in.

She had a disturbing dream about the bear on Swanson Hill. In the dream, she was lying on the forest floor again. As the bear ambled towards her, she was terrified and unable to move. She thought the bear was going to rip her up, but it didn't. It lay next to her and nuzzled her body and together they were warm. As they lay back to back on the forest ground, she could read its thoughts. It was a male bear and he had died on top of the hill after a long, happy life, he said, but he couldn't go to the stars and be reincarnated and come back and walk the earth unless he became part of the Skull House.

"You know about the house?" Lillie asked.

"We all know about the house," the bear said back.

Lillie wept tears of joy and promised she would come back for the bear when she could move.

*   *   *

Lillie awoke in the hospital hot, sweaty and delirious, the dream images of the bear still circulating through her thoughts. A nurse came and took her temperature and said it was 103 degrees and put cold compresses on her head. Lillie didn't care about the fever or that her whole body ached. There was one thought now: she had to get that bear from Swanson Hill.

She waited until Karen came the next morning to talk about it.

"You have to go get the bear's head," she told the young woman. "I know it's up there."

"You've got a bad fever, Lillie," said Karen. "Try and get some sleep. There probably never was a bear."

"You promise you'll check, though?" she said "I'm just asking this one thing. Please check. How hard is that?"

"Fine," Karen said. "I'll check. I'll let you know tomorrow."

Lillie reached out and grabbed Karen's arm and beckoned her ear closer.

"I want you to bring me his head," she said. "I want to see for myself. The bear wants to walk the earth again."

*   *   *

Lillie's strange dreams about the bear continued. She clutched a raft in open wa-ter, which she guessed was Lake Michigan, the only large body of water she had ever seen. The bear was behind her on a different raft trying to catch up. In an-other dream, she was locked in a room on the second floor of an old house which felt like a hotel. The room was completely empty and there was nowhere to hide. The bear was on the other side of the door, trying to get in. He wasn't clawing or making any other noises, but she was intently aware of his presence.

She woke in a feverish fit to see Karen standing in the hospital room shrouded in shadows and beeping machines. It was the middle of the night and only the lights in the hallway of the Bear County Medical Center were kept on. Karen had a large backpack with her.

"Is that it?" Lillie asked.

Karen took a few brisk steps towards Lillie's bed, unzipping the pack and reaching inside. The severed bear head she pulled out of the backpack was mag-nificent. Karen held it for Lillie with both hands it was so big and heavy.

"It was right where you told me to find it, on the top of Swanson Hill," Karen said. "It's perfect."

Lillie felt a sudden wave of relief and joy. She laid her head back on the pillow and closed her eyes, happy that she could clean the flesh off of the skull and put it in the house somewhere so the bear could go up to the stars and come back down to earth.

*   *   *

The fever broke the next morning. Lillie woke up in the bright hospital room with only mild sensations of the dreams of the previous two days. The nurse brought her some orange juice, which she drank while reading the *Bear River Dauntless*. A certain amount of clarity had returned. She was midway through her juice and a story about an upcoming community theater production of *Fiddler on the Roof* before she felt the dream bear return to her thoughts.

Lillie shuddered with slight panic because she couldn't remember what was real or not. Had she been on a raft? In an old hotel room? Had Karen been in the hospital room with the severed head? Lille couldn't be sure of anything. She also didn't want to reveal to the doctors, nurses and especially Karen that she didn't remember everything. The rest of the morning was spent fretting over the poten-tially embarrassing things she had said to people in her feverish fit.

Karen came to visit in the afternoon. The young woman was bright, smiling, carrying a stack of new magazines for Lillie.

"Jeez, you look a lot better," Karen said, pulling a chair up to Lillie's bedside and setting the magazines on table. "You looked like hell yesterday."

"I feel a lot better," Lillie said.

She desperately wanted to ask Karen about the crazy things she may have said, but didn't. Lillie hoped she would offer it up on her own. After a few minutes of chit-chat, Karen finally did.

"You had a heck of a fever," she said. "You were saying some weird stuff."

Lillie couldn't resist.

"Like what?" she asked.

"About how you needed that bear's head, about how it wouldn't be able to come back to life if I didn't. You were so sure it was there."

"Was it?" Lillie said meekly.

Karen became concerned.

"No," she said. "Like I said yesterday, it was a garbage bag filled with old clothes. I brought it here to show you because I knew you wouldn't believe me. Don't you remember?"

"Yes, of course," Lillie said.

The awkwardness was glossed over. Lillie was relieved. She felt a great burden being lifted. Her spirit was light and airy in the hospital room with the winter sun shining in through the big window. Karen had brought a DVD compilation of French New Wave cinema, with films by Truffaut and Godard, and was sliding one of them into the player. Lillie had seen them all before dozens of times but thought it was a perfect afternoon to re-watch them with Karen, who had never heard of them. They could talk lightheartedly about the movies and forget all about the bear on top of the hill. Lillie wouldn't have to worry about any bear's soul that day. The animals knew how to find their own way back to earth with or without her.

THE LETTER X CHOOSES HIS OWN ADVENTURES

AMORAK HUEY

1.
You grow up along an endless sidewalk, the Midwest
playing on a loop, all cornfield and heavy metal

and the regurgitated taste of desire. The circle
and the circle back. Familiarity is the first step

toward trust—trust the only path to betrayal.
It's the neighborhood that makes you feel safe,

the basement where light bulbs burn out first.
If biology determines outcome, hide under the bed.

If you climb into the back of the van
the story ends here. Another begins.

2.
You learn what it means to crave
while snuggling in the back row of American history

or posing like lovers on the bumper of a muscle car.
You share hairspray and cigarettes, curls of smoke

and vodka kisses. You have nothing
and share all of it. You believe in Manifest Destiny—

her body is a continent. If you don't answer
just this one phone call, if you aren't around

tonight, if someone else drives her home,
if it rains, if it rains, if it rains.

3.
You move away but cannot move on. The landscape
never changes. North Florida is eastern Indiana

with a short-term memory problem.
The only kind of anger worth holding in your fist

breaks like thin ice. It's not supposed to snow
this far south. How long since you cooked

a meal worth eating? You can
spend the night anywhere. A stranger's

just someone who hasn't fucked you yet,
unless the truth is the other way around.

If you decide no one will get hurt,
write the check. If you decide to run, run fast.

If you have to blame someone
there are plenty of choices.

4.
Every war belongs to someone else,
camouflage can't hide what matters.

The sand is different. The waste
remains waste. The blood is the same color,

the sun just as forgiving. You will tell people
you are becoming a man. You will suggest

your priorities have ordered themselves
at last. It is the clatter and the power

and guns. No point in pretending otherwise.
If the other guy shoots first, get it on tape.

If you do not like the results, rewrite it.
If you do not like the smell, too bad.

If you survive, remember to remember

how bright this sky, how beautiful this moment.

5.

A guitar in your hands and someone listening—
why did it take you so long to arrive?

You hope it's the music but again the noise,
the drowning out. It feels

like waiting. That's the beauty of song:
impermanence. If you forget the lyrics,

swim. If you wake up feeling trapped,
swim. If your dreams begin making sense,

swim. If you cannot swim, wrap your arms
around any limb that passes amid the swirl.

6.

It's the repetition that kills you. It's the repetition
that keeps you alive. It's not the job

but losing it. It's not the sense of purpose
but the way grass creeps onto the sidewalk,

given time and water and sunlight.
Having money in your pocket

always felt like an undeserved surprise
so its absence doesn't hurt. What hurts

is having people depend on you,
this too an undeserved surprise.

If you let them down, turn the page.
If you let them down again, turn the page.

7.

There is always more than one possibility

but that doesn't mean happiness.

Your father dying, your daughter in trouble–
these are synonyms for *helpless*.

The human body is smaller and more fragile
than you ever knew. If you are allowed to vanish,

do so. If a migraine is born behind your eyes, seek
comfort in the familiar grip of a hammer handle.

8.
Make a world of your own choosing.
A place to eat, a place to rest–

all else is indulgence. You cannot believe
everyone doesn't gamble like this.

If you are out of timeouts, hurry to the line.
If you are surprised by how much weight

you've gained, grow a beard.
If you are afraid of flying, double down.

9.
Everyone dies. What's ridiculous
is it startles us every time.

Cheat on your wife, buy a motorcycle,
pay your taxes on time–we control

only what we control. You can try
to make sense of the sections,

look for order, impose rules,
you can sign the lyrical contract,

sometimes you will guess right. Sometimes
the leaves fall, and sometimes they fall into place.

If the sidewalk appears to end, turn left.

If the sky is wide, the story closes here.

If your favorite shape is a circle, keep reading,
but do not say you were not warned.

THE LETTER X GIVES THE INSPECTOR FROM THE NATIONAL REGISTER OF HISTORIC PLACES A TOUR OF HIS CHILDHOOD HOME

AMORAK HUEY

The kitchen is hard for me to talk about. The front hall speaks for itself.
Anyone would feel this way, growing up with eyelashes like a girl,
spiraling half into love every time I walked past a mirror
or wrote my name in the snow. No such thing
as too many ex-lovers or too few escape routes,
it's the porch light left on until the bulb burns out.
Yes, we have let certain things go. It's the only way
any of us makes it through the day.
Yes, these curtains are knit from cat fur,
second-hand choking: my grandmother died
between the couch and the hamster cage,
and yes, all this woodwork is original: untouched
planes of white oak, all dovetail and craftsmanship
plus four generations of initials scratched
with the pointy handle of a spoon. My mother
will outlive us all, she's in the Alzheimer's wing
because it's cheaper there and she likes the soup.
This carpet is her fault. The chandelier as well,
so much wrought iron and guilt.
I learned to scavenge early, spelling came easy
and I'd give anything to go back
and tell a certain version of myself how much easier life
might have been if I'd worn blue jeans more often,
brushed my hair. That basement door has been locked for decades,
some places just aren't worth the effort,
I've been meaning to go through these boxes,
sort the scraps, stay in better touch with my siblings.
The fire damage in my bedroom has faded. I heard
she married well. Maybe she remembers
how we laughed at this bedspread,
its tiny cartoon lassoes and spurs and horseshoes–
the way we tangled uncertain limbs and whispered,
as if being overheard was the worst that could happen.

THE LETTER X SEDUCES THE ASPARAGUS QUEEN IN EMPIRE, MICHIGAN

AMORAK HUEY

Do you know what would taste good with that asparagus?
Come on, baby, let me touch your crown. Let's overcompensate
for my split ends, your untender ambitions. Let's steam
and sizzle and deep fry, let's swim in powdered sugar
and funnel our cakes together. There's no shape we can't shift,
no season too short for arts and crafts and friendly competition.
You be my time zone, I'll be your western edge, we'll stay
light all night and tell stories about our dazzling childhoods,
angle of sun against big lake, a million smaller lakes and lesser stars,
the dunes and don'ts of having hippy-dippy parents—
marijuana growing under the elms and metalwork in the shed,
all that welding: joining of unlike shapes
in the name of beauty, or its opposite. Stem my tide, stalk me
all the way home, ride this highway until we hit the water,
the thing about a peninsula is there's only one way to run.
This is our saving grace, our fresh water, our reason
for eating. Sand on your tongue is part of the experience,
that grit and godawfulness, quest for absolution,
if you weren't young here you have no idea
what winter is—how quickly the human heart freezes,
how hard the ice. Once you've used a chainsaw
there's no going back. Let's wait for the lighthouse
to glance our way, spin and cycle and our moment of clarity
when all this paranoia pays off, let's pretend our piss doesn't stink,
our fantasies don't sink beneath familiar chop and heave.
This crowd is watching us, we are the attraction,
everyone wondering what you see in someone like me.
They do not know the high cost of symmetry, the value
of balance in an imbalanced world, it's not the heat,
it's the economy—ask about my good side,
let's show off our skin, capitalize me, let's shock the tourists,
these people who think purple is for vegetables,
let's pepper and assault and coat ourselves in cornmeal,
you lift your sash and flash your big ideas,

I'll spin and sidle and offer my strong shoulders:
first Empire, then state, then all the world's a cage,
surf and ski and a bucket of homebrew pale ale. As good
a place to start as any, here. The woman who created Barbie
grew up across town, Dr. Rubik—the cube guy—
vacationed in a cabin on the bay next to the Ford estate,
we've birthed a half-dozen serial killers and a trio of test-tube babies,
the dentist who invented invisible braces, that one girl
from that gum commercial, you could look it up, but don't tell anyone
because I might have some of it wrong. All my angles
wrench askew, the eight-cylinder engine
is the new endangered species and the planet
has never been smaller. All the more reason to give in
when I beg, borrow, feel you up. Listen carefully: never
wake a sleeping bear, never snowmobile alone,
don't pick the mushrooms on the eastern side of the hills—
these are words to give away, the price of admitting
that I am the ex among the wise, and as soon as I saw your face
I swallowed all your secrets. I wrote them, lived them, lost them,
I dreamed you into being. There is no path that does not lead
to this particular sunset on the longest day of this year or any other:
your cheek touching mine, this sharing of the air between us.

LAST REQUEST
ASHLEY SWANSON

"Long time no talk, stranger," Eve's voice, feminine and upbeat as ever, radiated from the phone.

"Yeah, I know. Listen—"

"Now is actually a really bad time, Grace. Could I give you a call tomorrow?" My baby sister has a way of taking control of the conversation. I could hear laughter in the background. She was probably with friends. I could picture her bouncing brown hair and sparkling smile. With a personality like Eve's, she was always with friends.

"Actually, I'm with Fa—"

"Let me call you tomorrow. Tell Daddy I said 'Hi'!" she interpreted, attempting to wrap things up.

"Damn it, Eve. Shut up for two seconds."

A warm hand clasped mine. I looked down at our father lying in the bed next to my chair. He was weak. His shirt—which once was filled with the muscle of a farmer's chest—sagged around the hollow regions near his collar bone. A violent wheezing sound escaped his throat. His cough expelled several bright red drops of blood and saliva, which splattered on his tan blanket. I brushed them away, leaving small pink stains where the spittle had landed.

Eve's voice rattled angrily like a television in a distant room.

"Eve," Father's whisper jolted me back to my task. I brought the phone back to my ear.

"—have no right to talk to me that way. You—"

"It's Father." Surprisingly, she went silent. "He wants to talk to you."

I flipped the phone around and gently held it to Father's ear. Through labored breaths he whispered into the receiver, "Evie, angel?"

The response was garbled, but I could see that it caused a smile to stretch over his pale face. Wrinkles formed around his eyes. I hadn't seen him smile like that since the last time he saw her. His angel who only visited him on holidays.

"I need to talk to Evie," he croaked yesterday. I'd tried to track her down all day. I couldn't keep the pang of jealousy from my chest when he asked for her again today.

"I need her."

I'd been with him through it all: the tests, the refusal of treatment, the slow decline, and yet he needed her.

"Evie, I want to...see you. When are you...coming home?" Father's words sputtered out like bursts of air escaping a balloon. I could hear the voice on the other end of the phone, smooth as a dove's coo.

"Okay...angel...I love...you." A lone tear found its way down his ashen cheek. He looked up at me, his jaw locked shut. The tendons in his thin neck bulged at the effort. I took the phone back and placed it to my ear.

"Grace?" All the bravado had left my little sister's voice. She sounded small, as if the distance between us—the thousand miles between our Father's bedroom and New York—had somehow shrunk her voice. "How long do we have?"

My eyes drifted to Father's thin body; his chest sputtered violently for air, his eyes closing tightly as he fought off another cough through gritted teeth.

"Just get here."

*   *   *

I stand by the bay window in the living room, and stare past the front porch swing to where the long dirt driveway meets the gravel road. It's the day after Father's funeral. The sun sends down hot, hazy rays that cut through the early spring heat. Freshly tilled fields fill the landscape around our house with dark brown dirt, cold from winter's freeze, raised into even rows to bake in the sun.

It's the first truly warm day, and the heat mixes with the moisture of the thaw to make the air outside thick. The warmth hasn't quite infiltrated the lower layer of the house and so I stand, waiting in the stuffy luke-warmness of morning, hidden in the living room.

I glance down at my watch and note that Eve is eighteen minutes late. This is nothing new—Eve is always late. She is late for this like she had been late for our Father. He'd wanted nothing more than to see her one last time, but she said she couldn't move her flight up any further.

"I've got finals, Grace. Daddy understands," she told me when I called her again. She was studying fashion at the New School in New York City. Apparently, doodling designs for skirts meant more to Father's angel than coming to say good-bye. He passed away two days before she arrived.

I'd planned the whole funeral: picked the small arrangements of white lilacs—the flowers he and Mother had at their wedding—and the picture to be displayed near the closed black casket. He would have wanted the casket closed, wouldn't have wanted his friends and loved ones to see what had become of him near the end. But that didn't stop Eve from asking for the casket to be opened when she arrived.

"I need to see him one more time," she whispered, dabbing at the fat tears that caused her mascara to run. *You could have really said good-bye if your new life wasn't more damn important than your family.* I wanted to say it, but instead I was silent. I bit my lip and let her lift the casket lid and cry over him, letting everyone see our poor, dead Father.

Today, Eve is coming over to go through the small box of my mother's things that Father kept in their closet upstairs. It was his last request. Then Eve would be free to go back to the East Coast. Back to hats and scarves, and whatever it is that she did with her life in the Big Apple.

Movement pulls my focus back to the view from the window, down to the road. A cloud of dust billows behind a white Jeep as it careens toward our drive-way. It skids slightly, crunching gravel beneath its tires. It isn't Eve, just the mailman. I sigh and reach up to massage my temples. The faint pain of a growing headache threatens to explode into a full force migraine if I don't take something to stop it. I abandon my post as lookout and head toward the stairs.

For the first time in as long as I can remember the house is totally silent, void of Father's coughs, or most recently, the beeping of his monitors. Now my feet manage to find each creaky spot on the hardwood floor, creating a symphony of moans from the old house. I know each spot by heart—the warped board near the sofa, the weak spot under the rug.

I was the one who stayed after high school to help Father run things, unlike Eve. Though I thought briefly about leaving to go to college, I always knew it would be best for everyone if I stayed here. Eve may have been able to leave us in her dust, but I couldn't do that. This is where I have lived since I was born. I know its scars, and it knows mine.

There are pictures clustered at the bottom of the staircase: baby photos, my parent's wedding photo, old elementary school portraits, even an aerial view of our farm. In the middle of these photos, in a chipped gold-leaf frame, is a picture of four-year-old Eve. It was taken on the Fourth of July. She's eating watermelon and the slice she is holding is as big as her head. Her baby teeth grin up at the cameraman. Sweet, pink juice races down her chin.

"Look how happy my angel is," Father used to muse whenever he passed the picture. After high school graduation, when Eve ran away to travel before college, I'd sometimes find him standing at her picture with a distant smile on his face, running a finger over the frame.

He didn't see that his angel was ruining her best white sundress. He didn't notice how thoughtless she was being, dripping stains wherever she wished. No matter how much bleach I used, I had never been able to get that dress perfectly white again.

What I am sure Father did notice was something that I always noticed as well: When I look at that photograph and Eve's shining face, it isn't her that I see—it's her eyes. Her big brown eyes. My mother's eyes. The eyes that—because of her—I would never see again.

I feel the pressure behind my temples building. I need that aspirin. The burning gaze of Eve's picture bores into my back as I climb the stairs two at a time. The temperature rises with each step. I'm not sure if it's the quick climb or the change in temperature that is responsible for the beads of sweat that I feel forming on my forehead. The air is much thicker at the landing of the narrow upstairs hallway.

Light from a window at the top of the stairs illuminates the red carpet between two doors. The one on the left is my room; the one on the right, closer to Father's room, was Eve's. I can picture what Eve's room looks like: pale yellow walls dappled with pictures of her friends and exotic locations ripped from the pages of *National Geographic*. The room was mine until I was five. A few months before Eve arrived, my parents moved me into the old guestroom so that the baby would be closer to them for midnight feedings and diaper changes.

Eve's bedroom still sits exactly as she left it—something she could hardly wait to do. I expected Father to change it to a guestroom when she left, but he wouldn't have it.

When I asked what his plans were for the room, he replied, "It's Evie's room. I want her to feel comfortable when she comes home."

It had been almost a month since Eve packed her bags and left with a friend for New York City. She wasn't going to start school there until the fall, but that didn't stop her from leaving the day after high school graduation. She wanted to see the sights, travel around the East Coast. Eve liked to do what Eve liked to do. I doubt if she even noticed the catch of emotion in Father's voice as they said good-bye.

The harsh sunlight from the window aggravates the pounding in my skull. I turn my back toward Eve's door and go into my room. Where did I put my aspirin? I scan the small room quickly, checking near my white twin bed and the wicker chair resting with one leg on the braided blue rug. A pearl-colored lamp sits alone on the little wood end table near my bed—but no pill bottle. My eyes drift to the ceiling-height bookshelf near the window.

There, on the third shelf. Hastily, I cross to it and snatch it up, press firmly on the lid to twist it open, and pop three of the small pink pills into my mouth. My tongue forces them to the back of my throat and I swallow without water, letting them slide down like tiny dry stones.

A single pill clinks against the plastic as I set the bottle back on the shelf. Time for a new bottle. *Hadn't I just got that one this week?* I turn the bottle so that the label is facing forward, feeling the slick finish, when something behind it catches my attention.

My children's Bible. It's a thick book bound in sturdy purple leather. The pill bottle topples to the ground as I pull the Bible off the shelf, blowing away the thin layer of dust that has gathered on its top. I trace the words "Baby's First Bible" scrawled in big golden letters on the front.

My mother used to read these stories to me every night before Eve was born. She would tuck the stiff wool blankets around my sides and sit next to me, draping one warm arm over my thin shoulders, and read. The stories were all so elegant. The night before Eve was born, my mother read me the story of Joseph and his colorful coat. The pictures came to life. Her voice was soft and reassuring. I rested my head on her shoulder; Eve was still just the lump in her stomach, nonexistent.

It was just my mother and me reading stories. That's the last memory I have of her. That night, as my eyelids started to droop, my mother closed the book without a sound and rocked forward to get her round frame up off the bed.

"Good night, Grace," she whispered as she leaned down to kiss my forehead, her lips warm and smooth against my skin. Desperate to keep her with me for a few moments longer, I recapped the story in my head, quickly scanning for a place to ask a question: Joseph got a coat—a rainbow of colorful fabrics that seemed to twirl along with his happiness in every picture—his brothers were upset, he was sent away, and eventually he returned and his father was happy. I told her I didn't understand.

"But what did Joseph do to earn the coat?" I asked, as my mother perched on the edge of the bed causing the mattress to slope beneath her weight. She nodded slowly, taking the time to think about my question before responding.

"You don't have to earn a father's love, Grace," she told me, her voice as soft as the nightlight near my desk.

"Then why didn't the other boys get coats too?"

"Well, because parents can show their love in different ways." She leaned down to kiss my forehead but stopped when I asked.

"But the father in the story, he punished the other ones for being mean to Joseph, because he loved him best. Do you love me best?" My eyes scanned her face, inches from my own. My mother touched her palm to the top of her belly and looked down at it. I could see the rhythmic pounding as her pulse moved her hand up and down with each of Eve's unborn heartbeats.

"I love you both equally," she replied. Her eyes didn't leave her stomach.

"No, that's not right." The words were out of my mouth before I could filter them. My mother's eyes jerked to mine, not in anger, but concern. I rattled, "You said that parents love their kids different. So you must love one better than the other. You have to love one best. It can't be the same if it's different."

My mother lifted her hand from her stomach and placed it gently under my chin, tilting my face so that I looked directly into her deep brown eyes. I waited for her to share her secret, to finally admit that she loved me most. She licked her lips then leaned in even closer, lowered her voice to a whisper.

"Some parents might have a favorite," she started, and I knew that she was about to confess, "but for as long as I live, I will keep mine a secret." My heart sank. She stood up and waddled toward the door, then stopped and turned before she walked out, "but I think you know who it is." She winked at me in the dim light, her smile warming me like hot chocolate.

That was the last night I saw my mother.

I put the Bible back on the shelf and look out the window at the front yard. *Where the hell is Eve?* Nothing stirs. There's no breeze to move the newly green grass, or even a bird in the cloudless, pale sky—and no Eve. I sigh, and out of habit begin to massage my head, digging the tips of my fingers into the indents of my temples. Forget it. I head toward the door. *If Eve can't make the time to fulfill Father's will, I'll do it myself.*

It's a short walk to the master bedroom door, which sits ajar and undisturbed since his body was moved to the funeral home. I push the door open and walk inside. The room is dim. The only light peeks in from around the sides of the heavy blue curtains that cover the window. His bed is still unmade. The white sheets tossed aside from when the undertaker came. My eyes wander from the bed to the floral print armchair that was my perch for the last several months.

*   *   *

After my mother died giving birth to Eve, Father had a hard time adjusting. It must have been hard enough being a single parent to a newborn, let alone dealing with that strain while mourning the loss of your spouse. It was the two of us, Father and me. We had to lean on each other to make it through those times.

I remember one night when he came home from work especially tired from a frustrating day. I was washing dishes in the sink after setting Eve up with a variety pack of crayons and several sheets of white paper at the kitchen table.

"My girls!" Father smiled as he entered the kitchen.

"Daddy!" Eve squealed, hopping out of her chair and scampering toward his outstretched arms.

"Hello, Angel." He scooped her up and rested her on his hip. He turned and smiled at me adding, "Something smells wonderful, Grace."

"Thanks, Fa—"

Unable to be pushed from the spotlight for even a moment, Eve interrupted me, "It's all gone!" she cried out with a giggle.

"Is it?" Father asked, focusing again on the girl in his arms and faking astonishment. "Did you eat it all?"

"Yup!" Her eyes danced with excitement.

"You did? Well, what are we going to do about that?" he asked, quickly moving his hand into tickling position.

"I did! I did! I eats it all!" Eve cried out through fits of laughter while squirming in his arms.

"No, you did not," I cut in from the sink, drying my hands on the dish towel. My voice silenced her. She froze. Her deep brown eyes flicking from my face to Father's.

"I..." Her three-year-old voice faltered. She looked down at her chubby fingers.

"You didn't. We do not lie, Eve," I scolded her as I crossed to the oven, where I had been keeping a plate warm for Father.

"Grace," Father said, his voice suddenly soft. "It's okay."

Then looking back at Eve, he smiled and repeated himself, touching his nose to hers, "It's okay. We were just playing. Weren't we, angel?"

*   *   *

It had to have been play like that which made Eve the way she is now. Just thinking of it makes my head ache more. I pull back the curtain to let the sun pour into the room. All Father requested of us after he died was for Eve and me to go through my mother's box. Father was never good with figures, and so the responsibility of sorting the rest of the estate he left to me. I had a head for numbers and had been taking care of his finances since I was eighteen. He trusted that I would be able to handle everything accordingly. All that was left for Eve and me was that one box.

She was staying at a hotel in town. I told her that she could stay in her old room, but she refused, saying, "It's creepy, you know? Daddy died in the room next door. I just don't think I'd be able to sleep there."

She wouldn't be able to sleep in her own home? It was probably for the best. It was just me and Father for so long that it would have felt odd to have anyone else in the house.

"Hello?" I jump as Eve's voice floats up the stairs. With a quick glance out the window, I see that a taxi has dropped her off and is now pulling out of our driveway.

"Grace?"

"Yeah, I'm up here," I call back. The messy and unmade bed suddenly feels wrong, and I dash over to make it. I pull the thin sheets taut and tuck them snug under the mattress, then sweep my hand over it to straighten any wrinkles.

"Hey."

I look up to see Eve leaning against the doorframe. She's dressed for the heat in a brightly colored skirt that reaches just above her knees and a white tank top. Her hair hangs loose in brown spirals around her shoulders. I run my hands over my own hair which is pulled back in a messy bun. Eve looks refreshed and light, like maybe she was at the beach yesterday and not her father's funeral.

She practically runs across the room to wrap me in a tight hug. My head throbs.

"How are you doing?" She asks, pulling back to search my face with Mother's eyes. Those eyes steal my voice, and instead of responding, I nod. She nods too, but her eyebrows scrunch in sadness.

She steps back from me and wraps her arms around herself, moving them up and down like the heat of the room has evaporated.

"Well, I guess we should get on with it," she says. Her eyes scan the room as if she expects a ghost to pop out of every corner. "I have a plane to catch."

"Already?"

"Yeah, well, I didn't see the point in sticking around—"

"You never have," I interrupt before I can bite my tongue. I see the muscles in her delicate jaw clench.

"That's not fair, Grace." My mother's eyes plead with me.

"I'm sorry. I've just been on edge...with everything."

Eve nods sympathetically. My headache has intensified behind my right eye. Sharp barbs of pain radiate from deep within the socket. "Let's just do this, okay?

It's in the closet."

Eve nods again and stalks toward the closet. There's a rusty key in the closet's lock. I let my fingers drift over it as I pull the door open. Over the years since my mother died, Father got rid of all of her belongings except for one box. That was what we were supposed to sort together. Eve steps into the closet and pulls the long string that illuminates the single bulb hanging from the ceiling.

The walls are hidden by the row of hanging flannel shirts, dark work jeans, and Father's gray Carhartt jacket. The room smells like him, the way he smelled before the sickness—like a freshly harvested field.

"It's over there. In the back," I tell her, pointing at a cardboard box in the far corner.

"That's it? It's awfully little," Eve comments as she squats to open it. She reaches to pull back the flaps, but stops. "Uh oh," she murmurs.

"Uh oh, what?" I demand, walking up behind her and craning my neck to see what she sees.

"There's a hole. Look, the back corner is missing." Eve sits on the ground, and lifts the box, rotating it so I can see the problem. Something has chewed through the cardboard leaving a ragged edge around a grapefruit-sized hole.

"I think a mouse got it," Eve says, looking up at me. "Yuck, I hate mice. Did I tell you about my apartment in New York? We—"

I squat beside her and snatch the box from her hands, opening the flaps without a word. The inside looks like it's been put through a cheese grater. Papers and photographs are missing corners. A small pink devotional book remains intact, along with a journal, a red scarf, and one white lace baby sock with a yellow urine stain from the mouse.

"Wow. What a wreck. This mouse had a field day. I hope these documents weren't important."

"Important?" I snap, snatching the journal and scarf before standing up. "Damn it, Eve, this," I shake them in her face. "This is all I have left!" Instead of understanding, Eve's eyes fill with rebellion. She opens her mouth—I'm sure to attack me—but before she can speak, a folded piece of paper falls from the journal and flutters onto Eve's lap. I recognize the looping, graceful handwriting scrawled on it: *For Eve, on your first day in this world.* Eve's mouth hangs open in stunned silence.

A cold knot forms in the pit of my stomach. That can't be all. I shake the journal violently, waiting for another letter—my letter—to fall to the ground.

Nothing.

"She took the time to write you this?" I ask, reaching down to grasp the flimsy paper in my hand. Eve reaches out for it, but I hold on. "She had the time to write you this?" The soft buzzing of the light bulb overhead irritates my ears. I can feel my blood rushing, pounding through my veins. I imagine my mother in labor, forcing her hand steady, penning the letter as waves of pain washed over her. When else would she have done it?

"She had the time to write you this, when she was lying in bed dying?" My voice sounds like it's coming from someone else, a voiceover in a movie. "She wrote you. The daughter she never met." My words are getting stronger. I feel my fist start to clench, crinkling the note in my hand. Eve tries to grab it, but I yank my hand out of her reach.

I can't stop the words that are flowing out of my mouth. They bubble up my throat, mixing with saliva, making my mouth taste like vinegar.

"My mother. My mother died because of you and all that we have left is for you?"

Eve looks like I've punched her in the gut. Her eyes are wide, her mouth a shocked "o."

"She was my mother too, Grace. I loved her too," her voice quivers, small, quick tears now streaking her rosy cheeks.

"No," I say, shaking my head. My voice is calm again. I drop the objects in my hands, looking down on Eve as she sits like a wounded animal, cowering on the floor. "No," I repeat firmly, "she was my mother. If she hadn't had you, she'd still be here."

"Jesus," Eve's voice cracks. "Jesus, Grace. You don't mean that. You're upset about everything—about Dad. I know what you're feeling, but you can't mean that."

I let out a short laugh, clipped like the shot of a rifle.

"Feeling?" My head feels as if it's splitting in two. "Yeah, Eve, let's talk about how I'm feeling. What, you weren't happy with all of Father's love, so you need to steal my dead mother's, too?"

Her tears have stopped, but her eyes still look wet and frantic.

"How do you think it made me feel, being here every day, listening to him call out for you? His angel. You, who left him, left us, and still he wants you."

"Grace, I—"

"And all the while, through the cleaning, the bathing, the shots, he keeps asking for his angel, but she's gone. She didn't have to listen to him fade away. She didn't have to watch as he died and know that the last words on his lips were a cry for you. Damn it, she was my mother, Eve, mine. Because you stole our father."

My face feels hot. The color has drained from Eve's flush cheeks.

"Please, Grace." She reaches forward, grabbing my calf. Her eyes stare up at me. Those deep brown eyes cause my heart to flare. I take a deep breath as realization dawns on me. Father wanted her here. I shake my leg free of her grasp and back toward the door. Eve stays where she is on the floor. Her chin is quivering.

"All he ever wanted was for you to be here," I say slowly as I reach the door. My hand finds the doorknob and the rusted key. I slam the door shut and throw my body against it, yanking the key from the lock. The doorknob jingles. I feel Eve's fists pound on the wood as she screams at me to let her out. Then she must switch to slamming her shoulder against it, as the thumping grows louder.

I sigh and reach to rub my temples, but stop. I turn from the closet and leave

Father's room. Eve's voice grows fainter as I descend the staircase and walk out the front door into the thick afternoon air. My headache fades as I walk down the driveway, gravel crunching beneath my feet.

COTTON
JEFF VANDE ZANDE

AN EXCERPT FROM THE NOVEL *OTTO'S HEIRS*

Robby Cooper stands in the middle of a street in Fox Ridge Meadows. In the distance, a lawnmower buzzes. Sunlight glares off the windshields of the trucks in front of him. He shields his eyes. The six adjoined townhouses beyond the trucks are all identical, painted an olive green that is faded and peeling in places. The three trucks parked near the curb each bear the Busy Bee Painting logo, which is a smiling cartoon honey bee flying with a paint brush in its foreleg and a can of green paint where it would otherwise be carrying pollen. The same paint drips from its stinger. Just beneath the picture reads the company motto: "Oh honey, we'll treat you right!"

A prep crew of guys works on one of the units. Some use power drills to remove downspouts or shutters. Others tape sheets of plastic over windows. Another crew uses power washers to knock loose paint from the units that have already been prepped. The guys shout back and forth to each other above the noise of the tools. Robby watches them. He swipes the sweat from his forehead with his palm.

* * *

A red-headed man in t-shirt and jeans walks across the front lawns surveying the work. "You guys are going too slow," he shouts. "These guys are going to be spraying water right up your asses if you don't pick up the pace." He points at a young guy up on an extension ladder. "Although you'd probably like that, wouldn't you, Eric?"

Eric reaches into his front pocket as though looking for something and then pulls out his middle finger.

The red-headed man laughs. "All right, all right, just give me a little more hustle, will ya?"

A driver taps his horn. Robby jumps and then moves closer to the trucks so the car can get past him. He waves apologetically to the driver.

When he focuses again on the townhouses, the red-headed man is walking toward him. His paint-splattered t-shirt has the same bee on it that's on the trucks. His laughing smile is gone.

"That you, Robby?"

Robby nods and waves. "Hey, Ty."

Ty stops in front of him and crosses his freckled arms. A ghost of sun block haunts his nose and forehead. "Holy shit." He shakes his head. "I heard you were back."

"Been back for a few days." He looks at the guys working on the houses. "I don't recognize anyone."

"Pretty much a whole new crew." Ty looks back at his men. "Always lots of turnover season to season. Nature of the business." He points. "That's Steve working the power washer. He was on prep with you last fall." He turns and faces Robby again. "Terry Jones is over on another unit doing trim. Remember him?"

Robby nods.

"Moved him up, too. Making painting wages now." Ty watches his fingers scratch his upper arm. "Suppose I would have moved you up too if things had been different."

Robby sniffs in a breath and looks at the ground.

"I wouldn't go out of your way to say hi to Terry."

Robby shrugs. "I never did really know him that well."

Ty leans against the tailgate of one of his trucks and fishes a pack of cigarettes from his pocket. "You look like you put on a little weight." He shakes a cigarette up from the pack and pulls it out with his lips. "Wasn't much to you when you were working for me. Regular stick man."

"They got it so food tasted good to me again. They had good cooks."

Ty pulls a lighter from his pants pocket and touches a flame to his cigarette. He takes a drag, exhales, and then looks into Robby's face. "So, what are you doing here? Casing the place?"

Robby winces. "Just thought I'd stop by. I was on my way to my grandpa's. I called the office, and Shelly said you guys were here."

Ty takes another drag and then studies the cigarette between his fingers. "Your grandpa still in the same house?"

"Yeah."

"Going from your ma's place in Livonia down to Lincoln Park by way of Southfield sounds like a pretty fucked-up shortcut to me."

Robby shifts his weight to his other foot. He crosses his arms and stuffs his fingers into his armpits. He shrugs. "I wanted to talk to you."

Ty exhales smoke into the air above them. "Why? You looking for work?"

"I'd take it if you're offering."

Ty's mouth slants into a mean smile. He shakes his head. "Jesus, but you got balls."

Robby pumps his palms toward him. "That's not why I came. I'm just saying that I'd take a job if you have one...if you need someone."

"I don't." He points. "And if I did, I sure as fuck wouldn't hire your sorry ass." He drops his barely-smoked cigarette and steps on it. "You're just goddamn lucky I've had six months to cool down."

"I know. I—"

"I had five bids come through in the last couple weeks. It's got me in a good mood. Otherwise, I'd probably be picking your teeth out of my knuckles right now." He crosses his arms again.

Robby's face pales. He swallows again. "Jesus, Ty."

"Come on. Come on. I got work to do. What the fuck are you here for, Robby? Just looking at you is bringing all that shit back up." He pulls out his pack again.

Robby stuffs his hands into his pockets and shrugs. "I want to make amends," he says.

"What is that, rehab talk?"

Robby shrugs. "It's just what I want to do."

He talks around the cigarette in his mouth while lighting it. "How you plan to do that?"

"I thought I'd come back at the end of the day and clean all the sprayers for you." He looks at him. "Tomorrow, too."

Ty exhales and then laughs. "And that would make us even in your head, huh?"

Robby rubs his palm against his forehead. "The trucks, too. I'll wash all the trucks for you."

Taking a drag, he stares at Robby. "You stole my equipment. You took all the sprayers, all the power washers, and all but one of the extension ladders." He holds up a finger as he lists each item. "You left me with nothing, and you're telling me that you're going to clean some sprayers and wash my fucking trucks?"

A few of the guys stop working and look over toward their boss's raised voice.

Robby takes his hands from his pockets and shrugs his palms into the air. "Well, just...Ty. I mean, just tell me—"

He flicks his cigarette into Robby's chest. "Get the fuck out a here."

Robby brushes at the sparks. "Ty—"

Ty comes off the truck and shoves him back a step. "I mean it, you little prick. Get out of here before I tear you a new asshole."

He stands stunned. "I'm trying to apologize here. I'm trying to make—"

Ty grabs the front of Robby's hoodie in both hands and launches him into the street.

He runs slap-footed with the throw and windmills his arms to keep himself from falling. He stands in the middle of the street. "You got it all back," he shouts. "The cops nailed me before I even had the chance to try to sell it. You got all your shit back, man."

Ty takes a step toward him. "Are you doing this? Are you fucking standing there and arguing with me?"

Robby takes a few paces backwards. "Well you did. You got it back." A car comes and forces him to the other side of the street.

Ty marches across the asphalt toward him. "Did I, Robby? Did I get my fucking shit back?"

He stares at him. "Didn't you?"

Ty spits on the ground. "Yeah, sure I did...about five weeks later, asshole."

Robby rubs his fingers on his forehead and furrows his brow. "Five weeks?"

Ty looks behind him where three of his guys are standing by the trucks looking ready to cross the street. He gestures them away with a swat of his arm. "Get back to work. There's nothing going on here." He turns back, his neck red up to his ears.

"I don't get...Five weeks?" Robby pushes his fingers through his hair. "Why five weeks?"

He takes a step forward driving Robby a few steps onto the lawn. "Evidence, fuck-face. They held it all as evidence. I almost lost my whole fucking business because of you."

"But the lawyer had pictures. That's what he showed...he had pictures."

He points a finger in Robby's face. "I was in the middle of two jobs. I had bids in on three others. You know how much that fucking cost me? I had to let guys go...guys with families. I had to borrow money from my old man just to cover my loans. Half that shit I didn't even own yet." He plants his hands into Robby's chest and shoves him to the ground. "I almost had to shit can the whole fucking thing."

He tucks his legs up into his stomach and covers his head with his arms. "I'm sorry, man. I didn't know. I didn't. I was all fucked up."

Ty looms over him. "What I should do is call Terry Jones over here. He didn't get Unemployment. Had to move back in with his folks." He looks back over his shoulder. "I should call him over here so he can tell you about it." He glares back at him. "Maybe you can do his laundry for him or wash his car."

Robby's hair hangs in his face. "I'm sorry, Ty. I really am. At the time...at the time, it seemed like the only way." He sniffs in a breath and clears his throat. "I was really in a bad place. Like I was cornered—"

Ty hisses a laugh between his teeth. "So then you fuck me over."

Robby inches a pace away on his elbow. He flips his bangs from his eyes. "It wasn't about...I mean, I wasn't thinking like that. I was desperate. I wasn't thinking about what it would do to you. It just didn't feel like there was any other way out. I wasn't thinking straight, man."

Ty looks to his right. Robby follows his gaze. At the next house, a man stands in his yard staring at them. He holds a small stack of mail.

Ty reaches down to Robby. "Get up."

Robby takes his hand, and Ty yanks him to his feet. They look back at the man who lingers before going up his stoop and into his house. Ty shakes his head. "Look at that. You're still fucking making trouble for me."

Robby slaps at the dirt and grass stains on his pants. "I'm not trying to make trouble. I just want to try to make things right. I know an apology is nothing. It doesn't do anything. I want.... I mean, I'll work for you for free. Just tell me something that would even start—"

"Fuck off, Robby. That's what you can do."

"Ty—"

Ty shoves him backwards. "I said to fuck off. Disappear."

He looks at Ty's right hand squeezed into a fist. He closes his eyes and sticks his chin out. "Deck me, then. Knock out a few of my teeth. Break my nose. Whatever you want."

Ty looks at his fist and then unclenches it. Shaking his head, he turns and starts to walk away. "Stay away from the 40-bar, Robby."

He opens his eyes. "Ty? Ty, just hold on—"

"You come around me again and I'll file a restraining order."

*   *   *

Ty crosses the street. His guys shoot looks Robby's way while they work in slow motion.

"What is this," Ty shouts, "a break? Get back at it, goddamnit!"

A guy up on a ladder looks over at Robby. "Who's the douche bag, boss?"

"Nobody. Don't worry about it. Just get your ass back to work."

*   *   *

Jogging to his car, Robby brushes away the tears welling in his eyes. A washer fires up behind him and hammers away at the side of a house.

"You okay? Did he hurt you?"

The man who was watching them earlier is sitting on his stoop going through envelopes. Robby looks at the cell phone in the man's hand. He's quiet for a moment. "Yeah, I'm fine. Nothing I didn't deserve, anyway." He snorts in a breath. "He's got strict rules about respecting the customer's property. I crossed the line, and he let me know it. That's all."

The man looks over at Ty's trucks.

*   *   *

Robby slips into his car, starts it up, and pulls away from the curb. He pushes his wrist under his misted eyes and then grabs the wheel and snaps his car back into his lane.

The driver in the other lane lays on his horn and glares at him as he goes by.

"Fuck you," Robby shouts.

*   *   *

Robby drives on the Southfield Freeway. He pulls down his sun visor, blocking the light glaring off the back windows of the cars in front of him. Listening to WRIF out of Detroit, he hammers his thumbs on the steering wheel to the beat of Led Zeppelin's "Black Dog."

Glancing at the clock on the dashboard, he pushes the car up to eighty miles an hour.

His phone rings. He pulls it out of his pocket, checks the screen, and rolls his eyes. He turns down the radio. "Hey, Mom. I'm almost there."

"Your grandfather has called me three times already. Where have you been? You left the house an hour and a half ago."

He draws in a breath and sighs. "I went to see somebody."

Jimmy Page's solo whispers from the speakers backed by a haunting of drums.

"Who?" Her voice cracks on the "o."

"Just somebody, okay?"

Zeppelin fades out. Robby's mother cries softly on her end.

*   *   *

The Rouge River passing under the highway looks like a long mud puddle, choked into a channel between concrete banks. Robby's hand squeezes the steering wheel. "I'm not using, okay? Stop crying. I'm still clean. I just had to go see Ty...had to try to apologize. You can't think that every time—"

"I don't know what I'm supposed to think," she shouts. She breathes in a staccato breath. "You spend all that time in your room. You don't tell me anything. You sneak out—"

"Calm down. I didn't sneak. Okay? I didn't. I just left. You knew where I was going. I told you I was going to Grandpa's—"

"But then you didn't, did you?"

He switches the phone to his other ear and switches hands on the wheel. "I'm on my way there right now. You can't worry so much, Mom. You can't."

She's quiet a moment. "It feels like that's all I can do."

He exhales. "I gotta go. I'm getting really close to—"

"What did Ty say?"

He clears his throat. "Not much."

"What, though? He said something."

A semi begins to pass him on his left, a looming shadow. He tightens his grip on the wheel. "He told me to fuck off."

"Robby!"

"What?" He laughs. "You wanted to know."

Quiet a moment, she breathes through her nose and sighs the breath out from her mouth. "Honey, I'm sorry. I shouldn't have raised my voice like I did."

"Mom—"

"I think it's great that you're making an effort to talk to people. Tiffany and Ty weren't very receptive, but you at least tried. That's all you can do." Her voice is cadenced and comforting.

A grey semi-trailer streaked with rust rattles and bangs outside his window. Brown and pink cow snouts press at the vents. A mournful, long-lashed eye stares at him.

"I'm so proud of you. What you're doing...what you're trying to do. It isn't easy. But it's going to get better every day. It may not feel like it all the—"

"Mom!"

Silence.

"Please stop reading those brochures. Please. You've been saying the same shit to me since I got back."

She sniffs in a hurt breath. "I'm just trying to help."

He holds the phone away from his ear, squeezes it, and then brings it back. "I know you're trying to help. You have helped. You gave me a place to stay. You're trusting me with your car. All of that helps. It really does. But no more motivational shit, okay? No more talk about each day getting a little bit better. All of that...it makes me feel like I'm retarded, like I'm six years old or something."

"Okay," she says. "I'll try not to anymore. But I need to know what you need from me. Tell me that at least. None of this is easy for me, either. I'm just as lost—"

"Just give me a little breathing room. Don't stare at me like I'm going to relapse any time I leave the room. Just trust me a little bit. Don't think that you always have to be doing something or saying something to support me."

A motorcycle whines past on his right going at least ninety miles an hour. The rider threads the bike between cars, leaning his body to the left or right, making it look easy. Robby watches his zigzag disappearance.

"Okay," she says, "I can do that. But then I need you to do something for me, too." She pauses. "I need you to tell me how you're doing sometimes. I need you to let me know what you're feeling or thinking. Don't keep me guessing so much. I'm not talking all the time, but just sometimes, so I don't feel in the dark so much."

He nods. "I can try to be better about that."

The highway flashes from shadow to light to shadow as he passes under overpasses. The semi full of cows starts up an on-ramp toward eastbound I-94. The Southfield Freeway becomes Southfield Road. Allen Park homes line the side of the highway.

"Good," she says. "That will help." She pauses a moment. "So...what are you thinking or feeling?"

"Are you kidding?"

"Just humor me, okay? Just this time."

He takes a deep breath and puffs his cheeks as he exhales. "I think I'm doing all right. It's been a shitty week, but I'm hanging in there."

She clears her throat and sniffs a breath. "And...and no cravings?"

"Nothing I couldn't handle."

"Honey, you are doing so—"

"Mom."

"Okay." She laughs. "Okay, I'm sorry. I won't...I'm just glad to hear that you're doing okay."

He smiles. "So far so good. One day at a time, right? Each new day is a step forward. Breathe in, breathe out. I got to remember that today is the tomorrow that I worried about yesterday. My clean life is closer than I—"

"Okay, Mr. Smarty Pants. Just get to your grandpa's before he calls me again.

You know how he can get."

He nods. "Almost there. I'll talk to you soon."

"Okay, bye honey. I love you so—"

"Bye, Mom." He hangs up the phone and sets it on the dashboard. Leaning his head into his hand, he squeezes his forehead.

* * *

Reaching under the driver's seat, he pulls out an orange pill bottle. He holds it between his finger and thumb, balancing it on top of the steering wheel.

It looks to glow in the sunlight.

When he shakes it a few times, it makes the sound of a nearly empty maraca.

Arching his hips up from the seat, he stuffs the bottle deep into his front pocket. He flips his bangs from his face.

Rush's "Tom Sawyer" plays faintly. He turns it up and plucks the steering wheel with the first two fingers of his right hand.

He passes under the shadow of I-75 and out into the blinding sunlight on the other side.

I LIKE TOUGH SKINNY WOMEN

GABE HERRON

not as sexual objects
or objects at all
but in the same way an ice skater
likes centrifugal forces

    I like tough skinny women

if they smoke and curse

all the better
      and they don't necessarily
have to be boozers but I like them
better that way

      if they are boozers

all three is best
      smoking
      cursing
      boozing

and dirty too
don't forget dirty

I like:

loud
boozy
dirty
smoking
cursing
tough skinny women

I like them the same way Emily Dickinson—
                    liked the dash—

and it isn't a sexual thing
                    not in the least

in the same way a train whistle after midnight
makes you feel extra glad you're warm in bed

safe and loved by others

    is how I like tough skinny women.

MASSASAUGA
CAL FREEMAN

I decide to call the police on our son
and his friends. I am in a different city,
and they are playing beer pong
at our kitchen table. *The whiskey*
I was planning to drink when I got home
is entering them through their stomach capillaries
and teenagers are likely fucking each other
in the crowded rooms of my little house, I explain.
I have it on the good authority of a neighbor.
The cops do not show up.

*   *   *

A massasauga rattler
suns itself on a dry creek bed
and that dream lapses
into one about a dog pulling rats
from beneath the foundation
         of our bungalow
then puncturing their ear drums
with a curved fang

*   *   *

well-suited for this purpose.
The cochlea of each rat
is a mahogany room
where my wife sleeps
         without me.
Have you ever slept in a rat's ear? she asks.
Have you ever been deafened by a dog?

*   *   *

Yes, rat-deaf,
and massasauga,
big river mouth gathering dusk
but there is no rattle
where there is no threat
and I do not know
if we are animals at all.

*   *   *

On the plane back from Seattle
she fears that her ear will burst
with the changing pressure. Michigan
is a grey ream of paper below.
My eyes set each expletive down,
though I can no longer hear them in my bones.
At home I continue to drink
and my wife says do not die.

*   *   *

I think I say to them I feel bad.
I think I say to them what hurts.
I think I know what hurts to say hurts.
I think hurt believes me,
winces and blossoms, no hurt
all this house makes
out of dull coughs coughs up
abstractions grown so tender
after having lived through all our theories,
on parenting, on dying.
Our son draws a bath;
the copper in the ceiling swells
and makes a stunted sound.
He seems well as the future narrows.

Nothing Uglier Than Gold on a Corpse
RON A. AUSTIN

Handsome Charlie was beaten dead ugly, mouth pulverized to a mess of cracked teeth and bleeding gums, lips split, curling like old watermelon rind, tongue oozing out over a busted jaw, eyes swollen shut, round and dark as bruised plums. The savage dudes who whopped Handsome Charlie stole his looks, but at least they left his bling. Handsome Charlie was shining hard, plated in gold and platinum. Diamonds studded his ears and chains laced his neck, but none of that junk warded off this epic beatdown. And I didn't know what to do for him—I mean, I didn't even know if he was alive. I was eleven and had no 1-up in my cargo shorts. Social Studies never covered what to do in case of finding a dude slumped and dumped behind a run-down chemical factory. Like I said, I didn't know what to do for him, but D swaggered right into action, telling me, "Avery, my nigga, get his kicks."

I spat a severe, "What?"

"You heard me, fam." D nodded at the flawless, red Jordans on Handsome Charlie's feet. Of course a vain fool would leave a well-dressed corpse. "I told you get his kicks, those Jordans, *los zapatos, ándale.*"

To be real about it, I was kind of jealous. My Shoe Carnival sneakers stank of ultra-concentrated toe juice and were falling apart like bad paper-mache, but stealing a half-dead man's shoes was just plan dirty. I told D, "Na'll. I'm not do—"

D shoulder checked me and growled, "Scary-ass nigga."

D hunkered down over Handsome Charlie, yanked off those Jordans with a grunt, and he didn't stop. D's hands worked cleanly, efficiently like starved rats, snapping every bright morsel of shine off Handsome Charlie's body. D stuffed all that loot in his jeans and then cut me with a razor glare.

"You ain't snitching, is you?"

There were neighborhood legends of snitches being force fed nails and broken glass. I answered, "Hell no."

D draped a platinum chain over his arm as if he were a salesmen at a department store, and I was the fussy old lady looking to buy. The cartoon skull on his t-shirt leered at me. "If you ain't no snitch, take it."

"But I don't want it."

"See, I knew you was a pussy-ass nigga." D's smile was mean and playful. "Old hoe-ass—"

I snatched the chain off his arm and said, "Shut up."

He folded his arms and said, "Now put it on."

"What?"

"Put that shit on, my dude. I ain't fucking with you."

The chain felt wrong in my fist; it would feel twice as wrong on my neck.

D started in again. "Oh, then you a faggot-ass nigga, old—"

I wanted to head-butt D, crack his face like plaster, but I snapped that stupid chain on instead. Morals and nerve crumble quickly under the hammer of fifth grade bullying. And fair enough, the chain was too tight, fit me like a choker.

D considered me with a sort of cautious pride and snapped a gold chain on his neck. He told me, "On the real, though, you cool people, Avery. So I'ma let you live this time." He pulled his bike off the ground and swung a leg over the seat. "My old-head dropped this shit on me: open mouths welcome open graves. Don't forget, my dude." D shot down the alleyway, tires rumbling on the cobblestone.

That chain might as well have been barbwire, the way it bit into my throat, but I didn't take it off right away, fearing D would feel a disturbance in the ether, instantly know I had broken our contract. I turned my back on Handsome Charlie and swung a leg over my bike seat, but when I stamped on that pedal, the gear chain slipped. I fumbled the bike over and wrestled the slick gear chain—and that's when I heard Handsome Charlie breathing—I mean trying to breathe. It sounded like the dry rattle at the bottom of an empty spray-paint can. I'm serious. I should have turned and looked. One pitiful look might have kept his body and soul fused, but—what if his cuts and bruises were contagious?

I closed my eyes and imagined a gang of crows falling upon Handsome Charlie like dark arrows. They'd rip at him with super-strong talons and he'd come apart neatly as if he was a life-sized action figure, limbs popping free of joints like plastic. The crows would fly away and bury him on a mountain or something, a place with tough-ass stones and wild flowers—I don't know. They'd ditch him somewhere, and I wouldn't have to deal with it. But Handsome Charlie kept trying to breathe, and I just didn't want to turn around and ask what happened. Didn't want to see his eyes open in wet, snotty half-moons, like some helpless, newborn thing. Shame lashed me as I hefted my bike and ran.

*   *   *

I cooled out at the junk yard. Anxiety made the summer light harsh and gave scrap mythical aspects: ruined trucks were the exoskeletons of giant beetles, engine blocks all heads lopped off a hydra, dust-licked and rotting. A full-grown fox jagged across the oil-slicked asphalt, mange flickering like muted flame, yellow teeth jutting from muzzle, primitive blades.

A rodent's fear of predators and open spaces walloped me in the chest, and so I crawled through a section of industrial pipe and hid in the Grungy Van. The Grungy Van was a vortex of gross, reeking like mildew and butt-sweat. One time I found a King Cobra bottle full of dark piss sitting on the dashboard, and another time the console was stuffed with bloody gauze, shed like lizard skin (no need to talk about those used condoms artfully glued to the ceiling, dangling, flaking ecto-plasm). This time I found tin-foil origami glittering on the passenger seat, a crane, a frog, and a few star-shaped flowers.

Handsome Charlie might as well have been dying on a faraway continent, but dread rumbled through my chest, thudding hard, rattling nerve and bone. I unfolded the tin-foil origami, refolded it into compact squares, and then ripped the squares into tinsel. That elemental dread diminished, became a ghost-story dread, unpleasant but surreal and kind of exciting.

I could have pretended Handsome Charlie was an awful vision brought on by heatstroke and too much black cherry Vess if it wasn't for that stupid chain burning radioactive around my neck. My reflection glowered at me from the re-view mirror, dull and blurry, the chain a bright scythe edge separating head from shoulders—and I really don't know why, call me an idiot, but Goddamn it—for one hot minute I really thought I looked like somebody, a caliph mean-mugging for hieroglyphs, royal guardians at my back, a high-priest hexing my enemies, amber-eyed women serving me cheese sticks from an ivory bowl.

A grimy hand shot through the driver-side window, tore at my sleeve, and jerked me out of that daydream. Franklin, the junk yard owner hollered, "Boy, I done told you too many times 'bout bullshitting on my property!" Before inherit-ing the junkyard, Franklin got his jaw busted in an amateur heavyweight box-ing match against Grady "Sledge Hammer" Jones. The bones never healed right, leaving Franklin with the grimace of a Rock' em Sock 'em Robot forced into early retirement. The crooked planes of Franklin's jaw grinded as he said, "I ain't play-ing with you!"

I kung-fu parried his hand, combat rolled over the seats, drop-kicked the pas-senger-side door, and hopped on my bike. Franklin hollered "Hey! You little shit!" He didn't normally get so pissed when he found me loitering. Either threads in his battered hippocampus were unbraiding, unleashing sooty veins of rage, or he to-tally knew. Totally knew I was a lying, thieving coward, flossing a dead man's shit.

*   *   *

As I biked down Grand, the elemental dread resurfaced and mutated into guilt, infecting heart and head with paranoia. I expected pharaonic curses to fall out of the sky and split my skull like an axe, but necrosis didn't eat my flesh; that stu-pid chain didn't squirm to unnatural life and flash venom dripping fangs—nope. Nothing bad happened at all. Life bullied by. Fluffy shaving cream clouds replicat-ed endless screen saver patterns. Oil-drum smokers belched rich, sacrificial fat. Morning Glory vines throttled fences and barbed wire. Little girls traded secrets for Garbage Pail Kids cards and snorted big rhinoceros laughter. Bullet-sized fruit flies sprinted from neck to neck, sucking up sweat and perfume, all that summer nectar. Out front of the meat market, Miss Annette offered me a candy apple, delicate and pretty as blown glass.

I ate that candy apple in four giant chomps, planning to run before Miss Annette started rambling. Sugar lined my teeth, lush as fur, syrup melting on my lips. Miss Annette swatted at a fly then nodded at a couple of teenage girls sitting on the stoop of a ruined storefront across the street, cut-off shorts riding their hips, thighs plump, sizzling in the heat. Squinting fiercely, Miss Annette shook her head in a mix of open jealousy and admiration. She said, "Oooooo child, these girls be so damned thick, like they don't drink nothing but buttermilk." Wringing her hands, she gave a sorry smile. "Sho'll put a bony nag like me to shame, don't they." I shrugged and wiped my mouth. Miss Annette swiped a few sticks, speared a few apples, rapid-fire. She pointed a stick at me and pursed her lips. "Get a good one, now, you hear me? Trust and believe, a fast girl will get you killed." I nodded studiously and biked on.

I spotted D on the corner by the liquor store where dudes bragged, hitting a lick became legend. D held up the clutch of jewelry he stole from Handsome Charlie as if it was the head of a rival warlord. Neighborhood dudes crowded like D was a celebrity. D had those Jordans on and his shirt off, skinny chest straining with false pride, and he was talking all kinds of shit. "Pay the cost or get tossed, that's what I tell a pussy-ass motherfucker." D saw me and his eyes sparked. *Yo'!* he hollered at me. "Yo', my nigga Big A!" The neighborhood dudes cast their attention on me, expecting me to corroborate my role in D's fictions. If I was a different kid, I would have taken off my shirt and joined D, braying no lie, me and that cold-blooded nigga Big D, "we whopped that bitch-made nigga—Wham! Wham! Wow!—brains on the motherfucking pavement." But that wasn't me. I turned and biked through traffic, D's shouting like stones pelting my dusty hide.

*   *   *

Later that night a collage of bad dreams thumped through my brain. Me and D were on the corner in front of the neighborhood dudes. Big D held up a string of diamonds stretched in a lattice between his hands. Those diamonds fused with Big D's voice, winking rhythmically as he spoke, fiery rainbows breaking inside glacial walls. I couldn't hear what he said; it was all radio distortion, static grinding. In the next dream, Miss Annette was dragging a trash bag full of gristle and bone behind her. She shook her head and said "live and die like these flies," her mouth and voice out of sync, something inside the trash bag writhing. Next there were men with bricks for heads, their expressions all angry crayon scribbles. And in the last dream, Big D nudged me in the ribs and said speak on it, my nigga. "Tell these niggas what we be about, how we do. Go on, tell 'em. Tell 'em what's up. Go on." And so I tried to tell them how hard me and Big D were, but when I opened my mouth, nothing but bent nails, razors, and black scabs fell out, no brags, only a cloud of rust. Truthfully, Little D was just a punk-ass scrub who ripped off some helpless dude, and I was too much of a pussy do right. I woke up with tacks in my belly and a sense of urgency sumo-squatting on my chest, that stupid chain tighter than ever.

*   *   *

Of course Handsome Charlie was gone when I returned to where I had found him, but it was eerie, like he had never even been there, not a chalk outline, not a sock, no cop on the case—just up and gone.

I wondered if he was somewhere crumpled inside a drum of corrosive acid, flesh made jelly, bones disintegrating into Alka-Seltzer fizz. Maybe his ghost was stalking me, observing my weaknesses, plotting to steal my soul. Maybe God's hand came down, wearily batted away a few clouds, and pinched him up.

I stared at that patch of tall weeds where Handsome Charlie had lain and concentrated as if it was a Magic Eye portrait, like the weeds might shift and reveal a message, give me a definite answer. But the garbage and dead hornets and mean looking spines remained constant, random, plain meaningless. I wondered: maybe he had gotten up, walked away, and soon, he'd catch me in the street, a gnarly club in his fist, that stupid chain attracting him like a beacon—that stupid chain. I didn't want it in the first place, and all it did was brand me a coward. I tried to snatch it off and the clasp stuck, so I tore at it, threw it in the dust.

When I got home, I found the smallest laceration on the side of my neck, weeping blood. I cleaned it, slapped on a band aid, but it still hardened, became a scar. And it's not like anybody looks at me funny—to this day no one knows it's there. Only me. That scar is tiny, nothing more than a tooth-mark from a beast that bit but could not kill.

ONCE, THE NOMENCLATURE OF BOULEVARD & THOROUGHFARE TURNED COMMON

MONICA BERLIN AND BETH MARZONI

place, barely avenue, & street & road, & their names
familiar—Cherry or Oak or Maple—or ghost, &

all of it dead-ended. So, now we might as well
give in to evening's sigh at the screen door

because it will pass no matter & even the light
we meant to save will hurdle away & everything

soon enough. Now that the river's up
in the trees, we'll watch whole towns

build walls of sand—they'll hold,
or they won't—& we'll watch them hang

border to border on lines stretched
for drying out or giving in, this

a cartography of plea. We'll follow it
farther until the map drawn out settles

all our damn loneliness & what we build
to shore or against it or to measure

each interval called wait, that vocabulary of flat
& still, & believe that once we knew the names

to call. Once we called each tributary
as we crossed & maybe we could call back

Prairie or Vermillion but struggle to mouth
what's overgrown. Mumble Spoon & Edwards.

Choke back Red, & what's worrying

the banks of the Rock, the Wabash, the Rush,

all that, always, & then the Middle, the Grand,
the Cedar, & maybe we're in the trees again,

something all this soaking does. That vantage
stays & stays what's rushing; periphery becomes

the only passing, impassable until the rivers meet,
or until delta—that obstacle the river

puts in its own way. & because our bodies
season, because our bodies drought & winter &

now sudden flood, too, we stand long at any window
& what comes into focus is the Blue, the Lost, the Deep,

& you're back, So & So, turned on light in the doorway, mouthing
the Wind, the Root, the Echo, the Current, the river, the river.

RED BEERS IN DUBOIS
BOYD BAUMAN

Rhymes with new noise
of which
in this stoplight-challenged burg
of 150 souls
there was none
save a pack of three dogs
that nipped at one's tires
on all but the most brutal
of August afternoons.

Not at all
on the way
to the Falls City Sale Barn,
Dad would pull the blue pickup
and cattle trailer
onto the grass street side,
saunter into the saloon with his small charge
and order "a red one."

The tomato juice
poured into the beer
would bob and weave
in a mesmerizing DNA dance,
regather as a whole
for a brief second
before succumbing.

Clouds broke
over Dad
in similar fashion
as he hummed along to Porter Wagoner's
"Cold Hard Facts of Life"
thumping through the membrane
of the jukebox.

Farmers materialized
in the doorway flare
in uniform of
OshKosh overalls,
faded seed company caps,

occasionally bearing
the scars of a battle
with the power take off of a tractor,
the belts of a hay baler,
or the auger of a grain elevator,
western shirt sleeve flying
as a flag at half mast
as they gestured towards my father

while I caught a buzz
from these stoic men
animating before my eyes,
through the smoky air
catching glimpses of what
was lost,
sketching outlines
of the whole.

.5 ML
JIM WARNER

A purple and Nyquil colored
bruise began to form like a Oklahoma
thunderhead below the skin, a gradual
developing oil spill, sickly foggy and
green-gilled at edges. The needle
had gone straight through
the vein. It burned, like a single
drop of boiling water leaving an exclamation
mark in the bend of my arm. Both arms
had little punctuations–like a Hemingway
novel was being penned in the blood
they were drawing out of me every three
hours.

It was ten after four, too early
for lab techs to apologize. Most sorry's that
wake you this early aren't worth much
anyway. Most draw slightly more
blood.   Most apologies in bed anticipate
bad weather. I broke my arm when I
was twelve, it always aches before a real good downpour.

THE RIVER
DANE BAHR

AN EXCERPT FROM THE NOVEL *RIGBY SELLERS*

During the late summer of dry years in that valley of Iowa when the rains were unreliable the elm trees and bur oaks hardened and greyed with the dust of passing trucks on the county roads. All the green of the Allamakee Valley was dulled by that dust and a wilted look to everything appeared and the horses and the cows dusted in their pastures moved like ash blowing in a small wind. The little grass near the roads was short and brittle and the weeds rooted in the dry ground turned a dark green and pushed out along the dry earth. The leaves on the trees grew crisp and rattled on their branches in the hot wind. Ants scuttled in thin processions, dark rivulets on the tallow land, and grasshoppers clicked on their inadequate wings and ratcheted their long legs together in the narrow fields of bluestem. Tall clouds grew in the distance each afternoon, hopeful, but dropped their rains over another country, and the tractors crossing their fields drove the dust into the air. The evenings were golden and the settling dust gilded the sky. And the mornings were heralded with dew but the white sun quickly burned that away, and the river sank a little each day into its bed. The frogs huddled in their drying places and cried out wildly into the hot nights. The hardened prints of animals in the dry mud showed where the river had been, and the blanched logs of floods past told where it was going.

There was a saying among these people: A dry year will scare yeh to death, and a wet year will kill yeh. In the wet years when the pale blue of the sky darkened and the big clouds, heavy with rain, came from the south and did not skirt the valley, the country changed. The air grew muggy. The dry county roads became cratered, slowly at first as the new rains came gently, and the coming rain gave a sweet smell. Mothers would come from their houses and call in their children and the men working their fields would pause, hooking their thumbs in their denim overalls or stoving their hands into the hip pockets and face the darkening sky and sniff at the air.

The first rains cleaned the thin film of dust from the trucks and soon there was no dust at all. The county roads became gullied and sloppy with red mud and the trucks forded the slop. The men huddled with their arms crossed in the open bays of their barns and muttered crossly once in awhile as the rain pounded down. During particularly wet years a group might gather at someone's place and in the barn they would set up picnic tables and hold a kind of impromptu social as a talisman to the rain. The women would bring pies and the children would chase each other through the barn, someone might bring a fiddle or a guitar, and a few might even dance, but you could see in the hard faces of the men the worry they carried like religion, and their eyes could not lie. The women would steal careful glances toward their men, sharing their worries, as they served the pies to the children.

Two days of hard rain and the townspeople would watch the river turn brown as it climbed its banks. Three days and the mayor would close the smaller bridges on the outskirts of town and the townspeople would begin to sandbag the south end. Four days of hard rain and the river became a butcher. It would rip at its banks as it swelled and cleave the edges of cropland like a knife to brisket. The rain fell and the river would feed. There was nothing it wouldn't take, trapping pigs and cows and gnawing on timber girders until the bridges collapsed on themselves. Days of that and no ease. Dawn would come but only because the world still turned. But the east would not pale like their prayers had asked for. A dawn rising like dusk, and no sun and no relent, and the children would not run to play in it like they first did; and as the day became dusk the sky would darken and night would fall quickly and still the rain would come and the river butchering.

THICKER THAN WATER
DAVID McGLYNN

My father made an excuse about beating traffic, but I could tell he just wanted to get out of town. My mother wasn't exactly eager to hang around herself. We said goodbye in the parking lot of the Jack in the Box on Bristol, blocks away from the courthouse and on a busy corner where people were almost always waiting at the bus stop. We'd stopped parking in the garage after a man with a crowbar followed my parents to their car. He'd read about my brother in the paper.

"Wainwright said he asked for Chino," I said. "We should know soon."

"The Corrections Department makes the call," my father said, checking his watch. "Not a damn thing Wainwright can do." Brian's lawyer had told me the same thing: the best he could do was put in a request. That morning the judge said he wanted to ensure Brian would never harm another woman for the rest of his life, and ordered consecutive terms, one after the other. The judge added time for false imprisonment and unlawful entry because one of Brian's victims had been under eighteen at the time of the attack. All together, more than ninety years.

"Chino's about as far from home as here," my mother said. "Only about an hour." She glanced over her shoulder at the Jack in the Box. The wind stirred the exhaust of the line of cars slogging through the drive-thru and a brown arm passed white paper bags of food through the window. I could see, through the tinted windows, fleshy people-shaped lumps hunched over their trays.

My father extracted his keys from his pants pocket and held them in his palm as if unsure of their purpose. The hairless circle of skin at the top of his head was spotted with moles. We squinted at each other in the dusty July sunlight, my parents and I, no longer sure of what to talk about now that the trial was over. It's all we'd talked about for the last year and a half. My brother's lawyer told us family support might convince the judge to let the sentences run concurrently, so my parents had continued making the drive from Glendale, even after Brian had been found guilty. I'd juggled my schedule when I needed be in court.

A man was standing at the corner near the Thrifty station. He was watching us, or seemed to be. It was hard to tell. For a few months after Brian was arrested, Colleen and I had reporters follow us around. Some mornings I found strange cars parked on my street or in the lot outside the gym. A few called my office acting like potential clients, asking me about the difference between closed-end and specialty funds, and then, by the way, would I like to make a comment about my brother? My father thought the man who followed them in the garage was a reporter, too, until he saw the jimmy in the guy's hand.

My father unlocked the car and sat down behind the wheel. I opened my mother's door and she dropped into the passenger seat. The engine started up and a gust of chilled air hissed through the vents. "Give Colleen our best." She reached across her shoulder for the belt. "It's too bad we didn't see her."

"Don't blame her," I said.

"I'm not," she said. "I'm only saying we missed her."

"We'll come up to visit," I said. "Or you can come down." My mother pulled the door closed and looked up at me through the window. I felt like I'd been cut off from her, and from my father, too, as though they considered the entire experiment of parenthood a failure and had resigned their positions within it. My father shifted into reverse. He coasted through the parking lot, but then gunned the engine when he hit the street.

*   *   *

I made it to my car before the man, whoever he was, crossed the street. I headed west, toward the ocean. The stock markets had closed at one, so rather than go back to my office, I took my laptop to the Wahoo's in Huntington Beach. I lucked into a spot right in front, and walked down to look at the shore before going inside. The swell had blown out as the wind picked up, but it was still big. A white Lifeguard jeep cruised over the sand, and people were fishing over the pier rail. A quartet of teenage girls in bikini tops zoomed past me on Rollerblades, bouncy as a music video, their colored shorts riding high on their skinny tanned legs. The other men on the sidewalk noticed them glide by. I wasn't the only one.

The Wahoo's lunch rush was over. Only one other table was occupied by a group of dudes in tank tops staring catatonically at the surfing videos on the TV suspended from the ceiling. One of them, a young guy with his sunglasses perched atop his crew cut, dragged his eyes to me as I approached the counter. He regarded me with a cool detachment and went back to the TV. I ordered the Baja Rolls and banged out a few emails. My last email was to Colleen, asking what she thought about dinner. I didn't mention the sentencing. We hadn't talked about Brian since she'd stopped coming to the trial. Brian was a topic she wasn't interested in discussing. I didn't blame her, I really didn't.

Colleen wrote back: "I'm about to step into a meeting, but I'm not in the mood to cook. Want me to pick something up?"

I replied, "How about we go out? Bombón? 6:00?"

"Sounds great," she replied. "It will take our minds off things." I don't know what it was about the word "our" that so filled me with love and want that I considered driving over to her office and pulling her out of the meeting. I fondled the keys in my pocket.

I liked Bombón because it was dark and the booths had tall backs that were hard to see over. I asked for the booth in the corner and ordered a Grey Goose with an olive and sprinkled black pepper over the ice, a trick Brian had taught me. The first time Colleen and I ate at Bombón, when we were engaged, we had to sit on the same side of the booth in order to see each other's faces. It gave me a chance to rub her knee under her skirt, as far as she'd let me go back then. There was still something about the restaurant, the braised chickens spinning on the rotisserie, the heavy wooden slats of the blinds, the candle flickering in the jar in the table's center, that made the space feel erotic.

"We haven't been here in ages," Colleen said when she slid into the seat across from me. It was how normal couples sat in booths, couples that'd been together a long time, though we'd only been married for eighteen months.

Colleen wore a lavender blouse tucked into her skirt, a necklace that was a complicated tangle of silver wire and crystal charms. Her slender cross was buried beneath the wire against her skin. She looked like a lawyer, or else like one of my brother's victims. They all wore smart business jackets, barely a necklace showing in the collars of their blouses, a wall of polished vengeance occupying the row of chairs behind the prosecutor.

"I like this place," I said to Colleen. "I was in the mood."

I gave the waiter my empty tumbler, and asked for two glasses of wine. Colleen craned her neck over the back of the booth and scanned the restaurant. Turning back to me she said, "I checked the *Register*'s website at work. I saw the decision. How'd your parents take it?"

"We were hoping for concurrent."

She leaned forward and her necklace turned prismatic in the candlelight. "I know you were," she said. "But consecutive was the right decision. Those women deserve justice. If I'd been one of his victims, I'd want him to have a decade or two to ponder what he'd done to me. Just me, no one else."

I stared into my wine glass. "I don't like thinking about prison."

"He's sick, Bryce." She sat up, arched her back against the booth, pushing her breasts into to the cone of light. "Criminally sick. Maybe now he can get some help."

I thought of something the judge had said that afternoon: Brian seemed to have two personalities, a split the court couldn't reconcile. Brian had organized the Phi Psi 500 when he was at USC, and had tutored elementary kids in South Central. He still did charity work with the Boys and Girls Club. He had photo albums full of pictures taken with a long succession of former girlfriends, so it's not like he was starved for action. And yet.

The food arrived. Barbecued salmon for Colleen, the leg of lamb for me, pink in the center and smothered in a chunky red chili sauce. Colleen reached across the table for my hand so I could pray. We hardly touched except when we prayed over food, though the less I touched her body, the more I thought about it: her nipples in my mouth, her heels in the backs of my knees. These thoughts tended to sweep in at the worst possible moments. Like, for example, during the victims' testimonies—those awful weeks of crying and blown-up photographs of thighs and necks and breasts distorted by teeth marks and continent-shaped bruises—while Colleen sat weeping beside me with a wad of Kleenex balled up in her hand. I tried to stop myself from thinking this way, but I couldn't. After the third woman testified, Colleen couldn't take any more and stopped coming to court. She didn't even make it to the teenager, by far the worst of the four.

I met Colleen when a guy at work had invited me to check out the singles' group at his church in Costa Mesa, this place called The River. The River sounded more like the name of a radio station than a church, but Orange County has so many big churches—you can't heave an egg out a car window without hitting one—and they all seemed to have names like that. Harvest and Crossroads and New Song. I'd had my share of invitations, and plenty of kooks knocking on my door and leaving pamphlets on my desk. I'd never had much interest in it, but my friend promised that the women at The River were hotter than in any nightclub, so I said okay. Turned out he was right. Colleen had brown hair that she wore pulled back with a headband and eyes that didn't require much in the way of makeup. She told me she ran fifty miles a week and could ski Huevos Grandes at Mammoth as fast as the guys. I asked her for her phone number, but she wouldn't give it to me. She only dated Christians, she said. I told her I'd been raised Methodist, but she laughed and spun away into the big room where people were mingling. I kept going back, and before long I started going to services on Sundays. I volunteered to drive one of the vans for the mission trip to Rosarito. The more Colleen shot me down the more I got involved. I wanted her in a different way than I'd ever wanted anyone before her and I took this difference to be the hallmark of love.

I set my thumb on her wedding ring and bowed my head and gave thanks for the meal. When I opened my eyes, I noticed two suited men at the bar and our waitress staring at us. Colleen turned her shoulder toward the wall. "Maybe we should get a to-go box."

"It's fine," I said. "The food will be cold by the time we get it home. Let's just eat."

"Maybe they think you're Brian," she said. "His face has been everywhere lately."

"They don't," I said. "They know the story. Besides, it's not like walking over there and telling them I'm not Brian, just his brother, would make a difference."

"No," Colleen said, stabbing at her salad. "I suppose it wouldn't."

*   *   *

Colleen backed out first, but waited for me to pull out so she could follow me home. I rolled down the windows as I edged onto PCH, then hit the button to retract the sunroof and turned on the radio. Jackson Browne's "Running on Empty" was playing, and sea air flooded the leather interior, tinted vanilla from the air freshener the detailer had slipped beneath my seat. I turned up MacArthur. The road climbed toward Fashion Island, and beyond it, Irvine, where we lived. The sky over the ocean had gone red. Past Big Newport the wind turned warmer. Colleen's face appeared in the windshield whenever she passed beneath a streetlamp, and then disappeared again, as if in a slow-moving filmstrip. For a moment I forgot I was driving home to the house I shared with my wife on the day my brother was sentenced to nearly a hundred years in prison and imagined I was guiding to my apartment a woman I'd just met, something I'd done only a few times—surreal endings to nights out with Brian in the years between college and meeting Colleen and never once after.

The street lamps cast an orange glow against the white stucco that covered most of the homes in our neighborhood. The crenelated Spanish roofs tiles were as black as a mudslide. My neighbor at the end of the street, a retired guy whose name I'd never bothered to learn, held his garden hose over the cloverdales along his driveway. He looked, in his khaki shorts and canvas slip-ons, like a guy who spent a lot of time watching the news. The water evaporating on the cement gave off a pleasant aroma. I waved as I passed by his house, but he didn't return the courtesy.

Colleen dropped the mail on the counter and stood separating the junk from real stuff. She made two piles: my *Sports Illustrated*, her *Sunset*; my *Forbes*, her *Christianity Today*. Some of the envelopes were addressed to her married name, my name, but most, her cellphone and MasterCard and bank statements, still came addressed to her old name. She was in the process of getting it changed when Brian was arrested, just a month after our wedding, and like everything else, it got backburnered. Sometimes it felt like we hadn't fully cleaved—Colleen's word, not mine—as husband and wife.

An ad circular fluttered to the floor, the pages separating, and Colleen bent to collect them. The hem of her blouse came untucked from her skirt, exposing the skin on her lower back, her underwear a pink crescent rising above the black fabric like a slice of the moon. A current traveled down my chest. I stepped up behind her and wrapped my arms around her waist. I worked my nose through her hair to the skin on the back of her neck. She had a bodily, almost barley-like aroma, a little tang leftover from the barbecue sauce. "Mmmm," I said. "I could eat you up."

I felt Colleen's biceps constrict, like she was about to twist out of my grasp. I let go before she had to. She handed me my magazines. "I'm going upstairs to read," she said. She was already moving toward the staircase. "You want anything?"

"I'm coming up, too," I said. I thought about apologizing, but how could I put into words what I felt guilty about? *I'm sorry, honey, I wanted to fuck you like a stranger on a one-night stand?* It didn't sound right. It sounded a lot worse than not right.

"Take your time," Colleen said. I followed her to the staircase and watched her runner's legs carry her up, the wrinkled tail of her blouse against her hips.

*   *   *

On our first date, Colleen said she needed to be very clear about her boundaries. I was the first non-Christian she'd ever allowed herself to date. She said she'd once dated a guy for an entire year without kissing him. She wasn't opposed to kissing on principle, but she wanted to know for sure it was God's will before it happened. I told her I respected that because I did. She was the opposite of anyone I'd ever dated and I was on entirely unfamiliar ground.

Brian didn't get it when I told him that Colleen and I had gone on six dates and hadn't slept together, and that we wouldn't until we were married. We were down at The Sand Bar, near the Lido marina—a dive with windows full of neon signs and a long mahogany bar that catered mostly to the yacht mechanics and marina staff, bronzed college boys in white shorts and navy golf shirts. It was where we went to talk because the only women in the place were either past sixty or else the Botox-stunned trophy wives of the boat owners. "No sex?" Brian asked. "None at all?"

I felt, I have to admit, a little proud. My relationship with Colleen separated me from him. I was coming into my own, accomplishing something he couldn't.

"What about other stuff?" he asked. "Oral, hand jobs, that sort of thing?"

"We're taking it slow," I said.

"I'll say." Brian tore his napkin into a pile of wet confetti and scraped his bottom lip against his teeth. "Hey, maybe she's a dude underneath. You ever think of that?"

I started to laugh, but stopped and stared him down. He caught the look in my face and put his teeth away. I could feel my loyalties moving in a new direction. I suppose he could, too. "Relax, I was kidding," he said. He paused and picked at the torn napkin. "So. Are you into her religion now?"

"I'm getting there," I said, though I had, in fact, that week prayed to receive Jesus as my Lord and Savior. We were sitting on the sofa at her apartment. Candles were burning and a bottle of wine was open on the table. Colleen had a little yellow booklet with stick-figure diagrams and quotations from the Bible, a prayer at the end inviting Jesus into my heart. "Are you ready?" Colleen asked. I nodded and read the prayer aloud. When I finished, Colleen leaned in and we kissed. At a certain point, Colleen rolled on top of me and pressed her jeans against mine, and started to moan. Did this fall within her boundaries? I didn't want her to stop, so I didn't ask. At the end of the night, she rolled off me and we prayed again, thanking God aloud for saving my soul and for the courage of our convictions. After we said "Amen," we kissed one last time. Then I went home and felt sick for the rest of the night.

"Man," Brian said. "You're a stronger man than I."

I liked that he'd said that. "We just want different things," I said.

I hadn't slept well in a long time but that night was worse than usual. I lay beside Colleen, hot and restless. For a while I played a game with myself in which I tried to guess the time without looking at the clock. I guessed it was 12:15 and when I turned over to look, I was only two minutes off. I'd spent a lot of time looking out the window during the trial, and I'd gotten to where I could tell the time of day by the way the shadows fell over the sidewalk and the small patch of lawn. I don't know where this ability came from, but I wondered if Brian would grow to have it too, if he didn't already. Colleen's breathing was flat and restrained, and a few times I said her name to see if she was awake, but she didn't answer.

I was up before five. Colleen was still asleep with her back to me, her hair a mess on the pillow and her arm poking out of her sleeve. I filled the coffee carafe with water and scooped in the grounds, then dug my running shorts out of the dryer, slipped on my Adidas sandals, and walked outside to get the paper. The sky over the Saddlebacks was starting to lighten. I unrolled the paper on the driveway and looked at it beneath the streetlamp. Brian's picture was on the front page. He stood with his head down, his hands clasped together—as if to hide the body part that had caused him so much trouble. I hadn't seen the pose that way before, but now I did. I was in the picture, too, standing right behind him with my hand on his shoulder, looking into the camera. Brian looked contrite and pitiful, but I had my teeth clenched, like I was a second away from lunging at the camera. At the bottom of the article, it read: "Attempts to contact Brian Moser's family were unsuccessful."

I threw the paper into the trash, but they were on every driveway, each one rubber-banded into a roll like a fresh loaf of bread waiting to be devoured. I threw my neighbor's paper away, too, and then the next house, and without intending to, I'd turned the corner and was no longer picking up papers, I was just walking.

I headed toward North Lake, the lagoon where on weekends families paddled around in canoes and raced remote-controlled boats. Starting a family was the major reason we'd bought in this neighborhood. In the shadows near the houses, water misted over the shrubbery. The temperature had come down ten degrees from the night before and a lot of houses had their windows open. After Brian attacked his third victim, the police had warned residents of Irvine, Costa Mesa, and Newport Beach to shut and lock their windows at night. At the trial, the D.A. held aloft the tiny Swiss Army knife Brian kept on his key chain, the blade as sharp as a scalpel. He'd used it to cut through a window screen.

In an upstairs window, I saw a silhouette taking a shower behind a beveled pane of glass. I couldn't tell whether the body was a man's or a woman's, but it made me hungry again for Colleen. I watched the body turn off the shower knobs and reach for a towel, a dark flag waving in front of the glass. I put my hands in my pockets and kept looking. The window sash slid open about a foot, letting loose a puff of steam and revealing, as if by magic, a woman's soap-shined belly, a gem twinkling inside her navel.

When I was fourteen and Brian was sixteen, we broke into Emilee Helprin's bedroom. Emilee was Brian's first real girlfriend, and even though he never told me so, I'm pretty sure he lost his v-card to her. He called her every night and they talked for hours; he cashed out his savings account to buy her a pair of diamond earrings for her birthday. But the gift was too extravagant for a teenager, and

Emilee freaked out and dumped him. The plan was for us to steal her dresser drawers and leave them on her front step—a *fuck you* to the girl who broke his heart. Brian popped her screen and swung a leg through her open window. I followed behind. When I got inside, Brian covered my mouth with his hand, then turned me around to see the one thing I never expected to find: Emilee asleep in her bed. He'd told me the Helprins were out of town. Emilee slept on her side with her arms beneath the pillow and her feet outside the covers. She wore, I remember, a purple tank top. I could hear her breathing in her sleep. Brian stood over her in the dark, his lip beaded with sweat and a tremor in his chin. He leaned close to her ear and mouthed something I couldn't hear. The look on his face was one I thought about a lot while I sat behind him in court.

Brian motioned for me to go back outside. I crouched behind the juniper and waited for him. A car drove by and its lights flashed right into the black square of Emilee's open window. "Brian," I whispered. "Brian." A moment later he climbed out and we ran for the car, where he fished a pair of Emilee's underpants from his front pocket. They were white cotton and had a faded stain in the isthmus of the crotch. Brian studied them in the dome light. "You think she'll know I was there?" he asked.

"You better hope not," I said. I'd never been more afraid in my life.

"I hope she *does*," he said. "I want her to feel me in the room." He folded Emilee's panties and laid them inside the center console. I never knew what he did with them.

I looked down the street and saw two women running toward me. They wore bright tank tops and reflective belts around their middles and one of the women was holding a cell phone. I stared down at the sidewalk, hangdog and guilty, but I could feel them looking at me, either trying to remember my face or already recognizing it. The police had come to my house more than once after Brian's arrest. My breath caught thinking that I'd arrive home to find them there again, their lights flashing in my driveway, Colleen standing in the doorway, holding her robe closed with her arms. I hopped up to a jog: maybe they'd think I was out for a run, like they were, like all the people who lived in this neighborhood. Just a regular guy out for a run. Though all they had to do was look at my bare feet poking through the toes of my sandals to know better.

*   *   *

Two weeks later, Rick Wainwright called to tell me Brian had been sent to High Desert State Prison, in Susanville, six-hundred miles north and on the east side of the Sierras. Only Pelican Bay was farther away. Wainwright explained that High Desert was a reception center for new inmates and it wasn't clear yet whether Brian would be mainlined there or transferred out. I looked up High Desert on the net. The picture wasn't good: gang violence, racial strife, an inmate stabbed by his cellmate when the guards should have been watching. I worried about what might happen once word got around about why Brian was there. I figured it would take a week or so before he'd be able to call, and when the week was up I thought two was the better guess. When I couldn't take it any more, I called the prison myself. The woman who answered spoke with the same clipped officiousness as the guards at the courthouse. She told me inmates could make but couldn't receive calls. I'd changed my number, and I wasn't sure if Brian knew the new one. Rather than tell the woman this, I thanked her for her help. I was afraid anything I said might somehow affect him—the privileges he received, the protection the guards provided. "This is all still new to me," I said.

"When did the inmate arrive?" I heard a keyboard clicking in the background.

"I'm not sure of the day," I said. "A few weeks ago."

"Oh," she said, and the clicking stopped. "It'll be a while." She sounded slightly gentler, like she understood that anyone who called a prison had already heard his fill of disappointing news. "He's in reception. It takes several months. You'll have to wait."

"I've heard some scary things about the prison," I said. "Are they true?"

"It's prison," she said. Her patience had run out. "It's no place you want to be."

I hung up the phone and sat at my desk, staring at the receiver, my stapler and roll of Scotch tape. Colleen smiled in the chrome frame, her face turned to the side and her wedding veil pinned into her hair. I propped my foot on the edge of the desk, and stared up at the ceiling. The swirl of pinpoint holes in the tiles looked like muscle cells beneath a microscope. My computer monitor sat glowing beyond my toe. Rage waved in like a migraine, a flood of adrenaline that makes men decisive and reckless—the kind of rage that causes soldiers to climb out their foxholes and fire into the dark. I leaned back and kicked the monitor off my desk. An impulse I hadn't expected to act on until I acted on it. I looked down at the cracked screen, like a broken window into a darkened house, and felt something like horror.

I was standing over the monitor, holding my forehead when Jenny, the admin assistant, came rushing in. "I tripped getting up from the desk," I said. I leaned my hand against the mahogany surface. "Tried to catch myself and missed."

I could tell she didn't believe me. She bent to collect the monitor from the floor and her blouse fell open enough for me to see her breasts hammocked inside her bra. I'd been thinking about my brother, but now I was thinking about my wife. "Don't do that," I said.

She lifted her eyes to me. "Are you okay? Do you need something?"

"A different life," I said.

"Tell me about it."

Colleen and I went back to our couples' bible study at Andy and Robin Tully's. The River's website listed them both as Senior Pastor, even though Andy had the office at the church and was the one who preached on Sundays while Robin stayed home full-time. Their son, Dylan, was eight. In addition to the couples' study,

Colleen went to the women's group on Mondays. I hadn't been to the men's group since the trial started, but back when I used to go, I generally enjoyed myself. Some Friday nights the guys played dime and quarter poker or went to a Ducks' game. Before he was diagnosed with leukemia, Ray Magana and I used to mountain bike on Saturdays in Crystal Cove State Park.

The Tullys lived on the other side of Culver, in a coil of newer homes with palm trees and streets with Italian names. Their second floor balcony looked over a foyer and living area as stark and white as an operating room: a white twill couch on travertine marble, a glass coffee table perched on an area rug that looked like polar bear fur. Even the candle in the center of the coffee table was white, nestled down inside a bowl of glass marbles. I don't know how Robin kept it clean. The kitchen passed into a rear den where a poster of Derek Fisher—Andy's favorite because he was outspoken about his faith—suspended in mid-air, the basketball at the end of his outstretched hand, hung over the leather couch. Robin called the den the Man Cave, and the men's bible studies that Andy led met back there. I once joked to Robin that she should call the Man Cave the Bro Hole, and later that night Andy called me at home and quoted from Ephesians and asked me to apologize. Apparently Robin thought Bro Hole was slang for vagina. I apologized, but Robin never stopped being a little standoffish around me. Brian's arrest didn't help.

I handed Robin the dish I'd made: millet patties with quinoa and lemon zest, an unwrinkled sheet of foil tight across the baking dish. I'd found the recipe on a macrobiotic website, the only kind of food Ray was supposed to eat. The pot simmering on the stove smelled god-awful, like bacon turned to vinegar. Leslie Yearling's couscous cake was having a hard time holding its shape; a trail of grains dusted the plate and countertop. Robin set my dish on the counter, lifted the foil and lowered her nose to within an inch of the food. "Yum," she said to me. "You married a good cook."

"Bryce made it," Colleen said. She leaned her back against the counter, next to me. I caught her sweet, baby-powdery smell. "You should try his tiger prawn papardelle."

"Sounds delicious," Robin said.

It was clear the women wanted to talk, so I went to stand beside Ray in the doorway to the Man Cave. Dylan sat cross-legged on the floor playing Mario Kart on the flat screen. Same Mario from years ago, zooming along a beach or through the woods, running down toadstools and turtle shells. It only made sense if you knew the original. "So the guy in the red is Mario, right?" Ray was asking Dylan. As though he'd never played Mario Brothers before. "Who do you like better, Mario or Luigi?" Like anyone likes Luigi.

Ray leaned his weight on an aluminum cane with a big rubber foot, and a few colorless hairs stuck out the bottom of his Dodgers cap. His knuckles were the size of marbles, the back of his hand spotted with red scabs. He was down thirty pounds. "Hey," he said. His gums were swollen and pink.

"Hey."

Dylan's mouth was slack and his thumbs frenetically worked the buttons on the controller. He wore a Chargers T-shirt with lightning bolts on the sleeves. "Uh huh," he said. He steered Mario into a hairpin, made the squealing noise with his mouth. *Urrrr.*

Licorice, the Tully's black lab, looked in from the yard, slobbering against the sliding glass door. Andy stood before the grill, engulfed in white smoke, his Tommy Bahama shirt moving across his body like a flag in the wind. He saw me and used the tongs to lift an orange patty, the size of a hockey puck, from the grill. He waved the burger, or whatever it was, at me. He had a big toothy smile and hair good enough for a politician.

Will Yearling sat on the sofa with his head against the cushions, his eyes closed and his mouth open. His bald skull looked like an egg nested in the cushions. He wore his white shirt with the pilot's epaulets on the shoulders, skinny black tie loose around his neck. "What's with Sleepy?" I asked Ray.

"He just landed," Ray said. "Leslie brought him straight from the airport."

"And they came here?" I slipped into my best bible study voice. "He must have something weighing on his heart."

"Maybe he has a babe in Portland," Ray said.

"A purple rose in Cairo," I added.

"You know what I think?" Ray said. "I think he didn't want to miss the food." We stood together laughing like a couple of punks. Ray was, like me, a late convert; he'd come to The River after meeting Karin. On the Saturdays we mountain biked together we could talk about who we used to be without feeling like either of us was making a confession. The women we'd slept with before we met our wives and the pot we'd smoked in college. Ray had been arrested once, in Tijuana, for taking a leak on the street and had talked the Federales into driving him to an ATM so he could pay them off. He was the only one of the group I think I would have been friends with had my life gone a different way.

Dylan turned around and eyed us over his shoulder, a preacher in the making, then turned back to the game.

Scott McDonough came up behind me and clapped a hand around my shoulder. "Hey bro," he said. He massaged the skin between the bone and my neck. I didn't like it. "I've been praying for you," Scott said. "How you holding up?"

I played normal, like I didn't know what he was talking about. "Good," I said. "How are things with you?"

"I saw your picture in the paper," he said. I stepped away from his hand, into the Cave, and turned around to face him. In the bent sunlight streaming through the slider, Ray looked like a bent stalk of wheat. "I'm glad it's over," I said. Even though that, too, was a lie. At least I got to see Brian at the trial. Now he was in Susanville.

I walked back toward the kitchen where the women were still talking. I had the sense as I entered the room that hard news was being handed out. I could see

Robin's wide concerned eyes and her nodding head along with Leslie Yearling and McKenzie McDonough, Scott's wife. I hadn't seen Ray in a few months. He'd gotten a lot worse.

I looked around the corner for Colleen and saw Karin Magana with the same saddened and sympathetic look on her face. What surprised me, though, was that she and the other women were looking at Colleen, who stood against the counter, where I'd left her, though now her eyes were glassy and puffed. She was crying, shaking her head. The women had their hands on Colleen's arms and shoulders. Their voices were hushed and I couldn't hear everything they were saying, but I heard Robin say, "If you ever need to," and "You can always call us," and I heard Colleen say, "That means a lot to me." Robin glanced up, saw me, and let her arms drop.

"Everything okay?" I asked. I looked at Colleen. "What's the matter?"

"We're fine," Robin said. She stepped into the center of the kitchen, beneath the overhead light, conspicuously between Colleen and me. "We're talking a few things out."

"A few things out?" I asked. I shuffled forward another half step. I wanted Robin to move out of my way. "Honey?"

"It's okay," Colleen said. She tore a paper towel from the roll and dabbed her eyes. "It's nothing. We can talk at home."

"We have something to talk about?" The hairs on the back of my neck stood tall.

"Let's wait until we're home," Colleen said. She held one hand inside the other, near her waist. I stared at the photographs and the jumble of word magnets on the Tully's refrigerator. Among the chaos, I saw the phrases, Man of God and Living waters. "Did those magnets come from the Christian bookstore?" I asked.

"What?" Robin said. She turned to the fridge. Colleen lifted the paper towel to her eyes again. "Oh, yeah. Aren't they great?"

Andy Tully stepped up behind me, a plate of blackened pucks balanced in his palm. He slapped my shoulder. "Let's eat."

After dinner, Andy carried a wooden chair from the dining room and set it down between the couch and loveseat. Karin guided Ray to the chair and helped him to sit. Andy stood with his back to window and puffed his chest out and said, "The Gospel of Luke says that when Jesus was in Capernaum, the people brought to him all who were sick with various diseases, and He laid His hands on each and every one, and healed them. We're here tonight to lay hands on Ray. Ask Jesus to heal him, for He's healed many before."

Karin knelt down and placed her hands on Ray's knees. Andy laid his hand atop Ray's skull. I could see the tendons flex in Andy's wrist, his forearms turning pearly as they disappeared inside his shirtsleeve. A triangle of sweat darkened the pit of his arm. The rest of us shuffled into a circle around Ray. I set my hand on his shoulder and he looked up at me uncomfortably. I squeezed his shoulder, gently.

"*Oh dear Jesus,*" Andy's was saying, "*purge this sickness.*" His voice had dropped an octave and was a tick louder than usual. I felt Ray tense at first and then begin to relax, giving into it, letting it happen. We were his friends and we were praying for him; it was a good thing and I was supposed to be glad to take part in it. But I was having a hard time. Scott McDonough was whispering, "Hmmm," and Robin mumbled, "Yes, yes" every few seconds and I kept seeing Colleen's face in the kitchen, Robin's hands on her shoulders.

The last thing Colleen wanted me to do before we got married was share my faith with my brother. I understood the request as kind of test, even at the time. Colleen said that if I couldn't share the most important thing in my life with the people I loved, how would I have the courage to reach the unsaved of the world? She said I should ask Brian to meet me someplace familiar, a place we both liked, so I suggested The Sand Bar. I gave the bartender my credit card, and scraped the label off my bottle of Miller Lite while I waited for Brian to arrive. Never in my life had I been nervous to talk to my brother. I told myself that saving my brother's soul was important because he was my brother and because it was his soul. When Brian showed up I drew on my cocktail napkin and explained how I'd discovered the love of Jesus Christ. I didn't have my own words, so I used the words I'd learned from The River and from Colleen. I told Brian that knowing Jesus was the best thing that'd ever happened to me. It had changed my outlook on life, and I wanted to share it with him.

Brian listened with a pinched, quizzical look, then leaned back on his stool and slapped the bar. He laughed. "Man, you must want that pussy something fierce."

"You know what?" I said. "Forget it."

"I get it," he said. "She's hot. She's got you whipped. I don't fault you."

"And soon she'll be my wife," I said. I leaned forward, put my finger right in my face. "If you ever disrespect her like that again, I'll knock out your fucking teeth."

"Ooh, tough guy," he said. He was still laughing—we'd always laughed together here—as I moved toward the door. I had to go back the next day for my Visa. Brian had paid for my beer.

Brian called my office a day or two later, but I let the phone go to voicemail. He tried again the next week and this time left me a message saying he wanted to redo our beer; he'd listen to what I had to say and wouldn't pop off this time. I didn't return that call, either. He'd run his mouth too many times. My indignation felt righteous—Colleen, Andy, my men's group all told me it was righteous, Jesus says, "A man's enemies will be the members of his own household," and I wanted Brian to know where he stood. We didn't speak until Thanksgiving. He apologized again and I asked him to be a groomsman in my wedding, even though I'd already asked Ray to be my best man. "Of course," he said. If he felt slighted, he didn't show it. "Anything for my little brother."

In the Tully's living room—praying for a miracle that I had no faith God would grant—I wondered if my salvation had somehow come at Brian's expense. According to the D.A., he'd assaulted his first victim a few weeks after I left him that night at The Sand Bar. He attacked the second woman in mid-November, a week before we saw each other at Thanksgiving. The other two occurred during the months that Colleen and I were sampling wedding cakes and licking the envelopes on the invitations. Brian and I had once hovered around each other like two planets in an elliptical orbit—not good by The River's standards, but certainly less than evil. Perhaps the greater sacrifice would have been to keep going, as I had been, my old self in my old life. I was the one who'd broken away from him. Racing toward Colleen's radical goodness, I'd pitched my brother into darkness.

I shut my eyes and waited for the prayer, like a spell of nausea, to pass. I still had my eyes closed when Andy said "Amen." I listened to the word travel around the circle. I had a lump in my throat and the back of my neck was wet. Colleen touched my hand. "Bryce," she said. "It's over."

*   *   *

On the drive home, Colleen sat beside me with the empty baking dish in her lap. I waited for her to tell me whatever it was she needed to say, but she didn't say a word as I turned through the streets and pulled into the driveway. We stared together at the garage door as it slid open. I inched my way in and shifted into park. Colleen turned to me and said, "Ray's starting hospice care next week. They're bringing in a hospital bed."

I nodded but didn't speak. I sat with the engine running while Colleen got out. She paused between the headlights when she came around the front of the car and looked at me through the windshield. In her lighted face, I saw the obligation and uncertainty that had replaced intimacy. I cut the engine and followed her inside.

In the bedroom, I sat at the foot of the bed while Colleen stood facing the dresser, changing out of her clothes. The sheer strap of her bra stretched across her back, practically the same color as her skin. I watched her bend to open a lower drawer, her spinal ridge rising in her skin. I was still desperate for her affection, even now.

I stood up from the bed and moved into the space between the bed and the dresser, where she stood. Her bra was embroidered with palm trees. Colleen's eyes grew wide and she pulled her arms against her chest. As if there was a chance I'd hit her—though, for a second, I pictured it in all its gory splendor: my knuckles meeting her occipital bone, Colleen crumpling forward and sliding down the doorframe to the floor, whimpering with her face covered. The thought appalled me, but she was no longer someone I recognized, nor was I. I'd become as enigmatic to myself as my brother.

I stepped backward, out of her way. Colleen slipped inside the bathroom and shut the door. I heard the lock quietly click into place. "I'll be right out," she said.

Our life together felt like it had shrunk to this moment, an entire beach's worth of sand compressed into a prismatic lens. I couldn't see past it in either direction. I was afraid of what she'd say when the opened the door, and worse, how I'd react. "I'm going downstairs," I said through the door. "I'm going to watch TV."

*   *   *

I watched the Angels lose, then turned off the set and lay in the dark with my arms folded behind my head. I thought of my brother in his orange pants and V-neck, pacing his narrow cell for the next ninety years. Ray staring up at the dining room chandelier from his hospital bed. I heard the ceiling above me creak, Colleen moving around in bed. I thought to pray, but the only word I could muster was her name. Colleen, Colleen.

A woman's scream woke me up. A high, shrill terror that sounded at once like Colleen and not like her at all. I jumped up from the couch and stood in the dark. Gunshots rang out; car tires squealed; the scream again: "Help me! Please, somebody help me!" A faint blue light filled the stairwell.

Colleen lay with her arm draped over the edge of the mattress. On the television, a woman lay dead in a rain-slicked street. I didn't recognize the movie. I lifted the remote from the bed and turned off the TV. Colleen dragged her fingers to her chin and rolled from her side to her back. Her hair dragged across her face and fell inside her open mouth. She smelled like bacon, like Sunday morning. I slid the hair away from her face, and then stood hovering over her, wondering if this was the last time I'd see her this way. For an instant, I saw my brother standing over Emilee Helprin, wishing she'd wake up and sense his presence in the room. His deranged hope that she'd see his betrayals as a sacrifice, as somehow, impossibly, an act of love.

RADAR GUN
CHUCK RYBAK

J.J. hadn't visited the County Fair in years. An older woman, a friend of his father's named Loretta something, often took J.J. there when he was younger. He planned to make those trips with his father, but after picking him up for the day his father found other things to do—usually involving his motorcycle and a strawberry-haired woman dipped in full-body leather—so Loretta would volunteer to watch J.J. until his dad returned.

Loretta was in her late forties and sipped scotch or beer from a thermos while driving her black Corvette convertible. She'd let J.J. work the stick on the highway, yelling "shift" while stomping on the clutch. J.J., years away from legal driving, would pull hard on the stick with both hands and slam it into place like he had seen Burt Reynolds do in the movies. The car surged and he believed the engine responded directly to his hands, just like video game spaceships when he pressed "thrust." While he managed the shift, Loretta drank from the thermos or rested her hand on his knee.

The Corvette sped down the highway, a black missile, topping eighty, ninety, one hundred because Loretta—as she often yelled to J.J. over the rushing wind—didn't like getting stuck behind trucks. But trucks seemed to be all there were on the road. When speeding by, J.J. would pump his arm and look back, hoping the truck driver would acknowledge him with a ripping horn blast. The truckers rarely obliged. They must have been too high up to see him, or maybe they were jealous of the car and wished they could drive that fast. They should be jealous. He loved the Corvette and wished Loretta would pick him up at his house, just once, so his friends and the people on his block would see him slide into the white leather seat and then whoosh! Gone.

On the Interstate they zoomed past police cars where officers sat reading beneath dome lights, staring at clipboards and filling out forms while their radar guns pointed to the road. Looking down at Loretta's leg, J.J. expected her to relax and ease off the gas, but she never slowed down. She'd just turn to J.J. with her red and graying hair twirling around her ears, and her baggy eyes would sparkle while she laughed. J.J. laughed with her, excited, and he knew then that he was invisible, invisible! This surprised J.J. because he hadn't been invisible just before his father moved out, when the neighbors had called the police during one his parents' screaming fights. The officers had walked in the house and looked around, and one even talked to J.J. for awhile as he stared down at his sneakers. But not in the Corvette—when he rode with Loretta the police never pulled out after them.

*   *   *

Now twenty-one and long licensed, J.J. drove to the fair in the old Buick Electra his mother owned for almost a decade. She "donated" the car to him, his first car, and with duct tape and regular oil changes the old boat managed to hold together. The radio lacked a cassette player, but at least the power windows on the driver's side still worked. The Buick got him through nights of delivering Pepi's pizzas, and when J.J. pulled into the roped-off parking grounds his pockets were stuffed with a night's worth of tips, all singles.

J.J. arrived at dusk for the midway lights, when the world throbbed with life and opportunity. He walked and wedged through hand holders, through boyfriends shouldering the giant stuffed animals they'd won, and carnies calling out like sirens, singing for him to take his chances for a dollar.

A man with a sweatshirt tied around his waist safely landed two softballs in a tilted bushel basket while his wife and daughter cheered. The man loosened up his arms before attempting to land the third ball. As it had for him many times, J.J. knew the ball wouldn't stay, that the two already in the basket would band together and deflect the toss over the rim and into the dirt. In this game there was no safety in numbers. The ball did fall, and the man dug into his pocket for another dollar and another chance.

J.J. threw plastic rings at the tops of Coke bottles. He shot a clown in the mouth with a squirt gun until a blue balloon filled and exploded on its head. Exhausting handfuls of dimes, J.J. tried to center one on the Lucky Strike symbols stamped across a wooden board. Everything glanced, spun too much or too little, rolled off the edge. The missed chances washed over him while he contemplated the physics of success, the required speeds and angles, the tricks that only insiders knew. Maybe this is the night. His car was big enough for at least a hundred prizes, and he could drive home with a full safari, stuffed giraffes and hippos sticking their heads out of the side window and into the wind.

J.J. stopped at the end of the midway near the booth with the radar gun.

No one waited in line or tried their luck. The carnie smiled and didn't call out to anyone, not even J.J. Giant prizes hung above the carnie's head, among them a massive St. Bernard. J.J. didn't have a dog, but he'd always wanted one, especially a St. Bernard. He admired the legend of the dog, how they saved lives, brought comfort to contorted men freezing in the snow. The prize dog looked to be ten feet tall and had a brown, stuffed barrel tied around its neck. That's the one. He would drive home with that dog.

He walked up to the carnie, who stood scratching his rosy face and blond, curly hair, and asked how much for a chance. J.J. knew the game. Throw one ball and the radar gun recorded the speed. On the second throw, if you were within one mile an hour of the previous toss, you won a medium-sized prize, like a stuffed manatee or monkey. But if you hit it exactly, the same speed, you left with a giant prize, the type of prize that required a girl be at your side. The carnie, whose name tag read "Sully" in sloppy black marker, didn't answer J.J. He just pointed at the $1.00 sign. J.J.'s pockets, filled with greasy dollars, certainly held enough to win the St. Bernard, even if it took all night. Sully looked at J.J. with his green eyes and drank deeply from a large plastic cup of beer. "What do you say there? Are you up to it?" Sully belched.

"Sure," J.J. said. "I'm going to win that dog."

"Great," said Sully, looking over his shoulder at the St. Bernard. "Let me show you how easy this all is. You'll have man's best friend in no time."

Sully picked up a baseball and bounced it in his large palm, then from hand to hand, his eyes never leaving J.J. He wound up in a wild, backwards motion and then released the ball underhanded, as if he were playing fast-pitch softball. The ball smacked into a hanging plastic tarp with a squatting catcher drawn on it—the catcher didn't wear a mask and had crossed eyes and buck teeth. The ball hit his glove with a *thwack!* Fifty-one miles per hour.

"That's pretty good," J.J. said.

"Ah, that's nothing," Sully said, taking another swig of beer and grabbing a second baseball. "Here's the tricky, or should I say easy part." He balanced the ball between his thumb and index finger and this time threw overhand, like a fast-ball pitcher. "Thwack!" Fifty-one miles per hour.

"Wow," J.J. said, a hint of sarcasm in his voice. "I bet you can do that all night long, right?"

"Like I said, it's easy."

J.J. gave Sully a dollar and stepped up to the line, baseball in hand. He had played this game before and failed each time. Loretta had once walked the midway with him, stood behind him and watched him throw. One, two, three times J.J. tried to match his first throw, but the speed was always less, off by as much as five miles an hour. J.J. would flush with frustration, feeling that he was shrinking, moving backwards from where he wanted to be. Loretta had kissed J.J. on the cheek from behind and asked if he still wanted to play. She winked when she asked.

Now, strategy was of the essence and J.J. cleared the air from his lungs. Most people reached back and let fly, hoping to impress their girlfriends, or more importantly, believing that the same strength could be reproduced in the next throw. J.J. had learned that it never was. For J.J., an easy motion and repetition was the key, making the same simple throw twice in a row.

J.J. threw and the ball floated easily to the tarp, hitting and dropping with a soft "thud." He and Sully looked at the radar gun. It blinked back double zeroes.

Sully wrinkled his eyes at J.J. and handed him a second ball, saying, "Must of missed the eye there or something."

J.J. focused on the cross-eyed catcher and repeated his motion. Thud. Once again the reading came back double zeroes, blinking red. J.J. looked up into the

St. Bernard's droopy eyes.

Sully squinted, finished off his beer, then walked over to the radar gun that was positioned on a tripod. With his open palm, he gave the gun a good smack on the top and then on the side. He turned it off and on. Sully walked back to the line with a baseball in hand and hitched up his jeans. J.J. admired his determination. Sully's throw sent the ball whipping into the tarp with a sharper, louder "thwack!" Sixty-one miles an hour.

"All right then," he said, clapping his hands. "Now we're in business."

Once more J.J. stepped to the line and threw the ball, even hitching up his jeans for luck, and once more the reading came back: double zeroes.

*   *   *

Since J.J.'s allowance amounted to zero, the best part about going to the fair with Loretta was that she paid for everything; her pockets never emptied. J.J. could blow twenty bucks in fifteen minutes, no effort required. He would leave Loretta chatting in the Oktoberfest tent and tear off down the midway to the waiting games and prizes. He usually returned with nothing to show for his journey, but sometimes he'd come back with a Van Halen mirror or cheap tee-shirt with a decal still cooling from the steam press—he'd gotten one with a sparkling Corvette that had "Wrap your ass in fiberglass" written beneath the tires. Loretta laughed when she saw the shirt and another bill emerged from her pocket. The numeric corner peeked just over the lip of her tight pants pocket. A twenty.

"I'm having trouble with this one," she'd say. "Why don't you reach in there and get it."

J.J. hesitated, then stuck his hand into her warm pocket. Loretta turned her body, laughing, making J.J. reach deeper, down and across the top of her leg. At these moments she'd hold J.J.'s eyes and he would meet her stare. All of the music and singing disappeared and silence floated between them, the world expanding until it got so full it popped like the midway balloons and the beer tent again flooded J.J.'s senses. When J.J. pulled his hand from her pocket, the man across the table turned away. Loretta laughed, blew smoke in his face and ordered another beer, talking to whomever she knew at the table. Grasping the money and speeding off, J.J. just knew he'd return with a mammoth, King-Kong prize. Then he would be satisfied. He wouldn't need any more money and Loretta would marvel at what J.J. had won.

Waffle cones and cotton candy, fried dough and chewy taffy, any time he wanted. After nights at the fair J.J. always slept with a stomach ache, but his appetite ran as deep as Loretta's tight pockets.

*   *   *

"I think it's you," Sully said, pulling a dollar from his pocket to offer J.J. a refund. "I don't think it's the gun. You're just not moving." Sully, still holding the dollar, cracked open another beer which he had stashed behind his counter. He held the silver can in the air, ready to pour its contents into the plastic cup.

J.J. looked up at the St. Bernard. He wouldn't leave until he'd won that dog. He looked forward to stuffing the prize in his car, the effort it would take to make it fit.

"What do you mean I'm not moving?" J.J. said, waving the dollar away. "Look at me. You saw me throw the ball. Did I look like I was moving to you?"

"That's a good point. Maybe we should do a test," Sully said.

"What kind of test?"

Sully walked over to the tripod and the radar gun. He lifted the gun and brought it to the counter.

"Here," Sully said. "I want you to pour this beer into the cup and I'll clock it, clock how fast the beer comes out."

J.J. and Sully huddled over the plastic cup, intent, readying themselves for the midway's newest game.

"Are you ready?" Sully asked. J.J. nodded. "Go!"

J.J. poured the beer into the cup while Sully aimed the radar gun. The cup filled quickly, foaming and overflowing onto the countertop. They peered at the reading. A red "20" blinked back at them.

"This thing definitely works," J.J. said. "Here, give me the gun. I've got an idea."

Sully and J.J. exchanged the radar gun and the beer.

"When I count to three I want you to spin around," J.J. said, "fast, and then we'll see if you're moving or not."

"Good plan," Sully said, setting his beer on the counter.

Sully swiveled and cracked his back while J.J. assumed a firing pose, like he'd seen television policemen do when they shot up a paper criminal at the range. J.J. counted to three and pressed the trigger as Sully spun, wobbled, and caught himself on the counter. Sully breathed heavily, as if he had just sprinted down the midway and back. "Well?" he asked.

J.J. and Sully looked down at the gun. The gun blinked "09." Sully appeared relieved.

"I'm definitely moving," Sully huffed. "Let's try you now."

Sully counted to three and said "go." J.J. spun wildly, surprised a small crowd walking by, and then rushed back to the counter. Double zeroes.

"I've heard about this," Sully said, intently, "about people that don't move. My sister's into all that new age stuff—karma and stars and tarot and what not—and she says that everything in the universe is in motion, that all destinations are fated and waiting, but some things, some people, just don't move."

"Why?" J.J. said.

"You'll need to find a different booth for that," he said. "Maybe you're too heavy. Maybe you're out of gas. Hell, I don't know."

*   *   *

Rather than the Bumper Cars or Hell House, J.J. enjoyed the Skyride, sitting in the giant, covered seat that ran on cables above the fairgrounds, above blinking lights, the midway, swirling rides, lifting higher than even the Ferris Wheel. On the Skyride, you drifted slowly over the fairgrounds and midway barriers, glimpsing the backside of everything: the tanks, hoses, and power trucks that made everything go.

Each chair had room for two, or maybe an adult and two children. Ahead, you could see the dangling feet of the riders, and if they were tall enough, maybe the tops of their heads through the gap between the backrest and the roof. When you looked back—as everyone did at least once along the way—you could see those who sat in the lift behind you, gripping the metal bar across their laps or pointing to the action below them.

Loretta also liked the Skyride and wanted to ride at least once before they left. When J.J. leaned back into his seat so the carnie could lower the safety bar, the flesh of Loretta's arm cushioned his head, extending across the seat behind him. J.J. leaned back into Loretta because he often felt dizzy when the chair and his feet first rose into the air, rocking back and forth before finally settling down.

J.J. had devoured swab after swab of cotton candy, and although he knew his stomach would hurt later, he let Loretta keep sending him back for more. His cheeks were painted with streaks of the candy, red and green, layering over one another to reveal the flavors of each visit. He wanted a napkin and there were none on the Skyride.

"You have candy on your face," Loretta said, leaning close, inspecting the colored, sticky lines of sugar. "You're very messy."

"Sorry," J.J. said. "The cotton candy is really good."

Loretta leaned over J.J. and he kissed someone other than his parents for the first time. Loretta kissed him with her tongue, and J.J. tasted the cigarettes and beer of the tent. Her lips, the tip of her tongue, glided over J.J.'s mouth and breathed the candy back to life, wetting it back into flavor. Eyes open, J.J. felt his legs tingling and his blood rushed. Loretta reached between his legs, beneath his clothes, and soon his body shook, wet and pulsing. The midway rides swirled and trailed light, and J.J. could hear the riders' excited screams. When Loretta put her head down, he focused on the ride directly below, the one with swinging chairs attached to a spinning center by chain links, round and round, faces tilted upward as J.J. floated overhead. The faces were neon, flashing, a flipbook full of smiles.

"You are so sweet," Loretta said when she sat back up.

J.J. looked forward, down at the car ahead of them. A woman's face, still and pale, looked back. When the lift touched back to earth, the woman rushed out of the chair, a little girl clasped by each hand. She never looked back, and Loretta and J.J. walked the midway for another hour or so, invisible and undisturbed, watching fairgoers try their luck.

* * *

"Is this booth rigged? Are you just messing with me?" J.J. asked Sully.

"Messing with you?" he said. "I don't mess around with people for free and all I've got from you so far is one lousy dollar, and I'll probably have to give that back since you haven't really played the game yet."

"Let's try another experiment," J.J. said. "What can we do?"

Sully scratched his curly head. "Back up a little and flap your arms like a bird, up and down, as fast as you can."

"What kind of bird?" J.J. asked, backing up, closer to the flow of traffic moving past the booth.

"What kind of bird? Good question," Sully said. "Something big, something powerful, like a crane. That's it. Imagine you're a crane."

"Okay."

After a moment of stillness, J.J. flapped his arms while Sully pointed the gun at him, squeezing the trigger once, twice, three times. A crowd of teenagers, mostly girls, laughed and pointed. One of the boys, a few years younger than J.J., imitated him, standing behind him and flapping. The girls laughed louder.

"Well?" J.J. asked.

"Still zero," Sully said.

Sully handed J.J. the gun and stood up on the counter, flapping like a bird, flexing his knees and squawking. A crowd gathered, watching the red-faced Sully.

"I'm a hawk," Sully said. He screeched. "I'm a hunting red-tailed hawk."

"Twelve," J.J. said. "You got a reading of twelve."

Sully hopped down from the counter and took the radar gun from J.J. "There must be something we can do to get you moving. You can't just go through life not moving."

"How about I get a head start and run?" J.J. said. "I jog a lot and can really get moving when I need to."

"Perfect," Sully said. "Now you're talking."

"Should I pretend to be anything?" J.J. asked.

"No," Sully said. "Maybe you need to focus. Block everything out. Be yourself."

They stood in front of the booth, and J.J. walked off about fifty yards to give himself a good head start. The gathered crowd, close to fifteen people now, mutely chewed on candy and popcorn and cleared space as J.J. backed up.

"Are you ready?" J.J. yelled back to Sully.

"Alright, kid," he yelled. "Haul ass!"

J.J. took off in a sprint, pumping elbows and arms, lifting his heels to lengthen his stride. He puffed like a train, exhaled with a burst every few seconds until he flashed past the radar gun. The crowd nodded their heads and commented on J.J.'s form. Sully looked down at the gun, then back at J.J., then back down at the gun. "Twenty-five," he said, his voice trailing off.

"Let me see," J.J. said. "You're lying."

Sure enough, red zeroes blinked on the gun.

J.J. looked up to the St. Bernard. Its eyes looked wide with disbelief.

"Sorry," Sully said. "I just wanted to make you feel good."

"It's okay," J.J. said, putting his hand on Sully's shoulder. Sweat dripped from J.J.'s forehead.

"Hey, kid," a man called from the crowd. "How do you know he's not ripping you off?"

*   *   *

J.J.'s mother halted summer visitations once she discovered his father was dumping him off on Loretta. The night on the Skyride was the last time Loretta took J.J. to the fair. His mother continued to fight with his father, saying she thought he was actually with J.J., instead of riding around on his motorcycle with a girlfriend and a new group of friends that a kid just put a damper on.

"J.J.'s only eleven," he heard his mother say. "Why are you leaving him alone?"

"Loretta's forty-eight," his father said. "What are you worried about? He's with an adult. He's not alone and he has a good time."

*   *   *

"You're worried that I'm ripping him off?" Sully said, stepping forward. "I resent the implication. Would you like to be part of the experiment? Would that put your mind at ease?" Sully barked loud, so everyone could hear.

"Sure," the man said, handing the child in his arms to his wife. "What should we do?"

"I don't know," Sully said. All three of them stood in a circle, thinking, looking at the ground. Sully silently sipped his beer, then let the man and J.J. each have a sip until a girl with face piercings called out, "Have them spin around together, holding each other's arms, like a dance."

J.J. and the man looked at each other and nodded. Sully said, "It's worth a try."

The man wore a light green sweater which zipped at the neck. He rolled up his sleeves and flexed his knees, stopping in a slight crouch as if he were someone who knew a martial art. Following his lead, J.J. held out his arms and flexed his knees. It must be the right thing to do. After breathing deeply, J.J. and the tall man tightly gripped each other's forearms and solemnly faced each other.

"Are you ready?" the man said.

"Which way?" J.J. interrupted. "Which way are we going to turn?"

The man thought for a moment, taking a practice step in each direction. "Counterclockwise. Counterclockwise feels better to me."

The pierced girl asked them to pause so she could step behind Sully and see the gun. "We need a witness," she said.

"That's right," Sully yelled, his arm in the air. "We have a witness!"

Sully flashed a thumbs up and J.J. and the tall man flexed their knees once more. The man's wife said, "Be careful, honey, remember your back," but the man shrugged her off, rolled his neck, and started the spin. They turned slowly at first then gained momentum, faster and faster until the force threatened to pull the spinning men apart. From inside the spin, J.J. saw the crowd—at least thirty people now—watching with interest. The faces, as the two spun faster and faster, flashed and interchanged with Sully, the pierced girl, and the gun. They continued to spin and the man and J.J. began laughing. "Hang on, kid!" the man yelled. The sweater and shirt pulled from the man's waistband and his eyes widened, and J.J. saw joy in them as his own shirt ballooned with air and his hair flew across his face.

"Now," J.J. yelled to the Sully, "clock us!" Sully squeezed and held the trigger. The pierced girl peered over his shoulder and called out the numbers, one after the next, "twenty, zero, twenty-one, zero, twenty-two, zero, twenty-three, zero," until J.J. and the man tired, slowing to a stop before one of them could be hurled up and away into the nearby tents.

"This isn't a rip off," the girl said. "The kid's just not moving."

*   *   *

When J.J. and his mother moved again, they were closer to Loretta, and he could drive to her house in minutes if he wanted. He drove by on the way to other places, seeing the light in the upstairs window where he imagined Loretta sat with a drink in her hand, stirring the ice with her narrow fingers.

He hadn't thought about Loretta much until the night he knocked on her door, eighteen years old, the County Fair just a set of flashing lights eclipsed by J.J.'s taller body and broad shoulders. J.J. felt strong, like he inhabited his body and could control its movements, steer it like a fast car.

When Loretta opened the door she didn't blink, acted as if she had seen him just yesterday, and invited him in to sit down and have a drink. Her red hair had gone grayer. J.J. could see the battle being waged with coloring. She wore a pair of checkered pants, black and white, with each square no larger than J.J.'s fingertips.

"How are you, J.J.?" she said.

J.J. didn't answer and looked around the living room at piles of magazines, a dusty T.V., a shiny bar with glasses. "I don't know," J.J. said.

"Do you still like candy?" she asked. "You used to love cotton candy. Your sweet cheeks would get all sticky."

There was a pillow and a blanket on the couch, and J.J. realized that Loretta had slept there, maybe just that afternoon, maybe every night for years.

"Do you still have the Corvette?" J.J. asked.

"Yes," Loretta said. "Would you like to go for a ride?"

When Loretta pulled the Corvette out of the garage it was just as sleek as J.J. remembered. The body, perfect and seamless, didn't have a dent or spot, and the leather interior looked pure white, no tearing or cracking in the sun.

Loretta drove the old route, merging onto the highway. Not once did she reach for the gear shift. She didn't have to call out for shifts—J.J. listened for the engine's sigh when she stepped on the clutch, and then he shifted, looking straight ahead. "I hate trucks," Loretta said as she weaved around them, the engine effortless, "they're dangerous. You never know how long these people have been out on the road."

He saw the "No U-Turn" sign, the idling police cruiser with its parking lights on, the ceiling light shining on the trooper who looked down at a clipboard, scribbling something with a pen. The trooper didn't have to look; a high speed would cause the gun to squeal—the faster the speed the higher the pitch. They blew by and broke the radar's beam. The cry in the trooper's car reached out into the dark. Their speed and pitch was so high that only a trained ear could hear it, could recognize what had come and gone in a flash. J.J. listened to the Corvette outrace that sound until it died the road behind them. The cruiser never moved.

Back in Loretta's living room, she fixed them both a drink and asked him again how he was, how his father was, his mother, and how his first year at college had gone, whether or not he had a job. Off the living room, a short hallway ended at a single door. "What's in that room?" J.J. asked.

"That's my bedroom," she said. "I haven't been in there much. I feel bad, but I guess it's stupid to feel guilty about not being in rooms."

When they went into the bedroom J.J. tore at her clothes, tore to get at her bagging, cracked skin. Loretta just turned her head to the side, closed her eyes, and had her mouth slightly open while J.J. looked down at her and huffed through his clenched teeth.

When he finished, J.J. felt weak, looking away and through the slats of the drawn shade. "You're sweet," Loretta said. "A sweet boy." She licked his cheek as she had on the Skyride, softly, with the tip of her tongue. J.J. could smell candy, and felt that his body was frail, sticky and spent, the faintest trace of what was supposed to be a delight.

He left with nothing to say.

When J.J. finally first kissed a girl his age, a beautiful girl named Emma, he tasted ash in her mouth. When J.J. first slept with a girlfriend, in the back of his Buick, he felt more like a witness, on the Skyride, floating over the car and looking down at her awkward legs and his bare thrusts.

Loretta died three years later from liver failure at age fifty-eight. The fair was in town the day her obituary ran in the paper. J.J. hadn't been to the fair since he was eleven, but hopped in the Buick and drove out to the crowded fairgrounds, to Sully's booth and the radar gun.

*   *   *

The gathered crowd yelled encouragements to J.J., asked to test whether or not they themselves were moving, if their bodies, their chest cavities, contained energy and momentum. They lined up for the new ride, money in hand.

Behind Sully's booth J.J. could see a darkening field and a row of trees, the forest beyond that.

"Just one more time," J.J. said, looking up at the giant St. Bernard. He took the radar gun from Sully. He pointed it directly at his heart and squeezed the trigger. Sully could read the meter from where he stood and looked at the ground. Double zeroes. The pierced girl, again a witness, frowned and toed the ground with her foot. The man who had pin-wheeled with J.J. stood silently with his family, waiting for the line to move forward, waiting for his family to have their turn.

J.J. pointed the radar gun at Sully's chest and squeezed. The meter flashed "07."

"I guess you're moving," J.J. said. "Even standing still, you still rate a seven."

"You have to be moving in this business," Sully said. "That's all we do, town to town and city to city. Maybe it's left over from the trips, momentum, like I'm always slowing down."

"Maybe," J.J. said. "That makes sense."

J.J. pointed the radar gun across the field, at the shadowed tree line visible in the glow of the midway. The gun registered "03," and J.J. said, "Even those trees are moving three miles an hour, and they haven't traveled far at all."

"They could be moving," Sully said. "They move up and down. Branches and roots." They all looked at the trees—J.J., Sully, the crowd behind them.

J.J. handed the radar gun back to Sully and moved to leave.

Sully stopped him by putting a hand on his shoulder. "Hey kid," he said. "Go ahead and take the dog. It's yours." Sully walked to where the St. Bernard hung, lifted it down, and sat its giant body on the counter. It took a moment for the dog to balance. Sitting there, the dog towered over the fairgoers looked over their heads toward some danger in the distance. J.J. knew that if he pointed the radar gun at the St. Bernard it would register. He imagined the dog springing from the counter, dashing off to rescue a child trapped in a stalled funhouse. The gun could sense that. It not only detected motion, but the potential for motion.

"Please," Sully said. "Take it. You earned it."

J.J. shook his head. He couldn't take the prize. He needed it to be the return on one of his dollars, one of the single dollars he'd earned and could run out of if he'd lost enough times.

"Thanks," J.J. said. "I'll try my luck later."

He walked away, the crowd parting for him. He was moving but motionless, and he had raised the stakes for every person waiting at Sully's booth. The clenched dollars might be for amusement, but now there was a hint of fear to draw them in. He heard a woman whisper to the man next to her, "What if I'm not moving?"

J.J. made his way back down the midway toward the Skyride. After the operator lowered the bar, the chair lifted him easily, and J.J. felt none of the nausea he did as a boy. He rose into the sky and looked to the chairs ahead and behind him. He couldn't make out one person, not a shape or silhouette. Even the midway looked empty. The rides still swirled, with their light trails and energy, but J.J. could hear none of the thrilled screams, the chorus of joy. Soon, J.J. was over the end of the midway and Sully's booth. The fairgoers had gathered there, a long line soon growing into an arc and then a circle. Sully stood in the middle of the crowd, taking dollars and handing them to the pierced girl who had become his employee on the spot. Fairgoers ran and flapped. They twirled each other. Back in the group, away from the center, J.J. saw people practicing, dashing, a line of shadows doing jumping jacks. A voice rose up to him, a girl's voice yelling, "I'm moving daddy! I'm moving!"

The chair carried J.J. over the midway's edge and he could now see people gathering in the field, waiting for their turn at the radar gun. In the distance were the trees, the trees that moved while he sat still. He wanted to leap from the chair and run out to them, put his hands on them and hold them. Could he even catch them? The chair began its slow turn back toward the midway and parking lot, and J.J.'s stomach began to ache. He looked out across the lights and rides to the dark, motionless cars, evenly spaced in the makeshift parking lot. The empty space of his car awaited, space that he barely filled when he was driving.

J.J. tried to shrink down in the chair, make himself as small as possible. He couldn't. J.J. had grown and the safety bar pinned him in place.

OURANOPHOBIA
ELLIE ROGERS

Meteors aren't supposed to kill people, or even come close.
If you watch one without sound it looks like something
you might wish for since it's bright and straddles the sky.

A flash can fail a heart. You won't know it's too near unless
you hear it. It might burst eardrums, windowpanes.
A thin cover fends off the rest of the universe, defends

us from cold dark matter, hot stars, unlikely dead
rocks of planets, pieces of which career across.
Only gases compose a layer of safety, torn easily in grief.

Yesterday, I found a whole static skeleton, stacked bones
white as vapor trail, white as light can be. I clacked
calcium together, heard that this deer, when prey, could race

away at a pace that sates fear. Subdued now, its bones still
form a spine, a locking line, not prone, but sideways in moss.
Only the frame remains, carriage of a beast's hot blood and breathing

from birth to death. All that upright body gone, and still
some to go. I used to dream the dead would live in space. We'd
swing wide circles, become a caravan of hooves, irises, momentum,

heat returned, returning. It's hard to hear that meteor made
meteorite, and not think of your own bones someday ceased, desisted
ghosts of no orbit, a likely quiet collapse, the definite settling of dust.

LOUSY BIRDER
MICHAEL LAUCHLAN

I look for goldfinch and warbler
but find birch, sky, stream,
stone, leafmold, mud, and what
snow remains from a bitter season.
Love calls and a woodpecker's drill
mix with not-distant traffic,
with something I meant to do
and a dread I've long dodged—
soup-lines threading alley
by alley, over mountains and
decades. A snatch of talk
intercedes. Sun cooks a stump
on which I've been planted.
A flash of color crosses the sky.

A History of Sacrifice
BRIAN D. MORRISON

A farmer mid-harvest, sun blackening the soybeans with his shadow, dropped one leg knee-deep in a hole. No surprise, his next move, once free, was to fill it. But the fill dirt sank. So he tried covering it. Whatever shape the covering, the hole imbibed it, chugalug. So the farmer called the paper. The paper took pictures, people came to gawk.

One boy, Smartass, the farmer dubbed him, tied a rope to his father and hopped in. An hour of wiggle in the rope, and Smartass was back. Only he came out in the shape of the hole: a rectangle, one corner missing. Doctors were baffled; prayers were made. Some prayed to the hole. Then, the order came to excavate the field.

The hole grew wider, the town, darker. They found nothing, but people realized anything they didn't want to see again—a wobbly rocking chair, stained overalls, Ms. McCready's walker and wicked cat—could be given freely to the hole. The government built a fence, caged the abyss in a structure, which it ate. So people decided to praise the hole solely.

Bob the grocer lugged Ms. McCready to the edge and shoved, said she was a witch, gone to meet her maker. Police arrived. Riots ensued. They were brief. The government built a second structure beside the massive mouth, repaired the fence. The grounds were stocked with armed guards. Sometimes, teenagers who sneak close enough still heave their dispossessions, Smartass's signed likeness, a lit bag of crap. Every time, they expect the hole, its terrible quiet, to throw something back.

MIGRATION
SARAH HOWARD

It was four days after the Bluebirds had missed their last chance to go to a bowl game, and Dad was still wearing his jersey.

Lisa, his girlfriend, had called to tell me. I wasn't exactly surprised. The Bluebirds were our local college football team, and Dad had been a fan his whole life, through the triumphs and the lately-all-too-frequent tragedies. He hadn't even gone to school there, although you'd never know it by how devoted a fan he was. He always watched their games in the rec room in his basement, on the big TV over the fireplace, next to an air hockey table that had been used probably five times in total. When I was a kid, in our old house, Mom and I used to sit on the couch in the living room and watch with him as he yelled from his nearby recliner. These days, he watched alone. Lisa didn't care about sports and I was an hour away at my college, a tiny liberal arts school that theoretically had a football team, although I didn't know anyone who'd ever been to a game.

"I didn't want to worry you until after your tests," Lisa said. "But I thought you should know. He's not eating, not sleeping...just sitting in his chair, staring. I think he's only moved to go to the bathroom." Lisa was OK. Mostly I just felt sorry for her. She'd had to deal with more of his shit than Mom or I ever did. Mom and Dad had divorced when I was twelve. Until college, I saw Dad every other weekend and, more importantly, every other Saturday afternoon for the Bluebirds game. The weeks I hadn't gone over, I'd watched the games on the tiny T.V. in my room at Mom's, then called him after the game to "compare notes," which meant sharing frustrations about the game, often with raised voices. Football was the only thing Dad and I were able to hold conversations about and the only thing we really had in common. The fact that I could discuss strategy with him and wasn't just a "bubble-headed know-nothing," as he said, made him proud. Now, I was the only other fan he had left, and I hadn't been able to come up and watch games with him for years. I'd watched the last game in my apartment while studying for my finals, which had ended yesterday. I'd been planning to drive up to Mom's tomorrow anyway for Christmas break, so an extra night at Dad's trying to get him out of his funk seemed reasonable. As reasonable as thinking someone who's spent four days in the same chair in the same clothes wants visitors, anyway.

I packed my bags, grabbed my coat and got in my car, a beat-up maroon Geo that sputtered in the cold but eventually decided to start. Last week's blizzard had left all the fields and trees and decaying barns along the interstate smothered in white. On the outskirts of town, I stopped at a Sunny Burger drive-through, figuring that would cheer him up. I ordered our usual: a double bacon cheeseburger for him, two orders of fries, and a plain cheeseburger for me. My picky eating and particular dislike of condiments had long been a family joke. Once, when I was eight or so, Dad had picked me up from dance practice with a Sunny Burger bag awaiting me in the passenger seat. When I bit into the cheeseburger and gagged on an onion, ketchup curdling out of the sides of my mouth, he drove back to Sunny Burger in a fury, dragging me in with him.

"I asked for a plain cheeseburger for my daughter," he seethed. "Plain. Just the meat. The cheese. And the bun. None of this bullshit!" He pulled the bun off and held the toppings up to the face of the poor high school kid behind the counter. "Does that look plain to you?"

"N-n-no, sir."

"Better make another one then." I was mortified, but I did get a plain cheeseburger, an extra kid's meal toy, and the pitying looks of every adult in the restaurant.

My dad loved this story and used to tell it all the time, even after the divorce, when he still got out of the house regularly. I didn't like that Mom and Dad had split up, especially when people in town found out and gave me feigned condolences and looks with ten times the pity of that day at Sunny Burger. But I didn't miss Dad's outbursts, the fights he and Mom used to have long into the night, the days where he'd just sit in his chair and stare out the window. After awhile, things seemed to be more normal. Dad met Lisa, and when she moved in, he seemed a lot better, even happy sometimes. Then a couple years ago, the fall of my freshman year, he'd been injured in an accident at the construction site where he was working. The backhoe he was driving had flipped, somehow, and one of his legs had gotten pinned underneath as he'd tried to jump out. He still walked with a limp, even after four surgeries, and had been on disability ever since. Since he couldn't really do much anymore, he became even more immersed in the Bluebirds' weekly fate. All the anger and sadness I remembered from when he lived with Mom and I came back even worse than before. It wasn't just the Bluebirds that had failed him on Saturday. It was, in his mind, everything he had left.

*   *   *

I pulled into the driveway. Dad's house was a tan split-level, like many of the others on his street. All the neighbors' houses had elaborate Christmas light displays with backlit Nativity scenes, inflatable snowglobes, and signs to tune your radio to a certain FM station to hear accompanying music. Among all of this, Dad's house was easy to spot, with only a single row of white icicle lights around the roof, sections blinking off and on erratically, out of sync with each other. He never bothered to take them down, and usually forgot to shut the timer off until the middle of February. Strangely, though, the other defining feature of his house, the giant

Bluebirds flag normally waving by the front door, was missing.

I rang the doorbell and was greeted by Lisa. She sighed, frizzy blonde hair framing her tired brown eyes. "Hi, Meg," she said. "Thanks for coming. I'm really sorry again for bothering you."

"It's OK. I'm glad you called. His moods usually don't last this long." Normally he'd get like this for a few hours, or a day at most. Four days was concerning.

"This is the worst it's been in a long time. Since right after the accident. I don't know why, they've lost before. I know that's rude to say, but it's true."

I nodded. "Where did the flag go?"

"He had me take it down. It's the only thing he's said to me since Saturday. *Take down that fucking flag.* I just don't understand..."

That was what Dad had always said about Lisa in reference to the Bluebirds. "She doesn't understand. Not like we do." She would have been better off than us that way, except the thing about Dad and the Birds is you're either with him or against him, and you need to know what the right thing is to say about them at any given moment. Lisa doesn't watch, so she doesn't know, and that makes it worse for her when he gets this way. She seemed different this time, though, like she was finally fed up with him.

In truth, I was fed up with all of it, too. Since I'd been away at school, I had realized how much more peaceful it was to watch Bluebirds games by myself, and that the world didn't end if I had to occasionally miss one because I was hanging out with friends or doing homework. Mom, the only one of the three of us who had actually been a Bluebird, told me this was progress. Watching sports was fun, she'd said, but there were more important things in life. In contrast, Dad had become more distant, concerned I was abandoning him. Once he called and quizzed me on the numbers of the new freshman class until I'd finally snapped and said, "I don't know and it doesn't matter." He'd been more wary of me since then, and I'd had to work harder to say the right things, to assure him I still cared. Even so, Lisa and I both knew I still had the best shot of talking him out of his daze, especially since this one seemed to be the worst in years.

* * *

I took off my boots and descended the shag-carpeted stairs to the rec room. "Hey, Dad," I announced as I walked up behind him, seeing the top of his bald head peeking up over the recliner, his cane propped against its side. "I thought I'd stop by and bring us some dinner."

I could smell him even before I walked around the recliner. A horrible mixture of stale booze and B.O. No wonder Lisa had stayed upstairs. He was pale and even skinnier than when I'd last seen him on Thanksgiving weekend. "Hey, Dad," I said again, softer.

He looked up at me. He had huge bags under his eyes, but that wasn't the worst part. It was the blankness of them. He seemed lost in another dimension.

At last, he blinked. "Hey, Meg." His voice was scratchy, and he coughed to clear his throat.

"I brought some Sunny Burgers. I thought we could maybe eat and watch TV." I handed him the white paper sack with a winking hamburger bun surrounded by triangles representing the sun's rays. "Double bacon cheeseburger and fries, just like always."

He opened the bag, the smell of grease almost putting an expression on his face. "Good. Thank you." We were up to five words now. He was getting closer to pulling himself back into the real world.

I sat on the couch, unwrapped my burger and positioned my container of fries against my leg. I turned on the TV and he groaned in protest, startling me. "They've been doing nothing but shit-talking our Birds. Especially those fucking Parrot gloats."

The Parrots were from the Bluebirds' rival school, and since the Birds had lost, they had won the conference and made the top bowl game. When I'd been touring colleges in high school, Dad had said to me, "I don't care where you go to school, just as long as you're not a Parrot." The Parrots' school was in the next state over, and so Bluebird fans and Parrot fans were sworn enemies, mostly because they saw in each other what they hated in themselves. They were even both types of birds, although I had to admit I liked the classic blue-and-white Bluebird color scheme much more than the hot mess that was the green-yellow-and-red Parrot color scheme. And although the Bluebird mascot had recently undergone a stupid makeover to look more fierce and intimidating, the Parrot mascot just looked stoned.

"They've moved on, Dad. They weren't even talking about it on the radio on the way over." Instead, the local sports talk duo of Biff and Mad Mike were discussing the local pro basketball team, the Schooners, and their continuing losing streak. Nothing erases a loss like an even worse loser.

Dad grumbled. "It's never over, Meggie. You know that. They'll be holding it over us until next season starts. And even then until we beat them." As if on cue, the local news broadcast cut to commercial with a graphic proclaiming *Season Over: No Trip South For Birds This Winter* under some video of players cleaning out their lockers. They'd probably been waiting all year to use that clever phrase.

I flipped over to the Weather Channel when a thought occurred to me. I got up from the couch and knelt down in front of the cabinet along the wall. I pulled the door open and sure enough, there were all the VHS tapes, untouched from when he'd moved in. A quick glance at the stickers along the tapes and I found the one I was looking for, in Dad's messy, jagged handwriting: *Rose Bowl. Bluebirds Win!*

When I was six, the Bluebirds won the national championship. We all watched it together: me, Dad, Mom. It was nearly fifteen years ago now, but I remembered the moment vividly: Dad's loud victory whoops and fist pumps, how he almost knocked over the bowl of popcorn and beer cans in front of him, how he scooped me up off the couch and carried me around on his shoulders chanting "Go Big Blue." How Mom looked on with tears in her eyes. It was one of the happiest childhood memories I had, before the fights, before the divorce, before Lisa, before the bum leg, before the disability checks, before I was a suspected traitor. Back when it was just the three of us, a real family, like something out of a Christmas commercial. Now, the cozy family holiday moments were as obsolete as the tape I held in my hand. But that didn't mean we couldn't pull them out once in awhile.

"Maybe we should watch this instead." I walked over and handed him the tape. He squinted, and then his eyes lit up.

"What a great day that was. You remember it, don't you?" I nodded. "Sure, why not. Let's pop it in. The VCR's still hooked up, right?"

"Right where you left it." I put in the tape and switched the TV over to the right input. Were we the only people left that had a VCR hooked up to an HDTV? There must have been others like us, others who couldn't give up their memories just yet. I sat back down on the couch and grabbed a fry as the tape began. It was a little fuzzier than the old days, took a little longer to adjust the auto tracking, but soon enough there were the palm trees, the jazzy synth intro music, the red rose logo swooping in.

"Happy New Year, and welcome to sunny Pasadena, California, home of the Rose Bowl!" I'd heard the opening so many times throughout my childhood I'd memorized it. I looked over at Dad. He was still lost in his own dimension, but it was a better one, a pleasant one, one where he wasn't beaten down by life, but where he had conquered it. Where we Bluebirds stood above all, having flapped our wings to the highest of heights.

We watched in silence as the pregame introductions unfolded. The Bluebirds ran out of the beak of a giant inflatable bird, and blue and white fireworks exploded over the stadium to wild cheers as the fight song played. Then the cheerleaders led a chant of "Go Big Blue," thrusting their pom poms determinedly with each word. This felt like home.

I'd never really understood how father-daughter relationships were supposed to be. Every Father's Day, and on his birthday, when I went to look for a card for him, all the "To Dad—From Daughter" cards said stuff like "I'll always be your special princess, Daddy," and "You'll always be the number one man in my life." It felt creepy, like a throwback to when dads traded daughters to husbands for goats. Where were the cards for daughters like me? *Sorry our football team lost again, Dad.*

Dad and I were more alike than I wanted to admit. Sure, I didn't have the rage outbursts and I'd never broken anything in the house. But there were days when I didn't want to do much of anything, either. I'd watched the game on Saturday, textbook sitting unread on my lap. Afterward, I got into bed and stared at the ceiling for hours, not even wanting to call him and deal with it. When it happens I worry I'll end up like him, that it'll only get worse. But I felt OK the next morning, and was able to study and deal with life. When Lisa said he was still in his trance tonight, I breathed a sigh of relief, fucked up as it was. I wasn't bad yet. I wasn't him yet. I was still able to outrun my genetics.

Then again, here were the two of us, watching an old recording of a football game, not saying a word, not needing to. A smile emerged on Dad's face as the ghosts of Bluebirds past floated over him, and I sighed with relief. Maybe there would come a day when even this would stop working, when there would be nothing I could do to help. Maybe Lisa would leave, and taking care of him would have to fall to me, because there was no one else. Maybe, worst of all, someday I would be the one in the recliner, disconnected from reality. But for now, we could be in his dimension together. Things could still be OK.

"I remember saying it would never get better than this," Dad said. "It never really did, did it?"

The crowd cheered the referee's whistle, and my eyes began to sting.

THUNDERSNOW
ERIC BOYD

I know who done it. Them goddamn taters. I walked around the yard and started picking up pieces of the Camaro, wondering if, from above, they'd laid the parts out into some kinda cult symbols or something. I've lived in Fairplains all my life, born there, played high school ball there (and still go see the Trojans every week of the season; they ain't been much of a team in a while, though), and been working up at the meat plant in Ottumwa like my old man did. What I'm saying is, I'm here for the long haul—and no goddamn hippies could change that.

It was '74, I think, when the Maharishi folks—we call 'em 'taters'—moved in. A few years before I bought that beautiful blue car. The old Parsen's college had gone under and they bought the campus; most people in town didn't think too much of it—if anything we were happy the old college wasn't just going to rot away—but in '81, when the Maharishi people built these giant gold domes for their meditation, the town took notice. They're pretty secluded at the school; they got their own shops and everything on-campus, but they're still within walking distance to the town square, and those bastards do come in every weekend, if not every other night, to drink at the bars. The school don't let them drink, and normally I'd feel bad for a kid in that position—hell, I remember going to the Flamingo Lanes back in the day; I'd sit right down at the bar, that old painting of John Wayne hanging right behind me, and I'd buy a Grain Belt right there, no problem—but these hippie kids at the Maharishi school shouldn't even be allowed on the same damn planet as the rest of us.

They're all goofy. I seen a kid unzip his fly down by the lake and take a leak into one of them plastic collapsible cups. Don't you know, sure enough, he drank it. I couldn't help myself, I asked him what the hell he was doing. He said it was a spiritual practice. I don't even remember what the hell else he said about it because I began reeling in my rod to get the hell outta there. They're all like that, too. Maybe they don't all drink pee-pee, but they go around town and start trouble over the dumbest things.

It was a Friday night and I was at the HiddenAway on the square when it happened. I was just finishing up a fish sandwich when some of the students came in—two guys and a girl, and I'll be honest, I couldn't tell them much apart aside from one had long hair; those kids are on strict dress codes, like little peace na-zis—and it wasn't more than two minutes before they began on some shit.

"You don't have organic vodka?" one of the guys said.

"And not grain vodka," the girl hissed. "*No grain.*"

"You hear that," I cut in from the end of the bar, "The tater wants to get schnookered on potato vodka! Ain't that, uh," and I couldn't think of the word.

"*Ironic...*" the other guy finished for me. "That's the word you're looking for. *Irony*, like the fact that you're probably some idiot farmer, yet you're stupider than an ear of corn."

"What'd you say?"

"Irony again," he smiled. "The ear of corn can't hear. Ha." He didn't laugh. He said the word *ha*.

Louis, the bartender, looked at me. "It's alright Henry, leave it be."

To hell with that. I stood up. The guys creeped back pretty fast; the girl started to, but dontcha know they had her stay put so when I walked towards them, they knew I wouldn't swing right away.

"I can't believe I'm actually in a place with townies," the one guy said. He was the taller of the two, I could see that.

"I know, I thought that was just in movies," the other one laughed. They both had little rat eyes. "And look at him. I bet you're the one with that ugly gas-guzzler parked outside."

"That's a 1977 Z28 Camaro you little sonofabitch," I said, closing in. "I've driven that old V8 longer than you been alive, and you say one more thing of it I'll be driving it after you aren't."

"You take a single step more and I'll scream," the girl said with tight lips.

"Government cheese," I laughed. "Who you screamin' to? You're the ones aren't welcome here."

Louis stepped up. "Look kids, I'll serve ya, but I'll serve ya what I got. I got beer and I got whiskey. I can do a little besides, but that's the long and short'a it. You wanna stay? Fine. If not, go."

"We'll leave," the girl said. The guys looked relieved, like they were committed to prove how brave they were if she hadn't let them off the hook. "Jai Guru Diev!" she shouted. I don't know what that is.

They went out and Louis gave me a beer on the house.

*   *   *

The next morning I found the Camaro out on the lawn. It'd been taken apart, piece by piece, and spread out all over, pretty neatly. A part of me couldn't even get angry; I mean of course I was, but it was more confusing than anything else. Almost impressive. How the hell did they do that? I'd been up most of the night watching TV. I can't ever sleep. I even sat on the porch for a while before it got too chilly. Even if they'd had the time to do it, I don't know how they did it was so quiet.

I stormed all the way to that campus and, after getting the runaround by some little secretaries, found the dean. I waited in his office for an hour before he showed up.

"Hello Mister…"

"Campbell," I said. "Henry."

"Mr. Campbell, first off, let me apologize for making you wait. I was in my morning meditations. As soon as I was done my secretary had someone waiting to tell me you were here."

"That's cute and all, but you know why I'm here?"

"Your car, sir. I heard, yes."

"Then you know it was some of your students?"

"Mr. Campbell, I don't need to tell you that you don't, from what I understand, have any real proof of your claim; nor must I inform you that, in every one of the lawsuits this…town…has brought against the Maharishi and the school, we have won."

"Except the murder," I chuckled. The dean, long and thin like an insect, looked shocked. "You let that crazy kid into your school because ain't nobody else enrolled here but crazies. He stabbed one boy—didn't kill that one, though—and you let him in your own goddamn house to 'relax'. Well, maybe it was real relaxing for him when he took a knife outta your kitchen and stabbed some other kid. Better that second time."

"How do you know about any of that?"

"My wife, Laura, she was the nurse working the ER. She tried to revive that boy for over…"

"That issue was settled," the dean said quickly. "Mr. Campbell, whatever complaint you have regarding your car can be taken up with the proper authorities and whatever issues you may have with the school you can take up…elsewhere. At this school we are interested in global issues; things like world peace, things you wouldn't understand. We meditate here, twice a day, and believe me, it's benefitting even you. When we meditate, the good spreads all over town. If something's happened to your car, maybe you weren't allowing that goodness into your Self."

"What in the hell are you even talking about?"

"When we meditate it sends vibrations all over this town. Granted, some people…can't take it. They don't understand the good things happening within them and they fight it…But Mr. Campbell, if that sounds like something you're experiencing. *Don't fight it.* I don't need to tell you that Fairplain's suicide rate is nearly ten times the national average, and that's from people in town…Even some nurses, yes?"

He had no goddamn right to bring up Laura in that way, and how'd he know about that to begin with? I was ready to break his neck but before I could do anything he'd opened the door for me to go, then kneeled down in front of a painting of some bearded guy in a chair. He started praying. Two big security guards were waiting for me, hands bigger than briskets. I walked out, cursed the secretary, and started off. The guards didn't follow. Anyone on the campus that saw me looked away. I passed one of the big gold domes and spit on it. After that everyone that saw me really looked. Hard. One lady wearing Indian clothes tripped over herself when I walked by, then a bunch of students ran over and helped her up. They all started muttering something towards me but I couldn't hear what. I never felt so weird in my life. After that I went home and spent most of the day picking up the pieces of the Camaro.

I saw the three kids again that evening. I went up to the Kum N' Go to buy a pack of Winstons; as I was leaving I saw them sitting outside on the curb around the corner, next to the free air pump, all sharing a 40 ouncer of Mickey's.

"Y'know," I said to the girl, "there's grain in beer. Pretty sure that's all that's in it."

She looked at me as if I'd stabbed her. "Shut up."

"What are you doing at a gas station?" the taller guy asked.

"Yeah," the other one laughed, "because you don't have a car."

"You fuckers! I knew it!" I lunged toward the little bastard but he scurried away from me and I fell on the curb.

All three of them got up and took off. After they were a few yards away the girl threw the bottle towards me, but she didn't have the strength to toss it further than maybe ten feet. I watched them as they ran away and was sorta fascinated at how they were all perfectly in step with each other.

Once I got home I sat on the porch for a while, looking at the last photo of her I had left, the only one I didn't have the heart to throw away. It was a quiet out, barely even a cricket in the night. All I could hear was my holding back sniffles and the creak of the porch when I shifted in my chair. I looked up at the sky. It was cloudy. When I started to look back down at the photo I saw the three kids at the end of the lawn. Once my eyes focused, they weren't there. People have said I ain't been well since it happened, but I don't see things. That much is sure.

I decided to call John up. He's been the sheriff of Fairplains since I was a kid. He knew my old man and was like a second father to me. "John, I need you to do something about these damn taters."

"Henry you know I'd love to, but I was actually gonna come see you tomorrow. That dean gave me a call. What are you doing spitting on their magic domes?"

"Ah hell, are you serious?"

"Oh don't worry," John laughed. "If that weirdo had his way I'd be calling in the SWAT teams and sending you to GitMo or something. He told me that, aside from having to thoroughly clean that *entire building*, they're going to have to bring in some specialist that can take the 'negative energy' you put on the thing, if not the entire campus."

I was silent for almost a minute. I went over to the gun cabinet and took out my rifle. "They're fucked up, John."

"I know it, but what can I do? Every time the taters get pissed off something happens in town but I never have any proof. I heard about the car, but I don't have nothing on that; I've got twenty eyewitnesses on you. You'll get a citation and I'm sorry to have to even do that. I told the dean I could have you give a public apology and clean the spot yourself, but he sounded terrified at the idea of even looking at you."

I put the phone between my shoulder and head, started cleaning the gun. "Oh Christ. So you don't think you can dig anything up on those kids with my car? Don't you have video cameras and everything?"

"Com'on Henry, I got two cameras in the whole town. One pointed over the square we had to put up after someone put a clay weiner on that statue of the old mayor, and then one by the train tracks which don't even work. That's it. Unless they took a piece of the car with them and happened to cut through the square, I got nothing."

"But you can pull footage from around town, right? Like from Wal-Mart or anywhere else?"

"Yeah, sure, but I gotta have a reason."

"How about public intoxication outside the Kum N' Go?"

"I'll see what I can do."

"John," I said, "that dean up there, he mentioned Laura."

"What do you mean?"

"By name he mentioned her. He knew. He said it just to mess with me."

"God," John sighed. "Don't let it get to you. I'm going to pick up the tapes from the gas station right now. We'll talk tomorrow."

I hung up and went back outside; thought about taking the rifle out with me, but I didn't end up seeing anyone or hearing anything the whole rest of the night, not even a dog or a paperboy or a truck. It was like I was in some closed off bubble.

I got maybe two hours of sleep before I went to the station and paid my citation. Then I went ahead and filed a complaint against the girl for throwing the bottle at me. I had to declare that I feared for my life and I could barely keep the giggles back as I wrote that down. John said he probably couldn't do much about the bottle thing, but it'd at least keep the kids on their toes. As I was leaving he gave me a wink and I saw him letting the kids out the holding cell; he told them he didn't want to see them around town and that, if he heard about them drinking in public again, he'd hold them a helluva lot longer than a night. They nodded their heads as John spoke but they stared straight at me the whole time.

*   *   *

That night, I was in the garage, most of the Camaro sectioned into parts. Transmission, electronics, body, etc. It needed fixed, sure, but I couldn't even begin to imagine what putting the thing back together would be like. I finished off a six pack of Busch Light, grabbed another from the fridge, and sat on the porch, rifle in my lap. I was hoping those tater bastards might show up again. I'd give John and that dean all the proof they needed. Maybe three proofs if they all showed up.

I was halfway through the second six pack when I started feeling funny. Not the beers, though. My head got light and my body felt frozen and hot at the same time. It was familiar somehow. Suddenly I saw them. My hand started trembling on my rifle. I couldn't even see how many were out there, they seemed to fade off into the night. They all had their dress-uniforms on like they were going to class. Somebody rang a little bell—the same bell I dreamed I heard the night Laura died—and then somebody said, "Jai Guru Diev" again; they all started muttering. My insides turned in on themselves. It was like thundersnow going through me in the dead of winter, some dark thing. I couldn't explain it. My head bent down and I started gagging so bad that my eyes welled shut. Everything felt like a dream.

I picked up the rifle.

TITLE FIGHT
SAMUEL SAYLER

I've got a gold belt around my waist for the last time. Tonight, I drop it to some kid who sells more T-shirts than me. I've known about it for the better part of a month, but I still got the feeling in my stomach that this isn't right. I'm not ready to lose my title, and the kid ain't ready to win it.

A crowd is already forming outside as I walk into the arena. A few of them reach out to touch me while others throw drinks at me. Some of them are surprised to see me in a suit after so many years of wearing a leather jacket on TV. But if I'm losing my championship, I'm losing it with all the style of a man who earned the title in the first place. I don't think anybody can tell I'm wearing my only tie.

This is the third time in my career I've wrestled in the Archibald Coliseum. The first time, I made a fake Middle Eastern terrorist tap out "under the might of Uncle Sam's everlasting freedom." After the second time, I had to get two of my cervical vertebrae fused together. The third time is set to be my swan song.

Inside the arena, I look for my dressing room. That's one of the benefits of being in the business as long as me. The mid-card guys share a locker room, local guys and jobbers have to change in the hallway, but the star of the show gets some privacy.

"Seems like they keep getting smaller," says Earl Atkins.

Earl and I have been together since I wrestled in the independent territories. We first met outside Kansas City, back when I bleached my hair and painted the American flag on my face. The little bastard manages to sneak up on me every time I enter an arena.

He's looking at the new guys stretching in the hall. Tonight is like a job interview for them. One of them might have a long run with the company, but most of them will never be on TV again.

"How tall is that guy in the yellow trunks?" Earl asks. "He's gotta be five-eight. You might be the only one here over six-two."

"Corporate wants a new look," I tell him. "They're interested in smaller guys with more diverse styles. Figure this'll distance them from the steroid scandals. Don't think anyone's concerned about their mic work, though."

One of the arena's employees walks up to me and says, "Your room's down this way, Mr. Powers."

"Thanks," I say. He thinks Powers is my real name. Dumbass.

The room has three bottles of water in a tub of half-melted ice. Next to the water is a bowl of candy. Most wrestlers frown upon eating anything with flavor, but this is something I picked up from outside the business.

"There's blue candy," I say.

I can practically hear Earl roll his eyes from across the room before he asks, "So?"

"It's in my contract that I have a bowl of Marko Mints with all the blue ones removed."

Earl sighs. "We've been through this game countless times, with candy and without. Do you think it makes any difference?"

"If they didn't take out the blue candy, what else didn't they do?"

Earl lies on the couch, picks up the bowl, untucks his shirt, and loosens his tie. He's developed more of a belly since I met him, which I now realize I've helped him do.

"Lance," he says, "this is *Clash of Champions*. It's the biggest event for the World Wrestling Coalition this year. Did it ever cross your mind that you might have blue candy in your bowl because everyone else is too preoccupied trying to make sure the ring doesn't collapse in the middle of a match or the pyrotechnics don't burn the building down?"

I kick his feet off the couch and sit next to him. I hate it when he calls me Lance. Earl's been a groomsman at my last two weddings and knows more about me than anyone else backstage, but he still sees me as my character.

"You think you've known me long enough to call me Howard?" I ask.

"I think I've known you long enough to call you whatever the fuck I want."

I humor him with a faint chuckle and rest my right leg on the coffee table, careful not to tweak anything before the match.

"How you feelin'?" Earl asks.

"I'll make it through the night."

Part of the reason I'm losing the championship is because I've ruined my knee over the years. Aside from neck surgery, I haven't had any injuries that have required time off, but the knee doesn't have much cartilage left in it, and I'm starting to hear my bones grind against each other. Tomorrow, I leave for some fancy hospital on the east coast for surgery. By the time I'm healed, my contract with WWC will have expired.

"I've been talking to some of the guys in creative," Earl says. "I don't think they'll be done with you after tonight."

"There's nothing left for me here."

"Don't be stupid. Your in-ring career is over. Either you stay here and become a commentator, maybe even a road agent, or you can kill yourself making nickels back in the independents."

Earl doesn't see the problem. I'm a wrestler, and somewhere along the line, WWC stopped being a wrestling company. When I watched it as a kid, WWC was imaginative, creative. Most importantly, it was fun. They had characters, guys straight out of comic books. They were superheroes. Titans.

Now, I'm just a guy in a leather jacket. The kid getting my belt is just someone with a baseball cap tilted to the side. I thought I could be an advocate to return to the old ways, but I'm an artifact. Archaic.

"Remember when I won my first championship from the Minotaur?" I ask. "Whatever happened to that guy?"

"He's still with us," says Earl, eating all of the blue mints. "He just has less hair on his head and more on his back. And he lost the mask."

"Nobody wears masks anymore."

Earl never knows what to do when I get in a mood. When I was recovering from neck surgery and didn't know if I'd ever walk again, he showed me a documentary about crippled guys who climbed mountains and competed in marathons. I told him to fuck off and didn't talk to him for a month.

Earl speaks up. "Do you have the match figured out?"

I shake my head. "I like to improvise."

"Is that it, or are you so pissy that you won't even talk to Jason?"

I close my eyes for a second and take a breath. This isn't a conversation I want to have. "The kid botches every other one of his matches and can't sell a move. If we plan anything, it'll just go to shit. Better if we play it by ear."

"Some might say that failing to prepare is preparing to fail."

I shoot him a look. He isn't helping.

"No?" Earl says. "'Best laid plans,' then." He stands up and walks to the door. "You know, Howie, Jason Jaxx has to win the strap tonight, but you don't have to make it easy for him. Teach him how it's done. If he gives you any trouble, stiff him. Lay his ass out."

"Stiff's for guys who don't know how to do it right," I say.

Earl smirks. "Maybe you're forgetting how to do it in your old age." He opens the door, but before he leaves, he says, "Don't forget, you have a signing in an hour. They want you in costume."

Tonight, my costume consists of a studded leather jacket, boots, aviator sunglasses, knee pads, a knee brace, tights, and athletic tape around my wrists. There's a bottle of baby oil sitting on the table. When WWC first signed me, everyone was covered in this stuff, thinking it made them shiny or something. I never quite understood it, but I apply a modest coat for old times' sake.

The tights hanging in my dressing room are black with blue lightning running down the legs and "POWERS" printed across the ass. Creative has told me to wear these since I won the championship three months ago. Earl always told me that tights are tights and it doesn't matter what they look like as long as I can wrestle in them, but they won't cut it tonight.

In my bag is a pair of tights I had commissioned from a designer in Chicago. They're meant to resemble the original pair I sewed myself when I was working my way up the indies: a pink base (nobody wore pink, and I wanted to stand out) and "POWERS" in yellow down the legs. Earl framed the original blood-stained pair (I can't remember whose blood) for my last birthday. I keep it under my bed.

In the main lobby, the signing goes about as expected. Kids tend to stay away from the heels, so I mainly get adults in my line. They bring their over-priced memorabilia for me to sign, and some of them ask to take pictures of me pretending to punch them. Most of the fans realize it's a show and just tell me to have a good match, but a few marks come through the line and tell me there's no way I can beat Jaxx, and one lists the factors as to why, including how real men don't wear pink tights. They don't see the smoke and mirrors, and part of me admires their innocence.

A teenage fan holding a VHS tape of *Clash of Champions 2001* comes to the table. I think I recognize him from other signings and shows. There was a kid who looked like him and always had his mom with him when he asked me to sign his T-shirts and action figure boxes, but this is the first time I've seen him solo.

He hands me the tape and says hi.

"I haven't seen one of these in years," I say. "Where'd you find it?"

He must've come to at least four of my signings, but he's still nervous around me. He says, "My dad found it when he was going through old stuff for a garage sale." He can't quite look me in the eye. "He asked if I wanted it. I said yes, but I don't have a VCR, so I had to watch it at grandma's place. You had a great match. You and Rodney Rollins won the tag-team titles from the Pride."

"Let's hope I do that good tonight."

"You haven't worn pink tights since you signed to WWC."

I'm impressed with how much this kid knows about me. Most fans his age don't remember what happened on our show a month ago. I say, "I felt like a throwback tonight. Special occasion and all that. It's just something fun for the people who remember the old days."

"I liked your gimmick on the tape, back when you and Rollins were jocks who beat scrawny jobbers and called them nerds, but then lost to a couple midget wrestlers after the Pride interfered. That's still my favorite angle."

I'm supposed to keep it kayfabe with the fans—don't acknowledge the theatrics—but this kid isn't making it easy. "Email the guys in charge. If there's enough support, maybe we can bring Rollins back for a reunion match next year."

"Aren't you leaving?"

Shit.

"All the wrestling blogs are saying this is your last match with WWC."

Nobody's supposed to know about this. I've only told Earl and a few of the backstage guys. The plan was to let WWC forget all about me and I'd slide back into independent wrestling.

"I hope not," the kid says. "There aren't any other heels like you, and WWC doesn't know what to do with any of their faces."

The line's getting annoyed. I shouldn't have let the kid stay this long. Before anyone has to move the kid away, I ask, "You want a poster? Super fan discount. What's your name?"

"Carl."

"Spell it for me."

"C-A-R-L."

"Not like Marx?"

"No."

"One more time."

"Carl, C-A-R-L."

I sign his poster and tell him thanks for dropping by and enjoy the show. As he walks away, I see him laugh when he reads my inscription: Thanks, nerd.–LP.

Before the show starts, I have to pre-tape an interview. Marlene has been the backstage personality for a few years. She wanted to be an actress or a dancer, but could only get work with us. She made a low-budget slasher movie called *Don't Look Back 4* before signing with us. It's godawful, but you get to see her boobs.

I always feel stupid waiting backstage in my tights while the crew sets up the camera and lighting. The only thing worse is the redundancy of the interview. Half the time, someone shows a clip of me getting beat up and asks what I'm gonna do about it. The other half, someone shows a clip of me beating someone up and asking why I did it and what I'm gonna do. It's the worst part of my job. This is my *Groundhog Day*.

Before it's my turn, Marlene tapes a segment with Francesca, one of the few female wrestlers hired for her in-ring ability instead of her looks. Her interview is similar to mine, except slightly more sexist.

Francesca says, "After I get my hands on Princess, Marlene, no man in the Archibald Coliseum will want her!"

Marlene says, "Strong words from a strong woman," or some other statement that doesn't mean anything.

Promos have never been my specialty. As soon as I start talking, I realize that the only thing sillier than pretending to fight a man is a theatrical monologue about pretending to fight a man. Marlene is the first interviewer to figure this out about me, so she tries to carry the conversation and get me out of there pronto.

"Did they give you a script?" she asks.

"I skimmed it," I say. "Something about ripping Jaxx limb from limb, his mother won't recognize him, maybe some stuff about what it means to be a champion. It ain't Hemingway."

We shoot four takes because I never know what to do with my hands. Marlene tells me to hold the belt with one and point to the camera for emphasis with the other. I try to keep my demeanor calm and cool, be the guy you're not sure you should be scared of because you don't know what he's gonna do.

When we're done, I walk back to my dressing room. There's a TV so I can watch the show. This is supposed to be our biggest night of the year, and we're filling the card with kids who are barely out of developmental. This isn't storytelling–it's stunt work. The wrestlers don't sell the moves and are back up before the audience can tell what's happened. I lose track of how many times anyone kicks out of a finisher.

The worst part of *Clash* every year is the celebrity match. Business-wise, it's a good theory. We bring in someone from outside professional wrestling—usually a football player—to attract a new demographic. In reality, it's insulting. It tells us that corporate has no faith in its employees to carry the show and make the money back from the production—let alone make a profit.

This year has some former heavyweight boxer in the ring with "Brutal Byron" Buchanan. The boxer does a decent job for someone who's only had a few weeks of training, but he's got no showmanship and doesn't know how to get over with the crowd. Buchanan's a veteran of the ring, and he sells the match as best he can, but nothing has any impact. Tomorrow, the boxer goes back to his own world, and everyone will forget about the match within a month.

There's a 10-man tag-team match featuring the tag champs and the Midwest champion not defending their titles. The match lasts three minutes in order to make room for a surprise performance from a '90s rock band that I almost remember. I want to strangle whoever booked this show.

While Francesca is wrestling Princess in the only match tonight that deserves my attention, Earl knocks on my door.

"Time for the main event," he says.

Earl leads me to the stage entrance just as Francesca is heading to our dressing room. I tell her she did nice work, and she thanks me. When she's out of sight, Earl stumbles into another conversation.

"They're playing the recap promo," he says.

"I know how it works," I say. "Been through it a few times."

"Then you come out. Do something to get heat from the crowd. I dunno, maybe flip 'em off. Then Jason comes out, everybody loves him, and you attack after the bell rings, but while he's not looking."

"The champion goes out last. That's a rule."

Earl waits a second before changing the subject.

"Corporate wants to talk to you after the match," he says.

"Not much to talk about."

"I'm sure you'll find something worthy of flapping your gums," he says. "Williams tore a muscle in his leg, so I've gotta go help plan a new angle for the tag champions. Good luck out there."

"Thanks." I give him a smile for old times.

"Don't fuck up your knee."

My match is supposed to last a half hour, but the recap goes on forever, and I'm not sure if we'll have enough time for the match. I watch the recap on a producer's screen and can't remember doing half the stuff I see. If I can't remember this angle, what makes anyone think the fans will?

"Anything I should know before we go out there?"

I turn to see Jason Jaxx in his sideways baseball cap and ugly orange dragon shirt with the sleeves ripped off.

"Yeah," I say, "my right knee's been giving me trouble."

"I'll be sure to use plenty of rest holds," Jaxx says. "Fans love the excitement of a rear chin lock."

I turn back to the screen to see myself hitting Jaxx over and over with a steel chair. That part I remember.

"I guess a bum knee's sort of a badge of honor in this business," he says.

"No," I say. "It's not."

Despite his best efforts, Jaxx is failing to get on my good side, to get my blessing as the new champion. He doesn't realize that my opinion means jack shit. After the match, I could grab a mic and shoot on him, tell the crowd how WWC is going to hell or spout off some work about how I couldn't have lost the title to a better contender, but none of that would mean anything. Jaxx's fans will still love him, and the fans who complain about WWC will still watch it.

"Do you have any advice," Jaxx says, "for after the match?"

I think for a second about everything I could say to him. Everything Earl tells me to write in a journal to get it out of my system. I could go through a list of all the guys who had the title and inspired me to win it.

"This is a championship belt," I say. "Don't sling it over your shoulder like some *putz*. Strap it around your waist."

He nods as the recap finishes.

There's nothing but silence.

My music hits.

Showtime.

At the Last Farm Lands They Haven't Converted into Golf Courses,
KAITLIN DYER

a boy died at the end
of the street.
He was riding his bike at 5am
but no one stopped until 7.

I sat in traffic for an hour that day,
trying to get off the road. I kept staring at this one deer.
He dug and dug his hoof into the soil,

tearing beans up and gnashing
them in his molars.   The newspaper said
they couldn't find

the car
who hit the boy.

They failed to mention the earth
under his nails and the beans in his mouth

TEAM MOM
MICHAEL HILL

She used to take us to see the Twins
at the old Met Stadium, long torn down now,
home plate buried somewhere beneath
the Godzilla-like footprint of the Mall of America, where I imagine
lots more moms probably take their kids today.
But back in those pre-Metrodomian times, my mom
would load my brother and me up in her long, low-slung Ford wagon
and sail off down I-94, and then I-494, toward Bloomington,
where the Minnesota Twins hosted their opponents out in the open air.
One year she even got us there on opening day,
only to have our repair shop loaner die on us in the parking lot.
I don't recall how much of the game we saw or missed,
but I do remember being marooned out in the middle
of that endless, pot-holed sea of asphalt,
no cell phones for another twenty years, walled in
by more cars than I could begin to count,
and looking up at my mom, secure in the knowing
that, however it all panned out, she would find a way
to get us where we needed to be.

KINNICKINNIC
MICHAEL HILL

Standing thigh-deep in the Kinnickinnic River,
I lean forward, watching the drift
of my dry fly so intently
that I can see clear back to my childhood
and the pages of my dad's old *Fishing Facts*
magazines, splashed as they were
with the same sorts of tableaus
as the one I now find myself occupying.
Back then I was bent on untangling the mysteries of trout streams,
this one in particular, and had no inkling
of all the other existential snarls
that would soon enough divert my course.
Tonight though, with the early June twilight
silhouetting the leafy crowns of oaks and elms
and the hungry trout boiling the surface
in the mad frenzy of the Sulphur hatch,
I am filled with a sense of arrival. And the river,
right here where I left it, welcomes me
without reservation, offering up
eager tugs and dazzling aerial displays.
Yesterday my son caught his first trout,
a gorgeously-mottled twelve-inch Brook,
on a different fork of this same river.
It was also his first fish taken on a fly rod,
and the smile it brought to his face is what I expect to find
when I lift my landing net from the dark water
and get a look at the joy wriggling inside.

GETTING TO KNOW THE KENNEDYS
KEITH TAYLOR

It was the thing to do, so I volunteered to work for the Eugene McCarthy campaign in South Bend, Indiana. I worked out of a small office on Mishawaka Avenue in River Park. Either the McCarthy campaign in Indiana was poorly organized and they forgot about my office, or they decided they were unlikely to get very many votes in my blue collar neighborhood. Once they gave me a key, I never saw any one else from the campaign. Occasionally I would find a box of new campaign literature sitting outside the door, but that was my only contact with the larger political world. No one from the neighborhood ever came in. Once I called up the city headquarters in downtown South Bend and volunteered to stuff mailboxes with the campaign pamphlets that were gathering dust in my little office, but they told me I should never go out on the street.

There was a coffee pot in the back room. I learned to make coffee, and then I learned to drink it. And in that back room I learned to smoke. I would sit on the unopened boxes of campaign brochures, drinking coffee and taking deep drags on my Taryton ("I'd rather fight than switch"), until my stomach churned and my head was swirling. I felt very lonely and very old.

Most of us who worked for McCarthy were bitter when Robert Kennedy joined the race. We felt he had waited until our man proved that hatred of the war made Johnson vulnerable, and then Kennedy decided to come in on McCarthy's right. Despite our bitterness, everyone understood that Kennedy would probably win, and we became quietly wistful.

Kennedy came through South Bend once during the primary campaign. I joined the thousands of people who packed Notre Dame's Athletic and Convocation Center to hear him. My corduroy jacket was covered with pins: No War, Clean for Gene, the stylized Picasso dove, and the chicken-foot peace sign. I thought I might have some kind of confrontation with the Kennedy supporters, but they ignored me. I don't remember anything the Senator said. There was lots of laughter. And wild cheering. He never mentioned McCarthy.

Even while I was feeling bitter about Kennedy's appeal, I was laughing and cheering like everyone else. When he finished, I pushed back through the crowd, ran across the parking lot, and stood by the only road his motorcade could take. No one else was there. After half an hour or so, I could see the cars moving slowly through the crowd in front of the Athletic and Convocation Center. A couple of police cars led a white convertible. Held tightly by their security people, Bobby and

Ethel sat on the back of it, shaking hands with the young people who ran behind.

When they drove past me, I wanted to be part of it all, too. I ran as fast as I could. Everyone who had been following was out of breath, and I was suddenly alone with the Kennedys. I reached up and shook hands with Ethel, then Bobby. They were windblown, just like in their photographs, but they looked very tired. Their smiles were forced, almost unreal. Bobby's eyes were glazed. In this quick moment while I ran behind him, I thought he looked uncomfortable. Or maybe he looked sad. At the time I thought he looked like that because a kid covered in peace buttons was chasing him down a Midwestern street. I realized later that he hadn't really noticed.

"Good luck, Senator," I called out. He nodded and his staff pulled him into the car. They quickly accelerated and left me behind.

THE DEVIL'S DAUGHTER
LESLIE PIETRZYK

1981

My roommate arrived first, staking her claim. Probably someone told her do it that way, her *cum laude* mother or Ivy League dad or an older sibling or cousin in college. I had no one telling me anything. So I didn't know I should take the overnight bus to Chicago from Iowa instead of the one arriving late in the afternoon, meaning that I unlocked the dorm room door to see a fluffy comforter with bright poppies already arranged on the bed along the wall with the window, cracked open and grabbing the only breeze. Several dozen white plastic hangers holding blazers and skirts and blouses filled the closet with the door where F.U. wasn't gouged into the wood.

I rubbed my fingers along the grooves of those letters, imagining a deeply angry freshman girl digging a nail file from the clutter of her purse, carving those letters into the wood while at the library her roommate wrote a smart paper about Jane Austen or blew her boyfriend in a car parked by the lake or spray-painted acorns lustrous gold for table centerpieces at a sorority mother-daughter tea. I hoped my roommate wouldn't be that angry girl.

Also, I hoped I wouldn't be.

I admired the precise lettering—straight, even; a challenge creating perfect lines in the cheap veneer—and then slid open this closet door to find a handful of flimsy, misshapen wire hangers. I trailed my fingers along them, once, twice, noting their musical jingle, and then hung up my skirts, blouses, and blazer (singular). These items filled about a foot of space, even including my parka for winter. I bunched the rest of my clothes—T-shirts, underwear, jeans, socks—into two of my four dresser drawers, organizing furtively, as if I didn't want to be caught taking them from my duffel and trunk. Then I stared into my roommate's open closet, counting, adding up the pieces, trying to do the math to determine the algebraic equation that would tell me how many combinations of outfits were possible with ten blouses and nine blazers and sixteen skirts and three dresses and a handful of scarves and—

The doorknob jiggled and I had only enough time to slide her closet shut and grab my plastic-wrapped, Kmart blue-light special, markdown sheet-set before the door popped open and a girl with bright, turquoise eyes wedged her head sideways through the doorway and said, "Got any masking tape I could borrow?"

Her eyes were the color of things I'd seen in *National Geographic*: lakes, oceans, seas, vast skies stretching above plains and pampas, veldts and savannahs and deserts. Later, I learned they were colored contact lenses, which, for a long time, made me believe Jess saw the world in a bluish haze. "I'm Jess, next door, from Oak Lawn, comm studies major." She pushed the door wider, angling herself into the center of the frame.

I didn't want her to leave, so about her request for tape, I said, "Hang on, maybe," and I rooted in the chaos of crap at the bottom of my trunk, pretending I might logically expect to find a roll of masking tape when no one had told me that I should bring such a thing to college. Of course, apparently no one had told her either.

"Did you meet your roommate yet?" she asked me.

I shook my head. "Just her stuff, all of it," and I swept one arm in a wide semi-circle encompassing the glossy stereo system on the cinderblock and plank book-case and plastic milk crates filled with records and her half of the school-issued bulletin board tacked with photos of perky girls with waves of dark feathered hair, so many girls and so much hair that I couldn't tell if each was a different girl or if I was seeing the same one in a funhouse of mirrors, over and over, the same girl, my new roommate. Dangling off a plastic thumbtack was a strand of pearls like the pearls I owned, but I was guessing hers were real, unlike mine, which weren't.

"She's from Fort Lauderdale," Jess said. "Voice major. Already planning to pledge Theta, she told me, because she heard from someone it's the best house on campus. But so sorry to say there's no way they'll take her because she's Jewish."

I leaned back on my heels, abandoning the fake search for the imaginary roll of masking tape. It was a whirl of information, language foreign to me—not the words, but how it was put together, and also the whole. A sorority wouldn't want a Jewish girl? A girl with nine blazers and sixteen skirts? With three rows of wool sweaters stacked six or seven each? A girl so cavalier with pearls that she draped them over a thumbtack? I wouldn't be that casual with my fakes, which my moth-er and I picked out for my birthday at the jewelry counter at Younkers depart-ment store. They were thirty-percent off, but the saleslady acted like they were full-price, nestling them into a white box between two pillowy squares of cotton. I kept them still in that same box. There were maybe four or five Jewish kids in my whole high school, and no one treated them any differently. Though it suddenly occurred to me that if I wasn't one of them, how could I know?

"Not that I told her that," Jess continued. "But some guy at the comm stud-ies welcome this morning gave me the rundown. Probably I heard wrong." She slipped the rest of the way through the door and bounced onto my roommate's bed, puckering the red poppies. I recognized the stitching along the leg seams of her jeans: Calvin Kleins, crisp like how Brooke Shields wore them, and on top, a man's white dress shirt with the cuffs rolled higher than anyone would roll sleeves, up to the middle of her top arm muscle. The sleeves looked strange that way, but also purposeful, and I felt I was the one in the wrong for not understanding that purpose, which was a different wrong than the tightness I felt seeing my roommate's stacks of sweaters. Those sweaters spiked my gut with jabs of anxiety: I would never have enough, even if I could buy out a whole store, an entire mall. The sleeves, though, maybe I could learn—if I paid attention. If I paid attention, my sleeves could be interesting and purposeful.

Jess was looking straight at me with those inhumanly blue eyes, maybe following the exact path of my thoughts. I was hunched in front of my trunk, also from Kmart. It wasn't exactly made of cardboard, but it wasn't real suitcase material, leather or even plastic. A little like cardboard, but definitely reinforced, with two pull-tab metal latches and a lock that had bent both of the dinky keys that came Scotch-taped to the trunk's inside. It was a heavy and ridiculous piece of luggage, but I had liked an Agatha Christie book where characters traveled with steamer trunks on a train, and this wasn't that, but it felt close. If it wasn't this Kmart trunk, it would have been musty vinyl suitcases from a neighbor's garage sale. My mother said the trunk was practical because I could double it as a coffee table, putting things on it, "a TV or record player," she had suggested, without suggesting where those things might appear from. But the trunk wasn't practical to haul around. After my father left me at the bus station, a long-haired man with a lisp helped me heave it into the luggage hold in the belly of the bus. In Chicago, a man wearing a snowy white Navy uniform took one side handle while I grabbed the other, and we walked lopsided down the street to the El train, and together we lugged the trunk up the stairs and he pointed me to the correct side of the platform. But when I got off in Evanston, people streamed around me, unwilling to be drawn into my problem, so I dragged the trunk myself by one handle, pretending not to hear the screeching and bumping and clanging beating the metal stairs. I dragged it eight blocks on the sidewalk, to registration, including getting lost and trudging two blocks I didn't have to. When I found the registration line, some of the dads helping their daughters jumped in, and my arms ached enough that I let them, despite their daughters' eyes needling me, petulant, pouting for me to find my own father instead of hogging up theirs. Now, the trunk was a scraped-up, practically-shredded, banged-apart mess, barely a functional trunk, let alone a "table" where my roommate might stack her silvery-sleek stereo components. Much of the fake brass trim lining the edges of the trunk was bent and mangled, including a good six-inch prong forking up off the bottom seam. I'd already gouged my calf against it once, enough to bleed.

Jess shifted her weight, and the bed ground out a wrenching groan, like elephants getting strangled, a sure sign that my roommate hadn't actually sat on this bed before claiming it. Jess bounced again and again, making the bed screech, a tiny smile jiggling her face as if she knew exactly what I was thinking. I was wary of smiling back. I had no idea why she rolled up her sleeves the way she did or how her eyes were that dramatic blue; there were many things I didn't know, so many I couldn't even say for sure what they all were. I should not have come to this school, lugging a cardboard trunk behind me—yes, time to admit it was made of cardboard, time to admit I was a Beverly Hillbilly, not even a Joad.

I fingered the dangling metal strip then tenderly stroked my thumb along its razor edge, wincing at each jag. As she watched, I tugged, peeling the metal inch-by-inch off the trunk, the slow ratchet making me think of a dentist drilling deep, drilling to somewhere painful that would end up hurting real bad.

Jess laughed. Like the tinkly keys of a piano. "That's the most pathetic piece of luggage I've ever seen. It looks like it went through hell. Where'd you come from, anyways?"

"Hell," I said. "You got it. I'm the Devil's daughter, and he sent me to college here."

With one last tug and a hard twist, I worked the piece of metal the rest of the way off and so there it was, overflowing the palm of my hand. I looked at the horrible, twisted, meaningless scrap. What was I supposed to do with it? The garbage can was—yes—on my roommate's side, by her desk. I drew in a breath, a deep, calculated breath. I was here, wasn't I? And hadn't I gotten myself here, no thanks to anyone else? The Devil's daughter would know when to take a chance.

So. "I want to pledge Theta, too," I ventured. Trying out the new, unfamiliar word was like sliding chocolate on my tongue, that same lingering melt, that craving. "Since I'm not Jewish, I figure I've got a shot, right?"

Jess laughed again. "They'll love you, Devil's daughter," she said. "Because I love you already."

We were joking—both of us laughing, not meaning anything mean—but we shouldn't have been, because anti-Semitism was wrong-wrong-wrong, a sin, and those discriminatory Theta girls were evil—we knew that—and since neither of us was Jewish it was especially wrong to laugh even this tiny bit, even at evil Theta girls—and a week later, when my roommate actually was cut by Theta after a single round of sorority rush—suspiciously the only sorority of seventeen to do so during three weeks of rush, to cut her and her pearls and her sixteen skirts—and she flopped sobbing across her screechy bed, with Jess and me tag-teaming on how Theta was stupid, that she was too good for those stuck-up bitches—reciting every platitude she wanted and needed to hear because we all three of us knew that those platitudes kept us from the truth none of us could bear to speak—that's when I felt most terrible for those jokes with Jess. It didn't matter that my roommate and I already deeply despised each other, that I'd decided upfront to stay with her for the whole year anyway, partly because it was easy enough to avoid the room, easier than paperwork and chancing someone else's unwanted roommate, but mostly, really, truly I was afraid that calling attention to myself meant they would snatch away the financial aid. And Jess lived next door, after all.

That was later. What was right now, my guilty laughter with Jess and that awful hunk of metal heavy in my hand, the mangled trunk and my cheap Kmart sheets still shrink-wrapped in the package, were those words: *Because I love you already*. She had spoken them easily and simply, like tossing a beanbag to a child, so she couldn't have recognized what I did: that they were the words I longed most to hear. That it really wasn't so terribly hard to say them. It wasn't. That this was news to me was the real news to me.

So: Where *had* I come from?

THE PRETTIEST ONE
DENNIS VANVICK

My parents and I had just arrived at our new stucco house in Minneapolis when there was a knock at the door. I hustled down from upstairs. A small woman—gypsy dark and dangerously thin—stood on our stoop on the other side of the screen door wearing dark colors way too warm for a muggy Labor Day afternoon. There was nothing physically imposing about her. Even at thirteen I was bigger than she, but there was something strange about her eyes.

She'd wasted no time getting to our door. Our new, black 1961 Mercury that Mother insisted we needed to "make a good impression right off the bat with the neighbors" was still going through its clicking and clacking cool-down at the curb.

"Is your mother home young man?" she asked. The pupils of her black eyes seemed to have bled into the irises and obliterated them, leaving no discernible difference between the two, just blackness.

"Yes," my mother answered as she approached the entryway. "You must be my acting coach, Madam Romanov."

The Madam interpreted Mother's acknowledgement as an invitation and opened the screen door and stepped into the foyer.

"And you must be Estelle," the Madam's thin lips gave up an Indian corn smile. She spoke with an accent that I hadn't noticed earlier and extended a bony hand in a manner hinting at royal lineage.

"Yes. I was expecting you tomorrow, Madam, but I'm glad you're here," Mother said. "We have a lot to talk about. The unpacking can wait."

Well, not for all of us. Pops and I unpacked the boxes delivered by the moving company while Madam Romanov and Mother spent the remainder of the daylight setting the schedule for classes—four afternoons a week—and discussing acting. Over time things would've worked out a hell of a lot better for our family if I'd simply slammed that door.

This move to Minneapolis from Stanley, North Dakota was a tribute to Mother's doggedness in pursuing her all-abiding theatrical ambitions. After years of hectoring, Pops finally agreed to sell the house and hardware store in Stanley and purchase the same in Minneapolis. Mother preferred The Big Apple and The Great White Way, but settled for the lesser sophistication of Minneapolis and The Tyrone Guthrie Theater.

*   *   *

She bought my allegiance by convincing me that an eventual shot with the Minnesota Twins awaited me in Minneapolis. True, I had to leave my friends in Stanley, but she whispered conspiratorial assurances—out of Pops' earshot—that the big leagues were within easy reach. Mother would be a famous actress and I would be the best pitcher in baseball. Pops would be able to retire and get out of the hardware business which, incidentally, was his passion. The big Mercury zipped us by the coulees and waving wheat fields of North Dakota toward our new life in Minneapolis. I left a lot behind; cherry Cokes at the counter of Schmidt's Drugstore, skinny-dipping in the quarry outside of town and Becky Anderson—whom I never mustered the courage to talk to—and of course my friends. I lost all that and in return I gained some of the resilience that would be tested later.

I spent most of the trip in the back seat of the new-smelling car, reading movie magazines stuffed into a cardboard box, the last item Mother chucked into the backseat before we headed eastward on Highway 2. Underneath the magazines, near the bottom, lay her 1948 high school year book, touting her as the school's "Prettiest", which I imagine was easy for her especially as a member of a graduating class of twenty-seven. Listed below her picture were the other credentials that showed how assiduously Stanley High School prepared her for life on the outside. She'd been in the drama club, on the cheerleading squad, and won the lead in the school play. No mention of scholastic honors. Under "What's In Your Future" she unleashed an ambition to act on Broadway and shop at Saks Fifth Avenue.

When I wasn't reading I was listening to Pops and Mother chatting in the front seat or Mother singing what must have been the entire songbook of Rodgers and Hammerstein. Pops and I preferred Johnny Cash or Patsy Cline.

The only time she was quiet was when she was engrossed in primping with that ever present faux pearl compact, or working a pocket comb through her peroxide-blond hair, or patting blush onto her sharply angled cheekbones. She was as self-absorbed and unselfconscious as a preening bird or a cat licking its fur. When she finally touched up the last bit of eye liner, there was always a special moment where she tilted her head to that singular angle and the mirror became more of a portal into her glittering future than a reflection of her reality. From the portal, judging from her enraptured expression, she could feel the coolness of the Hollywood's sidewalk cement in her hands, or maybe hear the applause as she strutted the red carpet of the Academy Awards.

There was little primping for Pops. He'd shower, shave, and dab Brylcreem on his sparse comb-over in less than ten minutes. No dilly dallying, no drama, there were cartons to unpack and hardware to sell, ranging from lawn mowers and snowblowers, to penny nails and packets of seeds.

In Minneapolis, Mother spent more money to maintain a higher life style, forcing Pops—now in a bigger city with tougher competitors—to work longer hours, including evenings. I had tougher competitors too, with more curve on their curveballs and more blaze on their fastballs. My baseball dreams were soon torched. A neighborhood friend got me interested in tennis, faster moving and more suited to my athletic skill set and temperament. Plus, fewer boys signed up, so an athletic letter was almost assured.

Pops' evening work hours left Mother with time and wine glasses to fill and she often invited Madam to stay after their afternoon classes and they chatted, smoked, and drank wine for hours at the kitchen table. Madam–a widow, no family–was always available.

At suppertime, I'd often slip in to the kitchen to fix myself one of my two dinner entrees–a peanut butter sandwich or Kraft's macaroni and cheese. Mother was animated and gushing but my presence had the opposite effect on the Madam who fell into a silent and motionless funk; even letting her cigarette sit unattended in the ashtray and burn a long ash while she waited for me to finish my food preparation. There was no movement, even her head was stationary–yet those obsidian eyes tracked my every movement around the kitchen. When I finally exited with my food they immediately returned to their conversations, stale as yesterday's cigarette smoke. Madam was happy to let Mother direct the conversation as long as the wine flowed.

Madam listened with the same rapt expression, nodding rhythmically–brass cigarette holder dangling from her lips–whether Mother was talking about show business or celebrities or repeating her struggle to abandon the "one-horse" town of Stanley. Mother shared how lack of funds forced her to abandon plans for drama school and the bright lights of The Great White Way to marry my father, "the only eligible man left in town" she always appended, as a means of an explanation. I would find out later that there was a glaring omission in her self-serving history of Stanley.

"I'd just broken up with Gaylord," she'd say, "son of the town doctor, who left for school out east–Columbia University of The Ivy League, in New York City."

She said "doctor's son" and "The Ivy League" in a reverential tone, carefully enunciated. The timeframe she was mired in was the autumn following her high school graduation. All the other eligible young men had blown town, even the non-medical progeny of the town fathers, even the ones not headed for the Ivy League. Pops, five years older than Mother, waited patiently in the wings and in the hardware store, which had been in the family since North Dakota had been a territory. He became the sole proprietor after a tornado killed his parents by plucking up their car from the highway and flinging it into a wheat field. After the accident, Pops bought out his older brother Charlie, an attorney in Philadelphia who didn't want anything to do with the nuts and bolts of the hardware business.

Mother recounted their betrothal like a business deal, "Henry proposed to me almost immediately. I made him promise that we would sell the hardware store and move to a big city. He also agreed that the big city must have a reputable theater and that I could take acting classes. I needed to spend time in the theater scene. After all, I gave up my acting, my passion."

Long before we left Stanley Mother managed to find a one line ad in the Minneapolis Star and Tribune, available at Schmidt's on Sunday mornings, and telephoned Madam Romanov. Mother didn't bother to get references.

Madam always arrived by bus and didn't have an office, so Mother's acting classes took place in our living room. I was always forced to meet Madam at the bus stop and escort her the three blocks to our house. Mother's idea was to protect her from any malfeasants who might prey on the little woman, but truth was I always felt the opposite; more like I was protecting the populace of south Minneapolis from the wiry Madam. Part of it was appearance, the dark clothing and always the cape—god knows why she wore it—and a persistent feeling, so far unfounded, that there was something sinister about her. I always slipped my jackknife into my pants pocket before leaving the house. When she stepped off the bus, Madam fired up a Lucky Strike already inserted in a cigarette holder clamped between her Indian Corn teeth. We'd head out after a curt greeting and I'd walk a step behind which she probably viewed as respect. In reality I felt more comfortable when I could see what she was up to. If I was lucky I was upwind from her odor—a wicked blend of cigarette smoke and sweat, topped off with a cloying perfume which failed miserably at masking the other two.

When Madam stayed after class to join Mother for wine in the kitchen, her accent became even more extravagant—as outlandish as the scarves wrapped around her skeletal head. Her accent flitted around the globe like an over-nectared hummingbird or, more visually accurate, a drunken raptor. She dropped names like a Hollywood tour guide; the revered Brando made frequent appearances, as did Joanne Woodward and James Dean, to whom Madam purportedly gave acting lessons. "Too bad he died," she said, Madam could have arranged a lunch with him if Mother ever found herself in Beverly Hills. Yeah, sure.

The two of them usually emerged from the overheated rhetoric of the kitchen, around nine o'clock—about a half hour before Pops got home from the hardware store—faces flushed to the hue of hot house tomatoes.

Following months of acting classes and Madam's Big Apple rates—plus a sky-rocketing wine bill which Pops equated to that of a small Italian restaurant—my parents began a long running argument. When I was in my room, some of their hot air would often rise up the stairs...

"Did you get a résumé from her?...I'm not going to ask Madam for a résumé... she's legit... she doesn't like personal questions... focused on her art...C'mon Estelle, face it, Madam's a fraud. She's a cartoon character for crissakes...That accent alone should be enough to get her arrested...And when in the hell are you going to actually do some acting?"

At the end of these arguments, the basement door usually slammed shut, signaling Pops had surrendered and was heading to his workshop—his haven—to make gadgets and bird houses to sell at the store.

*   *   *

It was 1962 when Mother—after a year of acting classes—actually wrangled an au-

dition with a community production of *Cat on a Hot Tin Roof*. Intense prepara-
tions began as soon as the ink dried on the application form for the audition;
smoke billowed, wine flowed, and classes with the Madam increased to six per
week.

The audition was held at the community center in the late afternoon of an August day. Mother's hair and nails were done in the morning and after lunch there
was some last minute cramming in the kitchen. There was also a clinking of wine
glasses. Madam was the only invited guest for the audition. I attended simply
because I had a tennis match at another school and I needed the ride that Mother
would provide after the audition.

Mother didn't want me in the actual audition, "You'll just make me more nervous," she said, so I waited in the hallway leading into the auditorium.

My teenage patience had the shelf life of fresh fish and after about twenty
minutes I used my jackknife to pry open one of the side doors just a tiny bit.
Madam—a whiter shade of pale than usual—if that was possible—was seated center
stage in the fourth row, her terror-stricken face tilted up to the stage in the aspect
of someone in the street waiting for a jumper to step off the ledge of a high building; she didn't want to watch, yet was unable to force herself to look away from
the impending disaster.

I couldn't see Mother when her quavering voice began the reading. Her supposed southern accent sounded more like one of the Madam's—origin unknown;
a strange amalgam of sounds, slightly slurred and bearing no relationship to any
dialect found in North America. Maybe from a southern region of Russia, but certainly nothing heard south of the Mason-Dixon line.

The next afternoon Mother rehashed the audition at the kitchen table with
Madam.

"They offered me a non-speaking role? With my elocution, my range, they
want me mute? Can you imagine, Madam?"

Madam never missed her cue, "No, Estelle, that's outrageous."

"I would've been perfect as the lead. You've perfected my dialogue. Frankly, I
refused the role because it was an insult to my talent."

The Cuban missile crisis dominated the news in 1962, but to Mother it was
just vague threats by silly politicians. Her casting emergency was concrete and
all-consuming. There were desperate, wine-slurred calls to Madam. Tears fell.
Madam smelled opportunity and money, maybe even a little wine. Her rates sky-
rocketed. Mother needed "advanced classes" and she needed money to pay for
them. I remember well the summer evening she tried to get it.

I had just biked home from my first tennis tournament, eager to brag to Pops
about making it to the semifinals, even though at fourteen I was one of the young-
est competitors. He and Mother were at the dining room table. Their tense faces
warned me to keep my exploits quiet until later. I headed to my room, noisily
ascending and quietly descending to sit on a step and eavesdrop behind the door...

"No can do, Estelle. In four years the boy will need money for college and by

God he will have it," Pops said, with new authority.

"What about student loans?"

"I am not saddling our son with loans in order to give a better living to the Madam."

"Now Henry, we've discussed this many times. You know this is my life's work, my passion."

"If you're so passionate about acting, you shoulda taken that role they offered you. I'll bet even Brando started as an understudy."

Mother didn't reply.

"Estelle, we need money for the future. Are you going to die an early death or what?"

"But Henry..."

"No buts, Estelle, its over."

And it was.

There had been an unheralded, yet tectonic shift in household power. King Henry took the throne in a bloodless coup, unless you count the death of Mother's dream to act on Broadway. No more acting classes. Even wine would be budgeted. Long live the king.

After considerable griping, Mother finally surrendered, stating one more request to seal the deal, "Can I have just one more class with Madam to wrap things up and talk about what can be done to learn acting without a teacher?" Pops granted the request.

The next night the Madam showed up and I listened on the other side of the kitchen door. Wine and emotions poured forth unrestrained. Mother whined and moaned and cried to the Madam. Acting was not mentioned. When Mother's voice dropped a level, I put my ear closer to the door and heard something that I might have done better without.

"I never should've married Henry, but I missed my period right before Gaylord left for school. He claimed he wasn't the father. What choice did I have? I mean, Stanley wasn't a good place to be an unwed mother . . ."

The hoarse voice of the Madam interrupted, "Pregnant? Does Henry know he's not the father?"

"Heavens, no." Mother replied. "He'd leave me. So far he hasn't noticed Andy's resemblance to Gaylord and I pray he never will."

I spun away from the door and headed directly to my room where I closed the door and fell on the bed to cry quietly into my pillow. The resilience that took root when we left Stanley—and carefully tended to by my father since our arrival in Minneapolis—was still alive and well and intact. I didn't cry much. There would be no rage, no acting out. Of course I was angry with my mother, but I felt sure that she wouldn't be talking to anyone about Gaylord again and I buried my anger in a thick-walled vault.

The trauma was short-lived. When my mother finally called me to escort the Madam to the bus stop for the final time, I rolled over to my back, eyes dry. On the way out of my room I grabbed my pocket knife from the dresser. Somehow it was always reassuring to have it when I walked the old crone to the bus stop. Not to protect her, mind you.

We walked in our usual silence, neither of us caring enough about the other to even mention the weather–an almost mandatory civility in Minnesota. We passed Eldridge's Grocery and Jenny Lind Middle School to arrive at the corner of the park, across the street from the corner where she would catch her bus. The blood-red sun was deserting our part of the earth, fading below the line of houses on the other side of the park.

I wanted to tell her to keep her mouth shut about my parentage. I wanted to threaten her, to maintain her silence, but she spoke first, making a simple declarative statement, "You have influence over your father."

Yes, undeniable. She finally recognized my value. I was an only child after all, which sometimes grants the anointed considerable sway with both parents. I made no reply, waiting to find out where she was heading.

"You can convince him that your mother needs my acting classes, that I'm good for her, that maybe she can make money through acting."

Ah, sweet revenge. She finally needed me for something.

"Me convince Pops?" I said, trying to sound innocent in the dusky light. "Isn't that your job, Madam Romanov?"

She looked at me surprised at my impertinence for a millisecond before her expression hardened as she realized that the fourteen year old in front of her didn't really have a card to play in this game.

Her nose appeared almost beak-like now, perhaps because the wind off the flat park ruffled her cape in the manner of a buzzard's wings as it settles comfortably onto a carcass.

"You wouldn't want your father to know anything about your family complications would you?" She rasped out this *coup de grâce* with no trace of an accent. "You know, about Gaylord."

I said nothing.

"Well?" she said. "I know you're aware of your parentage. I saw the shadow of your feet at the bottom of the door." She made it sound as if eavesdropping was a capital offense.

Again, I stayed silent. The Madam said, "You're a disgusting rat-faced little shit."

Finally, something I expected her to say, something unfiltered as the Lucky Strike she lit up. Her apparently native accent seemed familiar to me, maybe New York City. The Bronx? A Mafia movie?

I grasped the knife in my pocket, turning it over until my thumb nail clicked into the notch used to pull out the blade. It was reassuring, yet I knew it wouldn't be used. I couldn't do that.

We paused at the curb before we started crossing the street to her bus stop. A bus was approaching the corner from our left and slowed to pick us up, the driver evidently thinking we wanted his bus, not aware that we were going to cross. I waved him on and he gunned the engine. I turned to find Madam stepping out into the street. I think I reached to stop her. She screeched as she fell. A low fluttering and snapping sound came from under the bus as it rushed over her.

Could I have prevented the Madam's death? No one will ever know the answer to that question—not even me.

After weeks of what I now realize was Mother's severe depression, a metamorphosis was triggered. She took to wrapping wild scarves around her head, took to using a cigarette holder, and even took to calling everyone "dahling." Even her jewelry changed. She suddenly preferred huge, dangling, connected hoops, in the style of the Madam. Gone were Woolworth's fake pearls. She even lost weight.

I made the mistake of asking her about her perplexing transformation, "Are you trying to be like Madam Romanov, or what?"

She answered with a stony stare, a chilling reincarnation of the absent Madam. I never broached the subject again. Pops and I endured Mother's idiosyncrasies. Public outings were embarrassing, especially for a teenager simply trying to blend in. The reasons behind her transmutation escaped me and not until much later did I understand the reasons behind it.

Strange, how we can't truly understand our parents until we are adults. Only by viewing them in the rear view mirror can we see them outside the role of parent and discover who they really were. I eventually realized that Mother was trading her dreams of becoming an actress, for a dream to be a doyenne of the arts in south Minneapolis.

Dreams still required funds and she petitioned King Henry for two items in order to pursue her new passion—a season ticket for the Guthrie Theater and yearly trips to New York City. Her requests were granted. Pops went to one Shakespeare play at the Guthrie and the next door neighbor filled his seat for the rest of the season.

Before Pops wrested control of our stucco castle, their disagreements were open, noisy. There was yelling and that basement door slamming, yet the problems themselves seemed transparent and somewhat understandable and eventually resolved. Now the discontent sunk below the surface, rumbling like a volcano, threatening to spew forth. In Mother's mind the villainous King Henry was blocking her path to the stage and fame and fortune.

I've been a bit tough on Mother. I loved both of them, though in different ways. I loved Mother because, well, because you have to love your mother. My love of Pops was a different case. I loved him even if he wasn't my biological father. I felt no connection to Gaylord, my bio-dad, and no urge to see him or contact him and no compunction to confront my mother. To me Gaylord was an almost-anonymous sperm donor and I wanted to maintain the distance at all costs. The truth served no purpose to me or Pops.

Four years simmered by to my senior year in high school. A third place finish in the Minnesota State High School Tennis Tournament, bolstered by my academic standing, gave me a choice of colleges. I selected Stanford because they offered me a partial tennis scholarship and it was comfortably removed from Minneapolis. Did I star on the courts? No, but it was a great experience. I played doubles on the junior varsity squad. During those undergraduate years, I spent summers in California, teaching tennis to young kids on Stanford's courts, and returned home only for the three weeks of Christmas break. Pops came out to visit me whenever Mother was on her yearly pilgrimage to NYC.

Following an undergraduate degree in business, I stayed on at Stanford, first as a teaching assistant and–after an MBA–as an assistant professor. That's how I managed to meet my fiancée, Marcie. She was a TA too, thankfully not an actress, and we were married in Palo Alto, both of us twenty-three years old. It was New Year's Eve, 1971. Before my parents arrived, I verbally sketched Mother's profile, so Marcie knew what to expect. They got along fine. Mother was still starring in her long running far-off-Broadway role as Madam and still wearing the Madam's garb, and yet my parents seemed to have reached some measure of détente. A peaceful coexistence now prevailed, at least on the surface, although I was sure there were still molten resentments percolating at some subterranean level. Our son–Andrew–was born eleven months after the wedding.

It was the winter of 1976, five years later, when Pops collapsed on top of his shovel one snowy evening in December. He was fifty-four. The driveway and sidewalk were clear of snow and he was beveling the sides–just the way Mother liked it–when a massive heart attack took him down. Marcie and I and our son flew in from L.A. the next day. My parents' final day together was detailed by Mother at the dining room table, "For breakfast he fixed perfectly coddled eggs and a Belgian waffle, just the way I like them. And in the afternoon we went to The Guthrie for a play and then dinner at The Criterion." She breathed The Guthrie and The Criterion, enunciating the words carefully.

"Sounds like a great day, Mother," I said.

"It was and, you know, we never uttered a cross word. The whole day!"

She emphasized, "The whole day!" as if any couple who accomplished a day without at least a skirmish or two deserved to have their names enshrined in *The Guinness Book of World Records*. And then she asked me to finish beveling the snow, "...you know, the way I like it, round the edges to the driveway, as if the lawn is covered with white clouds."

For the two days before the funeral, she talked to us about Pops, as his soul– presumably–took leave to zoom or flutter its way through the ether to the Lutheran neighborhood of heaven. We drank wine at the dining room table as she talked. We ate breakfast as she talked. We drank more wine at the table as she talked and I began to comprehend how the finality of death can sometimes filter out every scintilla of ill feeling that the living may harbor for the deceased. The canonization was swift. By the day of the funeral, Pops was a saint in Mother's eyes. Others at the funeral realized this truth long before his death.

Pops' oldest brother Charlie and his wife, Aunt Dolly, were behind me at the grave site as Pops' casket was lowered into the ground. I overheard my uncle's whisper, "He's free now. He's finally free."

Mother was also free, in a sense. Free to pursue her passion, free to become who she longed to be. Instead, she chose to become who she actually was. In the process, she jettisoned the theatrical pretensions, including accoutrements like the cigarette holder and the scarves. She took a job at an upscale menswear store downtown. She said she needed something to keep her busy.

She never dated–that I was aware of–and never remarried and she never returned to NYC, although I sent her money at Christmas to do so. She chose to use the money to come out to California for two or three months in the winter, dote on her grandson, and tell him all about the things he already knew or had been told about his grandfather.

MIDWESTERNERS IN PARADISE
WENDY VARDAMAN

Seventy-five degrees. No clouds. Light SW breezes. Everyone knows your name, smiles, and says *Hi Jimmy! Hi Susan!* when you walk by. Of course no one *has* to walk. You don't need it for your health, or to get around. Everyone is slim and beautiful no matter what! No glasses, no hearing aids, no walkers, wheel chairs, canes. And though it's a little hard at first to recognize your friends, partners, relatives, you catch on quick: a familiar wave, or lift of lip. And, if not, well, it hardly matters, because everyone's so nice. So pleasant to chat with, so attractive. And everyone has all the time in the world—eventually, you're bound to bump into everybody! Sometimes, you chuckle, thinking about that earthly life with its ups and downs—it seems so silly now! Everyone gets their hands back here. Siamese twins are separated, dwarves elongated, lepers patched and tanned, the snaggle-toothed awarded brilliant smiles.

And that talk about angels not being human? *Nonsense!* They take off the animal heads, the horns, the feathers and wings, and underneath the scary costumes, they're just like you and me!

It's like being in your *favorite* movie, but it never ends! Or the happiest birthday party with all the foods you like most but *better*, because you don't gain weight, you never get sick, and you get to *have* your cake *and* eat it too!

MORE THAN WE WILL EVER BE
MERI SHEFFLER

When I walked into our little kitchen, Jeremy was taking an empty skillet out of the oven, using two potholders with each hand. The countertops were crowded with sugar, flour, eggs, and milk. "What are you making?"

"A Dutch baby." He did not look at me when he replied. He inspected the skillet then dropped a pat of butter in it and swirled it around. "You ever had a Dutch baby?"

I looked at him like he was crazy but he was still not looking my way. He stirred batter in a bowl and hummed softly to himself. I said, "No. What are you talking about, Jeremy?"

"Dutch baby. You pour this batter in the pan, and it gets all fluffy, then after it cooks it collapses. Ends up kind of like a crepe. Or a pancake. Or something in between." Jeremy took a scraper and started pulling the batter away from the sides of the mixing bowl.

Something in between? Maybe that was me. Two weeks ago, I miscarried. It happened very early at only ten weeks, so early that I hadn't even managed to tell Jeremy that I thought I was pregnant. Now I tried to picture myself saying the word "miscarriage" out loud to him. The word by itself reminded me of the word "mistake." I had tried for days to imagine how the conversation would go, over coffee at the diner, in the car ride to church, on a commercial break during an Indians game. I waited too long to pick the moment, and now that seed of a new life became a thick stone between us. Should I address it as *my, our,* or *a* loss? Was it even a baby yet or just an idea in my imagination?

"It's kind of like Yorkshire pudding, the way it rises in the oven then falls and you're just left with the crust," Jeremy said.

I turned to look away from him and the batter, and I hoped that Jeremy's creation, which I could tell used a lot of eggs from the remnants of the bone-white shells that lay in the drain of the sink, tasted better than Yorkshire pudding. I never liked Yorkshire pudding. I never understood what it was, or what it was supposed to taste like. The name fooled me. I assumed it was a dessert or at least a treat to offset the thickness of the meat and potatoes. It was neither and I was disappointed.

I took a deep breath and changed the subject. "Don't forget we have to go feed Steve's horses tonight. And I don't know what we are going to do if his barn floods. There's a flood warning until this evening," I said. Steve was our boss, the director at the equestrian center portion of the college. He was gone for the weekend at a horse sale. "It might be flooding right now. Should we go check?"

"We can't go right now," Jeremy answered and finally looked at me. He held the filled skillet with two potholders protecting his long slender fingers. I fell in love with those hands when I met him. I remember the image vividly. He was on the back of a horse and I kept looking at his hands and the simple butter-smooth way they adjusted the reins. "I'm just putting the Dutch baby in the oven."

"That sounds horrible," I said softly so that he couldn't hear me.

*   *   *

Later that day, I went down the stairs of our hallway to the front door of the building. It had rained nonstop for the past three days. Our apartment was on Main Street and the Blanchard River crossed beneath the street about a quarter of a mile to the north. Normally, it ran far beneath the bridge that spanned Main Street, but with all of the rain water flooding the creeks and the tributaries, the river swelled and rose and started to overtake the land that was around it. Whenever there was a flood warning I would walk to the bridge every morning and check the level of the river. Today, it had not crested yet because the rain refused to cease. I opened my umbrella and pulled the zipper to my raincoat high under my chin.

Traffic on Main Street was very light because it was Saturday. I walked through puddles on the sidewalk, peering down washed-over allies and side streets. The one major side street between my apartment and the bridge was stamped with a road sign warning drivers: "High Water Road Closed." I imagined I would have to live in this town for a long time before I would understand and memorize its topography, what roads were higher and which were more prone to flooding.

When I got to the bridge I saw that the water was just five or six feet below. I felt a cold and familiar wave of panic run through my stomach as I gripped the edge of the railing. The river water was greyish brown, a dark khaki that swirled the mud from the banks into it like a thick gravy. I stood as still as I could and watched the water churn violently.

Three weeks ago, I saved a life. At that time it had rained for a full week and the river was just about even with the bottom side of the bridge. I was standing in the very same spot on the bridge looking out at the water when I suddenly saw a flash of yellow down on the bank of the river just yards away from me. I looked closer and saw a small blond haired boy in a yellow raincoat, squatting over his knees and playing in the river water. He was alone and he had a plastic cup and he was throwing cup-fulls of water in the air. He didn't have shoes on, and his feet were covered in mud.

I clearly remember that I wanted to scream at him, *There's sewer water mixed in with that river water!* He was in a different world, as I watched him unfold his short legs, slide into the water and grip the muddy bank with his hands. He was in that uncomfortable spot between the land and the water. He had already abandoned his cup in the river and it bobbed and floated far away. His small fingers pressed into the mud. I watched the cup nod in and out of the water drifting farther away from me until it was a speck and then it was gone.

Before I knew what I was doing, I dropped my umbrella and raced off the bridge and down the side of its bank until I was right behind the small, towheaded boy. I grabbed him by his armpits and heaved him out of the river water. He was screaming his head off. I kept pulling and dragging until we were back on the sidewalk, his soaked and muddy body lying on mine.

I was still holding him by the armpits as he struggled mightily against me. I was out of breath and exhausted and released my grasp. He jumped up and turned to me, throwing his finger at my face and running backwards.

"You tried to take me!" he yelled as he started backing away from me. I propped myself up as my elbows ground into the sidewalk and looked at him. We were both completely covered in mud.

"No I didn't! I saved you!" I said. He was running away from me, his muddy raincoat peeling off of his small shoulders.

I remember that as I lay there on the sidewalk, it stopped raining. The sky was still grey and cloudy but there was no more rain, just the thick humid still air that it left behind. I pulled myself up on my knees then to standing position. My whole body was completely covered in mud and rain.

In the weeks following that incident I often imagined that the boy ran home and told his parents that I tried to kidnap him. I was sure his parents would believe him. And then wouldn't the police have to take the words of a scared, small boy very seriously? I wondered if word spread and the small community worried that there was a kidnapper anonymously living among them. I avoided the glances and eye contact of people I didn't know, and then right away I would wonder if that made me seem guilty. I never told Jeremy about it because I knew he would think I had just overreacted that day, and now I worried that maybe I had. I stood on the bridge and watched the thick water churn and saw no flashes of color at all.

Jeremy was deeply engrossed in a movie when I walked in, and he didn't notice me as I made my way around the living room and into our bathroom, where I stripped and stepped into a hot shower. I cleaned the rain and guilt and fear from that small boy off of me with scalding hot water. When I finally felt cleaned, I left the shower, wrapped myself in a robe, and lay down on my bed. As I drifted off to sleep I saw a word at the forefront of the mixed faces and expressions that condemned me in my worst dreams: MISTAKE.

*   *   *

I slept for the entire afternoon. When I woke up it was late evening. Jeremy was in our room, putting his laundry away. He saw that I was awake and said, "Hey, we need to go feed Steve's horses."

I got dressed and we drove South down Main Street, away from the town and the flooded streets to the higher elevation of the country. I thought to myself that now I should tell Jeremy about the miscarriage, before two weeks turned into a month and the stone between us became a wall. As I sat in the passenger seat I saw the words I wanted to use hanging above me towards the roof of the car, dangling on the visor and plastered on the sunroof, out of my reach.

I opened my mouth to speak and the words that came out were "I never told you, but I saved a little boy from drowning in the river last month."

Jeremy didn't turn his head away from the road but he raised his eyebrows as he said, "Oh really? How did that happen?"

"It was when we had that big flood. He was playing in the water by the bridge and then started to slide in. I was on the bridge and ran over and pulled him out." It sounded a lot easier than it had felt.

"Huh." Jeremy turned the car down the long muddy driveway that led to Steve's barn. "Wonder where his parents were. Why would they be so careless to let their kid play by a flooding river?"

Maybe they didn't know. If they had only known what to do they would have been able to stop it from happening, I thought to myself. "Maybe," I said out loud, "they just made a mistake."

Jeremy laughed out loud. "Some mistake! Maybe some people just shouldn't be parents!"

My stomach felt like a void and my mouth felt dry, and I knew that no matter how hard I tried, I could not force any more words from within my core to come up through my throat. Jeremy stopped the car and we climbed out. Steve had two fat, old broodmares that were in foal and a border collie named Francine, who ran free on his land. We were supposed to bring in the mares from the pasture, feed them, and fill Francine's dog bowl.

It was almost dark. The place looked scary when the sun went down. I could hear the mares moving around in the pasture. I saw the deep mud mixed with strands of hay and of course everything was soaking wet. I followed Jeremy into the dilapidated barn. Even with the light turned on it was dark and dreary. There was an old tractor parked in the middle of the aisle, and on one side there was a stack of hay bales piled up to the ceiling. The stalls were on the other side of the tractor, almost hidden behind a mess of buckets and hose.

Outside the back door of the barn was the pasture and both mares were standing by the gate, ready to come in. They were covered in gray, dried mud and their manes were knotted. Jeremy and I checked each mare over and threw two flakes of hay and half a scoop of grain in each stall. Then we filled the dog bowl with dog food and also filled all the water buckets. As we turned to leave, Jeremy whistled for Francine. She didn't come.

Jeremy whistled again. Then he cupped his hands around his mouth and yelled, "Francine!"

The night seemed stiller and quieter than ever. I walked to the edge of the muddy turnout and sank to my ankles into the sticky muck. I called for her. Then

I heard the jingle of her collar as she came trotting in from the other side of the road. As she got closer, I couldn't see her but I could tell by the way that she was breathing that she was carrying something in her mouth.

Jeremy came up behind me, and we watched as Francine trotted towards us. "Damn," Jeremy said. "She's got one of the neighbor's chickens."

Francine dropped it at our feet, and Jeremy knelt down and held the squirming thing up. It was still alive but it flailed around in his arms, wet and frantic. Francine had a mouthful of feathers and her legs were covered in mud all the way from her feet to halfway up her torso. The chicken was making a noise that sounded like a cross between a grunt and a bloody scream, as if she were coughing from the bottom of her stomach. Jeremy searched its neck and sides for signs of broken skin but she was just wet.

I looked to the side of the barn and saw a dumpster. "We could just put it in there."

Jeremy still carefully studied the crying chicken. "No. We'll just bring it back."

"Why? It's not our fault. And I'm not touching that thing. No way." I took a step back.

"I am not going to leave a dead chicken at Steve's house for him to find when he gets back. Come on, let's go." Jeremy turned around and slowly walked over to the car. He reached in the back for a towel from beneath the seat and wrapped the chicken in it. It was a quivering mess at this point. He got in the car. I just stood there because I knew that if I followed him he was going to expect me to be the one to deliver the chicken to Steve's neighbor down the road. This was not my chicken and not my dog.

Jeremy, I thought to myself, it wasn't my fault. I opened my mouth to repeat the words aloud but once again the words flew away from me, up in the air, and I couldn't force the sound. Instead I stood motionless, mouth open and gaping as Jeremy started the car and began to slowly pull away. We were miles from the apartment. He knew I would not let him leave me at Steve's farm. I thought of the boy in the yellow rain coat that I pulled from the river, his scared and frantic body shaking and wet. I grabbed the door handle and got in without saying anything.

"Here." Jeremy tossed me the bundled up chicken. I held it with stiff arms stretched away from me.

"Hurry up," I said. We drove down the driveway and made a left. The road was completely empty. None of the lights in any of the houses were on. It was cooler, not as humid, but the air was still. In the car, wrapped up in the towel, the chicken looked like another baby. Her body vibrated, and I felt as if she were right between being dead and alive. She was shivering and shedding feathers everywhere. It would have been terrible if Francine had carried a small baby home in her mouth. I relaxed my arms and held her a little bit closer.

Jeremy turned down another road that was riddled with potholes filled with muddy water. "It's going to be okay," he said under his breath, more to himself than to me. I had no idea what he meant.

No, Jeremy, it won't be okay, I thought. Two weeks ago we were more than we will ever be.

I could see the chicken farm up ahead, looming with bales of straw and piles of manure. Jeremy rolled down my window and slowed down slightly.

"Throw it," he commanded. I held the towel tightly and leaned my upper body out the window. Then I let go, still clutching the towel. The chicken flipped around in the air. Its white feathers against the thick black sky looked stark and angelic, as it tumbled in the air that was filled with both night and tomorrow. As soon as I released it from the towel I wanted to reach towards it and grab it back to me. But it was too late, as it landed on the ground and rolled across the mud in a tangled, feathery heap. We drove away before I could tell if she got up and moved.

YELLOW
E. CE MILLER

You found a dead canary on the sidewalk and it made you think of her.

It was a strange thing to find in the middle of the city, especially this time of year when the wind is cold and dry and hinting at snow, and on this short stretch of Damen Avenue where there are hardly any trees and the air pulses curry and you can still buy a decent hookah pipe for less than thirty bucks. It was a strange thing, this canary, laying quietly still on the sidewalk, between a red aluminum box empty of free newspapers and a sign for the Number 50 bus. Its shiny, yellow-white belly was turned upwards, facing the sky. The canary was small and round and dead and you wanted to pick it up; wanted to cup the bird in one hand and stroke its bulbous, downy breast with the fingers of your other. But you didn't. Instead you stood there staring down at the tiny, yellow creature while people walking past you on the sidewalk turned their heads to make puzzled eyes at one another.

It didn't bother you, their expressions of judging confusion. You were still young enough to look like a college kid, some existentially-in-crisis, urban art student with your thrift-store dress and your tobacco-colored hair falling down long around your hips. Art students did weird shit like this all the time, stopping in the middle of the sidewalk to poke at dead canaries. Plus you were still just high enough from the night before that your sense of holiness hadn't worn off yet. You always felt holy when you were high—everything was always so goddamn holy, girl; you were holy and your friends were holy and that cute lady drug-dealer who wore the knit cap with the cat ears sewn into the top was holy; even though she wouldn't sleep with you because she said she didn't sleep with her customers. You told her she was the only other lesbian you knew, which was a lie and the wrong thing to say and she was unflattered and recommended you stop getting so high and go outside more often.

"Stop selling me drugs then," you'd said, and she laughed and made everything alright again.

"That canary is holy," you thought; and you thought about taking your shoes off and sitting down on the curb, but it was cold and your thrift-store dress was thin and you didn't want to push it.

The canary made you think of that last time you saw *her*—not your drug dealer but that girl, the other girl, the only girl, *your* girl, the first. That time when you said: "Every time I see a dead bird, for the rest of my life, I'll think of you."

You said it a long time ago.

You were a couple months out of rehab—some sterile, dorm-style, suburban rehab center staffed by graduate students and AmeriCorps volunteers and nothing like the granola-sounding centers you'd heard existed in places like Santa Monica and Salt Lake City. You were taking things one step at a time and when you saw her you knew you'd probably take a step backwards later that night.

She was walking towards you, so you looked down at the sidewalk and said: "No shit, there's a dead bird." And it was there, right by the tip of your black-and-white checkered sneaker. You kept looking down for what felt like a long time, running your tongue over the rough edge of your front tooth, which was newly-chipped but you couldn't remember how.

When you finally looked up she was standing there, smiling. You smiled back a slow grin and then caught yourself, because your tooth was not chipped the last time you'd seen her.

You were not so skinny either. Your hair had been thicker. She was visibly surprised and in trying to hide it she made her surprise more obvious.

You wanted to tell her you were okay.

You wanted to be okay and maybe if you could convince her that you were okay then you would be.

"Want to go for a walk?" you said. You'd been wandering around the Northside, one of those neighborhoods with all the brownstones and the black iron gates, waiting for something to happen though you weren't sure what. She was on her way somewhere and there was a ring on the hand she'd slid into the pocket of her jacket but she said yes anyway. You didn't walk far. She was cold and asked if you wanted a drink; there was a small, Irish-style pub up the street. You told her you'd just gotten out of rehab. She didn't hide her surprise that time.

"For what?" she asked.

"I was drunk," which was a lie.

"We were all drunk," she said and you laughed, but you hadn't meant it.

Instead, you sat on a dugout in the batting cages of some abandoned baseball field in the middle of the city. It was too cold for baseball and too cold for sitting on a metal bench.

You told her about the dead birds.

"I see dead birds everywhere," you said.

"Maybe there's something in the water." She looked bored. You didn't want her to be bored. Maybe she didn't believe you. You stood up suddenly.

"Well," you said, and then nothing. She stood up too.

After you left the batting cages you walked west even though your apartment was east—she was heading east and you didn't want her to think you were following her—and you saw another dead bird on the sidewalk. "No shit," you said.

It might have been the same one. You couldn't remember.

You took out your cell phone; snapped a picture. It was dusk and the flash reflected off the bird's eyes. It looked unnatural. You took another. Uploaded it into a text message that said: "Every time I see a dead bird, for the rest of my life, I'll think of you." You wondered if she still had the same phone number.

She responded quickly.

"Well," she'd typed, "It's good to have traditions."

You weren't sure how to take this. You remembered her as someone who sometimes said things without thinking about them, so maybe what it meant was nothing.

For the next few days you sent her messages. One more bird; lots of: "No birds today." She was friendly at first but eventually she stopped responding.

You continued to send her pictures of dead birds, maybe two a week, leaving the birdless days filled with silence.

Then it snowed in the city and there were no more dead birds for months.

You still went on long walks. Looking. Waiting. Taking things one step at a time.

*   *   *

Later, after she is married and moved away and you live in another part of the city, working at a coffee shop during the day and telling yourself "only beer, beer is legal" and then getting high anyway at night, you see a dead canary on the sidewalk.

A flash of bright yellow against the sidewalk.

It is clean, unharmed-looking. As though it just climbed down out of a tree and wanted to take a nap in the sun on the sidewalk.

You take a picture.

You try to remember what step you are on.

You are taking things one step at a time.

You think about sending her the picture.

Sketches Preliminary to the Portrait of an Art Dealer

J. WEINTRAUB

"You have no idea how difficult it was then, and how ruinous! Profiting from living artists has never been easy. But in Chicago? Back then? Impossible!"

This was my second interview with Racine, and both had begun with the same complaint.

"No idea," he repeated, his vague eyes still wandering, toward the left and the blank white wall where a Clifford Stimmons once must have hung. He seemed to prefer the emptiness to my features or to the reproachful glare of Thomas Hart Benton, who was scrutinizing us both from behind his easel.

One of Sotheby's curators had warned me about Racine's "fixed, piercing stare, as calculating and unnerving as that of a Tennessee horsetrader." But whenever he turned his eyes toward me, they were cloudy and uncertain, the eyes of an old man, enfeebled by sickness and age.

Yet still he seemed pleased by my presence there, even if it was only because of my interest in the life and work of another. Although Racine had achieved some prominence as an art dealer and critic in the fifties and sixties, he was now primarily known for his support of Clifford Stimmons, and for anyone hoping to do work on the artist—in my case one of a series of studies on the lives of contemporary American realists for *Arts Monthly*—an appointment with Charles Racine was obligatory. In fact, many now believe that without Racine's patronage, Stimmons would never have produced most of his great portraits nor even lived as long as he had. "We all owe an inestimable debt to Charles Racine," the director of the Nelson-Atkins Museum declared some years ago at the opening of the *American Life Studies* exhibit, "for his contribution not only to the world of contemporary art but also to the heritage of America's heartland."

*   *   *

"He needed to be protected," Racine told me. "Economically and socially. You must understand, isolation was necessary to Clifford's art. He was a meticulous worker, preparing drawing after drawing, and once he began a canvas he could progress only through a rigorous technique of accumulation and excision. Outside interferences, obligations distracted him, and his exclusive arrangement with American Artists gave him the security and protection he needed. Besides, he drank less when he was alone and at work." (Clara Stimmons had another view of Racine's motives, attributing her father's isolation to Racine's fear that

Stimmons would eventually be seduced away from him by another dealer or be tempted by the easy profits of clandestine, private sales. Late in Stimmons' career, there had been discussions about a New York show in cooperation with Midtown Galleries, but there were disagreements over commissions, and before they could be resolved, Stimmons had become too ill to travel, ensuring that his reputation would never extend beyond the Midwest during his lifetime.)

Racine's American Artists remained Stimmons' exclusive gallery throughout his productive years. The space had been located just off North Michigan Avenue, near Bonwit Teller's, and Peck & Peck, and the high-fashion boutiques that then catered to the wealthier tourists and residents of the Gold Coast. In the publicity stills Racine showed me of his gallery, clusters of elegant women in wide-brimmed hats and Chanel gowns—all of them, he said, hired from modeling agencies—were grouped around the paintings, admiring them. But the black-and-white glossies could hardly do justice to the vivid coloration that was the signature of Stimmons' art—the complex pastels and play of light that transformed paint into flesh, the deep and occasionally sinister backgrounds that propelled the figures outward from the canvas, the multitextured impasto layered onto the faces of his subjects like so many years of wisdom and experience or, as in most of the portraits, vice and decay. Miniaturized as they were in these photos, the pictures resembled tiny mugshots, a criminal history written in the faces of the previous generation of Midwestern businessmen and industrialists. A model in one of the publicity shots seemed transfixed by the predatory gaze of a McCormick heir who now trains his manic eyes on all who enter the Art Institute's American Wing, and on the day the portrait was donated to the museum, the subject's widow was heard to remark "I understand now how the Rockefellers could have destroyed the Rivera mural so easily, and how satisfying it must have been." Her complaint has since been echoed by many families who could not prevent what they considered to be scandalous libels of distinguished relatives from hanging in museums around the world. "A slanderer brought into faddish fame, by leftist idealogues," wrote the Tribune critic of the Art Institute's seminal show several years after Stimmons' death. "A Goya for our age," declared others with more liberal credentials.

*   *   *

The Art Institute show assured Stimmons posthumous fame, particularly after it traveled to the Guggenheim. But by then American Artists had long since closed its doors. Despite his wide network of social contacts and his distinguished and expensive collection of American realists, Racine could not prevent Midwestern collectors from traveling to New York to buy their art, even when they were in search of a Benton or a Grant Wood. "Or to London and the Marlborough for their quaint rural landscapes." he complained to me. "Or to Paris for those neo-Impressionist knock-offs perfect for that space just above the buffet. And, of course, for those with more contemporary sensibilities, a Fifty-Seventh Street address and a dealer with a Central-European accent was essential to valorize taste!" The only buyers who seemed to stray into American Artists were new homeowners looking for waves breaking on beaches or sylvan glades. "With deer," added Racine. "Very important, the deer."

But Racine hardly needed a gallery after the Art Institute show. He owned almost all of Stimmons' important work, and two or three sales a year, carefully controlled in the auction rooms or directed to the right buyers, were enough to make him a wealthy man. For years he had been showing his holdings from his own apartment, and still displayed on his living-room walls—equidistant from each other and illuminated by tracklights—were the rolling, chromatic landscapes and self portraits of Thomas Hart Benton, the stark brown and yellow fields and seasoned clapboard farms of John Steuart Curry, Peter Hurd, and other American regionalists. Purchased at inflated prices, the works of these once popular artists had been acquired by Racine to lure collectors into his gallery, without, apparently, much success. "After so many years, they're still a hard sell," explained Racine. "But I have no intention of unloading them until I see the right price. Patience. That's the name of the game. Patience unto death. And beyond."

*   *   *

He was wearing a black pin-striped suit with a red silk tie and matching socks, and a scarlet handkerchief crested from his coat pocket. This was, I had been told, Racine's customary outfit when he walked the floor of American Artists, and when he led me into his bedroom to view the last of his Stimmons' collection, I noticed ranks of black suits hanging in his open closet, separated here and there by candy-striped shirts, some with pink collars. A row of tasseled black leather pumps, similar to the ones he was wearing, stretched across the closet floor.

The few Stimmons' portraits he still owned were lined up along one side of his bed on an otherwise bare wall and, like the paintings in the living room, were illuminated by track lights. He admitted that they weren't of the best quality. "Too much rancor in them," he said. "A flaw in his later work. A little stiff, too. Almost caricatures rather than essays. Of course, they weren't painted from life. In those last years, anyone wealthy enough to have Clifford do his portrait knew by then that he risked having his soul flayed before his very eyes. Inferior, yes. But if I wait long enough, they'll fetch a good price. Like holding them hostage. The longer you wait, the higher the ransom." He smiled at the aptness of his metaphor, knowing that the price of a Stimmons' portrait often climbed to unexpected heights as museums bid against families intent on preventing the public display of a beloved parent or sibling transformed into a monster by the art of the painter.

"Of course, I shall have no trouble selling Clara when the time comes," and I followed Racine's eyes to the painting over his bed. If the other portraits in the room were studies of sinners on their descents to hell, this was a view of one of the blessed, comparable to a Botticelli virgin or a Bellini saint. "It was my idea. I told him to paint her. The daffodil was my idea, too." The daffodil shimmered with color as if it were the only source of light, yet despite its splendor and its central position in the portrait, the viewer's eye was inevitably drawn to the countenance of the five-year-old girl staring down at the flower in her hand, her face a vision of youthful longing and innocence. I had seen reproductions of the work before, but despite its surprisingly small dimensions, I was still awed by the intensity of its life juxtaposed against the tranquility of its emotion. "It is a glorious piece," said Racine as he turned toward the door, beckoning me to follow him from the room. "But after all these years, I'm finally beginning to tire of her," and a month later, Clara with a Daffodil was sold to a Japanese collector for one of the highest prices ever paid for a modern American portrait.

At about the time of the sale, I finally managed to arrange an interview with the subject of the painting. Clara Stimmons was the only surviving member of her immediate family, having lost her mother, her step mother, and, finally, her brother who, like his father, had died of alcoholism before reaching middle age. I met her in her studio, a third-story loft on the northernmost edge of River North.

I was surprised to learn that she also lived in the space, since every utensil, appliance, table, and chair was covered with thick incrustations of paint. Piles of rags and clothing, empty coffee cans and glass jars, dirty brushes and scrapers, flattened tubes and used palettes contributed to the kaleidoscope of random color. Rejecting the figurative style of her father, she declared herself to be "an experimental field colorist," and it seemed that if an empty frame were propped up anywhere in her studio, a painting would emerge within.

Only her canvases disturbed the composition of the space. These vast, horizontal expanses of muddied tones could be distinguished from the ground of her studio by their general murkiness. Whereas her father had layered paint onto canvas until character was revealed, Clara Stimmons did not seem satisfied until the accumulation of pigment ended in an inert dinginess, and I doubted that any dealer would handle such indecisive work except to traffic on her name.

*   *   *

Fortunately, she arranged her own sales, refusing to show her work with a commercial dealer. "I'd burn in hell before doing business with any of those leeches," she said as I settled against the window sill, one of the few surfaces seemingly free of new paint. She had been cleaning her brushes, and she was now rubbing her hands raw with a mottled rag.

"But dealers support artists, too," I said, prodding her, "investing in them when they're young. Racine, for instance..."

"And overseers feed their slaves. Racine baited his trap, and Dad walked into it. Freedom to paint, as long as Racine told him what to paint and the painting belonged to him. I suppose at the beginning there was some kind of synergy there, and I'll give Racine credit for recognizing Dad's genius for portraiture. He loved doing those things, exposing a person's soul bit-by-bit, whether it was innocent or shameful. But eventually the deal soured, particularly after I was born and Mom got sick..." She paused, looking down at the rag in her hands as if reflecting on her own contribution to her father's servitude. "Being dependent like that, mortgaging your artistic labor for the roof over our heads, the canvases, the paint, the booze. I sometimes think that Dad drank because of that damn contract, because Racine owned everything."

She raised her eyes to mine as if expecting another question, but before I could react, she asked me, "How many gallons of Winsor-and-Newton orange do you think you could buy, how many families could you support, how many national debts could you pay off with that obscene windfall Racine just received for my portrait? Another Japanese industrialist, I understand. They've got my brother and my Mom's nude, too." The last comment was spoken with the bitterness of someone whose youth had been ravished by East Asian pirates.

"It's a great painting," I said. "Your portrait with the daffodil." She smiled, as if I had been complimenting her. But there was none of the plump innocence of that childhood left in her face. It was lean, like that of her father who had descended from a line of Great Plains farmers, and although she was barely fifty, her hair was steel-gray and her complexion ridged and leathery as if she spent the days plowing fields in the heat of the sun. "Racine said it was his idea for your father to paint your portrait. The daffodil was his idea, too, he said."

*   *   *

Her smile disappeared. "Don't you see? That was his game. Racine used our portraits to get commissions from all those wealthy friends of his, and after seeing my brother's portrait or my step mother's, how could they resist? And since that was the only way Dad could make any real money, how could he refuse? But he hated all those pigs. 'The rich have spots on their souls,' he used to say, and that's what he painted. Of course, most of them couldn't handle Dad's brand of truth, so Racine usually managed to buy the paintings back at cost. Eventually the commissions dried up and Dad had alienated every wealthy art collector within a thousand-mile radius."

"But why would Racine jeopardize his own business by encouraging such commissions?"

"I told you!" and she flung the rag down to the floor, a spray of dusty pigment sprouting up from the impact. "My father was a genius, and Racine knew it! He just had to wait, and he didn't have to wait very long." The deep ridges extending down from the corners of her mouth began to quiver. "He knew Dad was dying, and yet he refused to hold a show or publicize his work or do anything to establish his reputation in those last years. In the meantime, he was buying up all of Dad's early paintings at cut-rate prices and paying him less and less for his work since none of it would sell. Those last years were horrible. Dad trying so hard to leave something behind for us, but he was always so slow and the work became more and more difficult for him. Drinking more and more so he could work harder and harder and die sooner and sooner. When he realized that Racine would fight to keep it all, he spent the last months of his life on that one final masterpiece. It's one of his best, too. At least of the darker portraits."

"Which one do you mean?"

"I mean *The Merchant of Art*. I guess your friend Racine didn't have that one hanging over his mantlepiece, did he?"

"*The Merchant of Art*?" I thought I knew of every one of Stimmons' finished pieces, but I had never heard of *The Merchant of Art*.

"A remarkable likeness. It should do for art dealers what the character of Shylock did for the Jews," she said.

"I can't recall seeing it in any of the catalogs."

* * *

"Racine compiles the catalogs. We tried to keep it out of his hands, but it was part of the settlement. I've got the preliminary sketches, though, both pencil and charcoal, one almost as fine as the finished portrait. Dad usually threw out his studies, but he died before he could destroy these. I doubt if Racine even knows they exist, but they're safe, somewhere where he can never get his hands on them." She smiled again. "Quite a predicament for a greedy lizard like Racine, isn't it? The portrait's a masterpiece, as good as anything my father ever painted, in an evil sort of a way, and the Japanese would probably pay another fortune for it. But if he puts it up for sale, there's likely to be publicity and reproductions, and that's the last thing a man like Racine, with his bloated sense of self-worth, would ever want. I'm sure he's got it locked away somewhere. The lawyers probably know where. Maybe they'll let you see it. They're the ones who handled the details. Talk to them."

I was planning to talk with Richard Bennett anyway, and I made an appointment with him the next day. Bennett was Racine's personal attorney and had been lead counsel in the litigation over the Stimmons estate. Racine had instructed him to be frank and open in his discussions with me, since, as he said, he had "nothing to hide."

"Mr. Racine has nothing to hide," said Bennett as soon as I sat down before him, in front of his desk. "Here. He asked me to give you this," He handed me a photocopy of the final Stimmons-Racine Artist-Dealer Contract, but since it was prefaced with a page of "Whereas..." clauses, I slipped it into my briefcase for later reading. "It's equitable and tight. I drafted the original myself, and since it was renewable every two years, we had ample opportunity to refine it to everyone's satisfaction." He smiled, looking down at me as if I, too, were a party to the contract and bound inextricably to its provisions.

"I must admit, it was an interesting exercise," he continued. "There aren't many contracts of this kind, at least not in this country. It's primarily a nine-teenth-century French instrument. But I suppose that's quite appropriate since Mr. Racine has far more in common with the great European dealer-patrons of the past—Durand-Ruel, Vollard, Kahnweiler—than with modern gallery owners who are now primarily agents or speculators. Of course, with each termination date I advised my client against renewal. So much exposure upfront with so little in return. A generous monthly stipend, a rent-free studio, the best materials. And the gallery expenses, too—rent, insurance, publicity, catalogs, shows, cocktails. A contract like that can easily drain working capital, and, in fact, it did, I believe, contribute to the demise of American Artists. Moreover, the total exclusivity that such extravagance buys is a condition ripe for conflict. Legal and binding, but always subject to resentment once the fruits are about to be harvested."

"You speak as if Racine never profited from the arrangement."

"The greater the risk, the greater the rewards. In this case, the risks were very great, particularly when you consider how unfashionable figurative art was during Stimmons' lifetime."

*   *   *

I recalled the wide swatches of color on the walls of the firm's reception foyer and the geometric collages lining the corridors—the kind of dull, neutral abstraction, without character or content, that businesses so loved to display and which was so instrumental in driving painters like Stimmons into commercial art and teaching. A pair of safe Lichtenstein lithographs decorated the walls of Bennett's office, giving it—in combination with the minimalist furniture—a vaguely contemporary air.

"In fact," Bennett continued, "if it weren't for the commissions Charles Racine arranged, Clifford Stimmons would have earned precious little from his painting. That and the stipend alone enabled him both to support his family and practice his art. He was a drunkard, you know, and virtually unemployable. I'm sure you've heard the stories about those life-study classes he tried to teach. The bottom line is that he would have accomplished very little without my client's patronage and without the contract that caused so much needless friction after Stimmons' death—just as I had predicted and even though the contract was air-tight."

"But you settled out-of-court."

"Against my advice!" Bennett was becoming irritable, as if I were seeking loopholes in his professional credibility. "All finished paintings belonged to my client. We laid claim only to those which Stimmons signed, an act indicating that the artist considered them in a state of completion and therefore subject to the provisions of the contract. There's precedent for that conclusion. *Rouault v. Vollard*, the Civil Tribunal of the Seine, for instance."

"And yet Racine still settled."

"You could say that my client is a generous man. If, instead, you prefer to seek venal motivations, you could say that my client preferred not to have the paintings displayed in court, exposing them to both physical damage and premature public valuation."

I had read a report of the proceedings, and I agreed with Bennett that the family did not have a case. "I understand that for a certain unstated sum the family agreed not to contest Racine's ownership of the six signed portraits and one still life found in Stimmons' studio at the time of his death."

"Correct. And afterwards the family complained in the media about the insufficiency of the amount and the meanness of my client, even though they had no standing whatsoever."

"There does seem to be one discrepancy that perhaps you could explain. I've checked all the catalogs and relevant sales records. I can only account for the existence of five, not six, of these last portraits."

"There's always been some confusion about the still-life. It may have initially been mistaken as one of the portraits and then later repeated as a still-life."

"So *The Merchant of Art* was not the mysterious sixth portrait?"

*   *   *

"You've been visiting with Clara Stimmons, haven't you?" Tinges of dark pink appeared on his cheekbones and across his brow, a war paint of sorts applied for serious confrontations. "And perhaps the Venus de Milo's arms were part of the hoard, too—unlisted, of course—and the head of the Victory of Samothrace. Rumors and innuendo abound in the world of art. It is a vindictive and clannish set, and you have to be prepared to deal with wounded sensibilities, eccentricities, delusions of grandeur, and world-class egos."

"As well as considerable sums of money."

"Extremes of wealth and destitution." Bennett arose, indicating that the interview was over. But first he would deliver a closing argument on behalf of his client. "It is true that Mr. Racine has earned a considerable amount of money from Stimmons' work. But only after decades of seeing his investments produce nothing. Moreover, he has given generously to public collections, contributed his time to the Humanities Council and the artistic community, and funded several fellowships for young artists. Throughout his life he has been primarily motivated by his devotion to the arts, and although I am not at liberty to reveal the details, the city of Chicago and several Midwestern institutions will benefit greatly from his estate. There are both positive and negative aspects to his relationship with Clifford Stimmons and his family, but I think the former far outweight the latter, and I suggest you balance them both carefully before laying claim to the truth."

"That has always been my intention," I said as I shook hands with Bennett. Yet if I were to report the truth, I would certainly have to see everything that Stimmons painted, particularly in his last days, and before submitting anything to my editor, I was determined to arrange at least one more interview with Racine.

But several months passed before I could meet with Racine again. He had been hospitalized twice, and after his housekeeper accompanied me from the foyer to the living room, I quickly understood why he was reluctant to be disturbed. Perched on an elaborately carved chair, the size of a medieval choir stall, he seemed more frail than ever, his black suit billowing and rumpled as if it had been flung hastily over a pair of pajamas. Adjacent to the Empire settee on which we had sat for our previous interviews, this huge, ornate chair disturbed the simple harmony of the room, but its thick seat cushion seemed to allow for both comfort and ease of access. A mahogany cane, the head of a dragon jutting from its top, was looped over one of its arms.

*   *   *

His eyes were still distant, and since Racine was sitting several feet away to my side, he easily averted them from me. His responses to my questions, too, were distracted and meandering, but he still seemed eager to testify about his past, an old warrior reminding posterity that his victories may have been bloody, but they were victories nevertheless, and he did not seem to mind me asking about the last frenzied months of Stimmons' life.

"He needed the money, you see, otherwise he never would've renewed his contract that last time. But that was always the case, wasn't it? As much as he grew to despise his dealings with me, he still appreciated my name on the bottom of a monthly check. And how he would rage if it was only a day late! That last year, he was especially difficult. But I suppose it was because he was working so hard, as sick as he was. Some of the finished pieces were good, some not so good. You've seen most of them here. Too much anger. Artists can be such spiteful children. But two or three were still works of genius, of a blistering sort. The human frailties that all of us share, clearly evident. That's why I value art almost above everything else. Great portraiture is always a record of imperfection. What keeps us human. Of course, Clifford himself was far from perfect. He wanted to cheat me, you know, there at the end, holding back those last paintings, not releasing them to me as was his legal obligation. But he was badly advised."

"Badly advised?"

"I pay for the best legal advice, as you know, and it's usually worth the money. He was told that if he willed the paintings in his possession to his children my contract would be invalidated by his death. That may be, but it was pride that did him in. Pride at what he had accomplished all that last year, as sick as he was. Near the end, on one day, he signed all those canvases. Proud, glorious flourishes. Not like those tentative chickenscratchings in the corner of so many of his commissions. All seven canvases in one day, and as soon as he signed them, they were legally mine."

"Seven canvases? According to your catalog to the Art Institute show, there were only six."

"Yes, six. The still-life. Sometimes it gets confused with the portrait listings. It's in Brussels now. One of his only still-lifes. A handsome piece, and it brought a handsome price, too."

"Seven agrees with the listing in the settlement report. Six portraits and a still-life. Surely Mr. Racine, you know the importance of establishing attributions as early as possible, especially for an artist whose work is a scarce and as valued as his is. If, as you say, you value art above everything else—"

"I said *almost*. I said 'almost above everything else.'"

"Nevertheless, it's essential..."

*   *   *

"That's what the Mayor said at the reception honoring me for my donation of the McCormick portrait to the Art Institute. That's what he said, and it wasn't my position to contradict him. But when Mrs. Potter claimed the same thing, that I would sacrifice everything for art, I was compelled to disabuse her of such a notion." I would have thought that this anecdote was another of Racine's meanderings, one of the several digressive journeys we had taken during the interview. But for the first time that afternoon, he was leaning towards me, staring directly into my eyes.

"You know Mrs. Felicia Potter, don't you? The dry goods heiress? She's still alive and collecting, and many years ago I almost arranged to have her portrait painted. But she declined, and at that same museum reception, she told me that we would never have remained friends if Clifford had painted her as he had McCormick. 'But you'd be famous,' I said, 'and immortal.' 'That would have been a fame I do not covet,' she replied, 'and a scandalous immortality!' I then reminded her that the painting would be worth fifty times what she would have paid for it. 'There are more important things than money,' she said, 'like my reputation, and our friendship which you would have sacrificed if my portrait looked anything like Mr. McCormick's. But I suppose you'd sacrifice everything on the altar of art, wouldn't you.' 'No,' I replied. 'Not everything.'

"She didn't believe me. 'I suppose you're one of those people, she said, 'who, given the choice of saving the Mona Lisa from destruction in a fire and a child overcome by smoke, would rescue the painting.' I told her again she was wrong, and she laughed at me. But she was wrong, you know. Dead wrong," and he raised his chin into the air and sniffed twice as if, proud of his choice, he were complacently inhaling the aroma from the smoldering pigments of a priceless masterpiece.

Two months later he was dead. The remaining paintings in his collection were donated to the Art Institute and the Museum of Contemporary Art, and a commemorative medal was struck in his honor, the phrase *ars longa, vita brevis* winding twice around its circumference. *A Complete Catalog of the Portraits of Clifford Stimmons*, edited by Charles Racine and the curator of the MCA, was published the following year. The listings had been compiled during Racine's final illness, but it probably had not been a difficult task since Racine kept scrupulous records and never lost sight of a painting that had once been in his hands. I ordered a copy of the catalog as soon as it was published, but, as I had expected, there were no surprises, nothing new to add to the canon of one of our century's greatest artists.

KANSAS
MARK PATRICK SPENCER

Infinite Hell. 1994.
Driving.
Not bottom to top, side to side.

Not stopping was the best plan.
Ricky's eyes were glue,
and there was nothing to see.

Ted's asleep in the back seat.
I'm sure we're goin to die in Kansas.
Hit scan on the radio, and it never stops.

Radio stops an hour later.
Rush Limbaugh is bent out of shape
about "gangster rapper" Nine Inch Nails.

An hour after that,
we're the ones that are stopped.
In podunk Colby, Kansas.

Cop doesn't like the Kentucky plates.
His car says K9 Unit, but there's no dog.
His girlfriend is in the front seat though.

Sitting on the guardrail
I'm wondering if she can
smell our weed.

Billboard says there is a
two-headed prairie dog
at the museum.

"Get in the car and don't stop til you cross the border"

No fuckin problem
Thanks for not checking
under the passenger seat.

Dumb ass Ted says
Salina is at the state line
He was only off by a few hours

This state will never end.

DOWNSTATE SUMMER

MARK MAIRE

Hot wind funneled through endless rows of corn,
the sound like Bible pages fluttering,
hammock swaying side to side, no one home.
Two friends, we trawled deserted nighttime streets
in that Aspen wagon, since it had air,
stopped off most nights at a bar called Danny's.
Too hot for strong stuff, we drank club soda.
The jukebox played "Gloria," "Key Largo,"
"Highway to Hell," then circled back again.
Straight line highways led in four directions,
each one the same, indistinguishable.
In barns, cows languished, suffering the night.
We just wanted out, but didn't know how.

THE THIRTY-THIRD DEGREE
FRITZ SWANSON

*Who is more visible than God? This is why he made
all things: so that through them all you might look
on him.*

—Hermetica 11:22

My wife made this argument: "There's never a good time to start your life."

Ten years later, time was standing still. We were just holding on. We had a ramshackle house, a baby girl, a son who was just shy of three.

He and I were sitting in the tub. He had his pirates and I had Magneto and we were exploring for buried treasure. The shark had joined the pirates, and I was tired after a long day at school, so I had Magneto stand on the edge of the tub and oversee the operation.

"I big boy," my boy said definitively when I said he shouldn't splash.

I agreed and I said, "You'll grow bigger every day, and someday I won't be able to fit in the bath with you. So let's not splash."

He dropped his chin and thought for a moment.

He splashed one more time to test, and a bit of water got on one of my books sitting by the tub. I think it was *The Cloud of Unknowing.*

I'll admit, at that moment I was angry.

"I grow bigger bigger bigger?" he asked. He held up both his hands with the fingers spread out. He meant 'ten big' by this, because that's his biggest intensifier.

And, regretting the flash of anger, I said, "Well, not bigger forever. You'll grow big, and then you'll be a man like me, and then you won't grow for a while." He looked up at me, from the other end of the tub. He held a small rubber shark that had been mine when I was little. I added, "And when you get very old you'll even shrink a little bit."

"Get smaller?" he asked. I nodded.

"Yeah, a little bit." I decided explaining osteoporosis wasn't worth it at this point, given the fact that we were still working on water displacement, and all that resulted in was him pulling his bottom out of the tub really quickly and turning around to see if he could catch the "hole" in the water that caused the waves.

As I toweled him and prepared him for bed, he stood still, which was very unlike him. He did not bounce in bed, but just lay his head on my shoulders as I told him more about Jack and the giant.

*   *   *

The next day was my birthday. Thirty-Three. It was November wet and November cold.

I updated my Facebook status from my office computer on campus: "FGS Has ascended to the 33rd degree. The high priest leans in, his skin papery and dry, and he whispers, 'Osiris is a dark god.'"

For the rest of the day, I happily harvested best wishes.

"LZ: Happy birthday! May you and Osiris party like rock stars in the underworld!"

I replied, "If someone offers you a free cedar chest crafted to your exact dimensions, I recommend you turn down the offer."

"KFK: Happy day! Seems like everyone was born in November. What is it about March?"

I replied, "In like a lion, out like a lamb."

I actually blushed after I hit 'post.'

*   *   *

Later that same day, before I taught, all the adjuncts had to sign up for classes for the next semester. Full time for a semester is three courses.

I looked down at my list of choices.

"This is it?" I asked, smirking at the two classes on the list.

The secretary, who was effectively my boss, grimaced and looked at me with pity.

"It's a trickle down," she said, nodding and frowning.

"But, with the economy, I thought enrollment is up?" I looked out her window and was greeted by the blacktop and smoke stacks of the roof of the enclosed computer quadrangle. There were an enormous number of crows. One hopped along, blithely, on one leg.

"Oh, it is," she was saying, "freshman enrollment is up by twenty percent. And that's good. But graduate school enrollment is up, and junior/senior retention is down." She sat down to show me some figures. "You see..."

I thanked her profusely, and left feeling hot all over my body. My face and cheeks especially burned as though I had a fever. I was lit on fire.

A whole class, gone.

In the hall, outside of my office, there was a young woman from one of my seminars. She said, "I'm sorry, Professor. I overslept." She handed me a late assignment and slunk away, which was good because my initial urge was to slap her across the face.

*   *   *

On the drive home I phoned my wife. She had lost her job last year. Half our income gone, now another cut.

She took the news well. She said, "We'll be fine. We'll manage."

"It's six hundred sixty dollars a month. Less." I said. I swerved carelessly around a mouse in the road. He stared at me Hamlet-like, and when I swerved, he darted, and I crushed him despite my best efforts. "Shit!" I barked.

I could hear screaming.

"We're having a hard day," my wife said calmly. Then there was the sound of many objects tumbling to the ground, and my wife covered the mouthpiece to yell "Get on the couch, Buster!"

"Don't worry," she soothed. "Try not to think about what we made before. We'll make this work."

*   *   *

Home was a huge, old house.

My boy was sitting at the table. She was standing above him, our baby girl on her hip. They were all eating the remnants of two hot dogs.

"I think we were hungry," she said to no one in particular as she swayed her hips, rocking our little girl.

But when she had returned the girl to the carpet in the living room, he slid out of his chair. As I slipped off my boots I watched him smirk and sneak around the corner toward the living room.

"Buddy?" I called.

Even at three, he had a detailed understanding of dramatics. He stood up on his toes, he raised his arms and dangled his fingers. He tiptoed, and whispered "Sneak, sneak, sneak."

Without patience I marched in my socks into the living room just as he broke into a run. Before I could reach him, he had pushed his baby sister over from her sitting position so that her head struck a wooden Waldorf stacking toy.

And then he made his escape, running into the kitchen and out into the dining room. "HEY!" I barked, and raced after him. My face was hot, my cheeks burning red, and as the girl wailed, I grabbed him by the shoulders and spun him around fiercely.

"Owie! Owie! Owie!" he wailed.

"Why did you do it!?" I shook him. "Why!?"

"It accident!" He whined. "It accident."

"It was not an accident. It was on purpose. Why?" Each sentence was sharp. He crumbled in my hands.

"I not know," he cried. "I not know." His face was red and hot.

I let him go.

He offered his arms to me to kiss. I kissed his biceps where I had held him. He calmed down, his face eased.

"I grow small?" he asked.

I sat down by him. "What?"

My wife came in cuddling our daughter. "Not this again, buddy." She shook her head.

"What?" I asked her.

"He won't let me give his baby toys to his sister."

"Why?" I asked him. "Why can't your sister have your old stacking toys?"

He burst into tears.

"He's saving them," my wife said.

"For what?"

"For when he's a little boy again." And then she repeated a phrase to him that she seemed to have been saying all day. "I'm sorry, sweetie. You'll never be a little boy again."

But this time he stood up and ran at her. He punched her in the stomach and he screamed, "Dad said! Dad said!"

I grabbed him and I wrapped him in my arms, and though he struggled and screamed, I just held him against everything in the world.

I carried him to the couch. He lay there. I kissed his forehead. I said, "You'll never again be as little as you are."

"You said," he mumbled.

He was waiting to be a little boy again.

I ran my hand along his cheek. On the other couch, my wife sat with her face in her hands, our crying little girl at her feet.

*   *   *

In the morning, the fog is dense. As I proceed through the swamps and farms toward the city where I work, I slow down progressively, cutting my speed by half, and then by half again. I can't see ahead, I can't see behind.

In the tendrils of the fog there is a deer. But has he stepped out into my path, or have I drifted off the road toward the wood?

As the deer shifts, he turns to look at me, to stare into me, and I cannot decide if I should accelerate or brake.

WATCH OUT FOR LIONS
REBECCA MCKANNA

FIRST APPEARED IN *SO TO SPEAK*

It happened in the morning before school. When Delia went to the bathroom she found brown stains on the crotch of her underwear. It was a mucky color, nothing like the bright red she had always pictured her period would be. And didn't a continuous stream of blood leak out of a woman on her period? In the sanitary pad commercials on TV, the model always held a test tube in a manicured hand, pouring a stream of blue liquid onto a clean, white pad.

Delia rifled in the cabinet under the bathroom sink, trying to find the panty liner she had hidden behind the rubbing alcohol and hydrogen peroxide. She had kept the wafer-thin thing tucked away for two years—ever since the school nurse handed them out in fifth grade. That was the day Delia and the other girls had endured their teacher saying "heavy flow" and "monthly visitor." She could still remember the way the woman said the word "vagina," like it was the name of a disease or a gloomy European city. Since that day, Delia's best friend had gotten her period, but she had never longed for it to happen to her. Now that it had, she didn't feel grown up. She didn't feel happy. She felt like her body was rebelling against her. Something was happening to her and she couldn't turn back.

Two years ago, before Delia's mom left, the two of them had perched next to each other on the guest bed. Her mother was already sleeping in there and not in the master bedroom with Delia's father. Earlier that day, Delia and her mother had watched a movie where a teenage girl lost her virginity. When the character rose from the bed, there had been rust-colored stains on the white sheets.

"When you have your period, you'll be a woman," her mother had said, staring at her chapped hands, ravaged from delivering mail through Iowan winters. "You'll be able to have babies. You can't be stupid and get pregnant. You can't have sex."

Delia knew her mother had gotten pregnant with her when she was nineteen. Her mother told her that she wasn't an accident. "You were a beautiful surprise." But if she truly felt that way, Delia knew they wouldn't be having this conversation. When Delia's mother had finished talking, Delia went to her room and sat alone with a burning face. She felt ashamed, although she didn't know what she had done wrong.

Sitting on the toilet, the panty liner adhered into place, Delia thought of her mother. The last time they spoke, her mother had called from Olympia where she was staying with a friend from high school. She was working as a temp and thinking of taking courses at the college there. Delia had never been to Washington or any place farther west than Sioux City. Still, she pictured it as a place full of evergreen trees, a place that smelled like rain and cedar.

"You know I love you, right?" her mother said after the updates, the sound bites of their lives, had begun to falter.

"I love you, too," Delia had said, and she could hear her own voice echoing through the bad phone connection. She didn't like the way she sounded–tiny and broken–like someone who would always be waiting.

*   *   *

At the breakfast table, Delia and her father didn't talk. He read the newspaper, and she stared at the back of the cereal box, reading about how a bowl for breakfast and lunch could help you be swimsuit-ready in a month. Her father worked at one of the three banks in town, helping other people get loans. She used to think he liked his job, since he spent so many evenings there. But since her mother left, he returned home promptly at 5:15 p.m. each day. Delia missed those evenings when he was gone. She and her mother watched foreign films her mother checked out from the library or cooked dishes from countries neither would ever visit–pad thai, veggie sushi, or japchae.

Delia looked out the window into the backyard, watching a rabbit jump across the snow. During the summer, a cat had tried to eat a nest of baby bunnies. Delia had heard them screaming, and her father had come outside with her.

"Where did their mother go?" Delia had asked.

"The cat scared her away," her father said.

"What if she doesn't come back for them?"

Her father was usually a practical man. Someone who didn't sugarcoat things. She expected him to say that life was cruel and that sometimes mothers left their babies and didn't return. Instead, he stared at her for a moment before saying, "She'll come back."

But the mother rabbit hadn't returned, and although Delia and her father tried to care for the orphaned bunnies, making a bed for them out of an old crate and feeding them with an eyedropper, all five died by August.

*   *   *

In the car ride to school, she and her father listened to a shock jock named Ray Randolph. He pulled stunts like having men sniff women's underwear to see if the men could guess which woman was a vegetarian. Her father used to get a sheepish look on his face and switch the station if Ray got too crude, but now that Delia was thirteen, he no longer seemed as concerned about Ray's influence.

On that day's show, Ray was having male callers and *Playboy* Playmates answer the same trivia. The segment was called, "Are you smarter than a centerfold?"

Delia stared out the window. The November sky was gray, and birds feasted on the remains of corn stalks in the farmer's fields. She and her father lived five minutes away from Eldridge Junior High, and each morning and evening they drove past the same farmland to get her to school.

"Darling," Ray said, talking to one of the playmates. "For the listeners, let me tell you, this girl is gorgeous. Blonde hair, blue eyes, long legs. What's your bra size, honey?"

"32D," the woman said. Her voice lilted. She sounded like someone who was pretty, somebody who would pose in *Playboy*.

"And how much do you weigh, sweetheart?"

"110 pounds," the woman said.

Delia tried to picture the woman, but it seemed cartoonish. A skeleton with giant water balloons for breasts. Still, Delia knew women like this existed. She saw them on TV and staring at her from the covers of magazines. At sleepovers, these women peered out of issues of *Penthouse* and *Playboy* and *Hustler* that girls smuggled away from their fathers' or brothers' hiding places under mattresses or in the back of closets. Delia had found a few issues of *Playboy* in her father's nightstand once, and she had traced the lines of the women's bodies with her fingertips. Their smooth, tanned skin. Their hairless vaginas. Their large, gleaming breasts. Delia herself had only the buds of breasts, a small swell that she accentuated with padded pink push-up bras. But while her father liked to look at the giant-breasted *Playboy* models, he could barely bring himself to hug Delia since she turned twelve. Instead, he jumped out of her way when she passed too close to him in the kitchen or the hallway. She knew she needed to tell him about her period. She needed him to buy her a box of pads. But she knew he would turn red and stammer, and then there would be even more of a gulf between them.

"Dad," Delia said. He glanced from the road to her face, and then Ray's voice cut through the car.

"Darling, you're just killing me," Ray said. "This girl is sex on legs."

Delia's father reached into the center console to grab his portable coffee mug. There were coffee stains all across the lid, because her father rarely washed it.

"What were you saying, Del?" her father asked.

"Okay, darling," Ray said. "Here's your first question. Name the four Beatles."

Delia's father cocked an eyebrow at her. "Can you name them?"

"Ringo, John, Paul," Delia furrowed her brow.

The playmate's voice was hesitant. "John, Paul, Ringo and..."

A buzzer sounded and Ray laughed. "Sorry, darling. Your time's up. You forgot George."

"You and the *Playboy* girl have something in common," her father said. "I've clearly been remiss as a parent when it comes to your musical education."

She rolled her eyes. "I just forgot."

Delia's father pulled into the middle school's parking lot and got in line behind all the other cars taking their turn at the circle drive to drop their children off. Delia watched the students' breath puff in the cold air, as they exited their parents' trucks and cars.

"It's Okay," her father said. "Everyone forgets George." He patted her arm with careful, staccato taps. "What were you saying earlier?"

"Nothing," Delia said. "See you later."

*   *   *

In homeroom, Delia's hands smelled like the metal of her locker. She liked the rusty scent and rested her head on her palm. Everyone wanted to talk about Jessica Weatherly, a fellow seventh grader who had pierced her eyebrow with a safety pin at lunch the day before.

"I heard there was blood everywhere," said Travis Schulz, shaking his shaggy blonde hair out of his eyes. "That chick is crazy."

Travis straddled the line between popular kid and burnout. When Delia was little, Travis' family lived next door, and the two of them played together every day, while their mothers talked in the kitchen. Every now and then, Travis' mother would cry and then Delia's mother would cry, and then the two of them would play the radio loud and light fresh cigarettes until they were smiling again.

"My mom hates my dad," Travis said once. "So does yours."

"No, she doesn't," Delia had said. "They're married."

"My mom says your mom hates Iowa."

Delia knew her mother, who had grown up in northern California, didn't like Iowa. She had heard her comments about the backward people, the lack of culture, the regrets she had about eloping with the son of a farmer she had only known for a few months.

Still, she didn't like hearing Travis say those things. "She likes it here," she told him. Then the two of them grabbed cherry popsicles from his freezer and sat on his deck, listening to the breeze through the cottonwood trees while the melted red liquid dripped onto their furry, summer-tan legs.

She and Travis didn't see each other for a few years after his parents divorced and he and his mother moved closer to town. When they finally saw each other again on the first day of middle school, each pretended not to know the other.

*   *   *

In first period, their history teacher told them how the Egyptians prepared bodies for mummification by pulling out the corpse's brains. They'd insert a hook into the dead person's nostrils and yank out their gray matter. Then, convinced the heart contained a person's soul, they'd leave the organ in the body so the mummy could move on to the afterlife.

Delia thought about her heart pumping inside her. She could feel her heartbeat when she put her palm to her chest, but she didn't think her soul lived there. As she considered this, she shifted in her chair and realized her underwear was damp. Delia got up to grab the bathroom pass. In the hallway, the rubber soles of her shoes squeaked against the pale tile, the squares the same blue as the belly of the dead fish her father brought home to fry on summer weekends.

In the bathroom, she saw fresh blood soaking the thin panty liner. She stuffed a wad of toilet paper between her legs and left the stall. There was a dented, white metal machine on the wall that sold pads, but Delia didn't have a quarter. She walked down the hallway to the nurse's office. She paused in front of the closed door. A laminated anti-smoking poster hung at eye-level. "Think smoking makes you look cool?" it asked. "Think again." On one side, there was a pretty blonde woman. On the other, stood the same woman, only lined and aged from smoking. The poster pointed out the deep grooves around her mouth, the yellowed teeth, the sallow skin. In the side where the woman was pretty, she was waving to a friend. In the side where she was ugly, she was alone.

Inside the nurse's office, the nurse was standing behind his desk talking to Travis, and Delia's science teacher, Mr. Folks. Delia had developed a crush on Mr. Folks their first week of classes. He was in his late twenties and wore black-rimmed glasses, and when he pointed out the bones on the skeleton that lived in their classroom, he always held the skeleton's limbs so gently.

"This is the fourth time in two weeks he's gotten a headache during my class," Mr. Folks said, as the door clicked shut behind Delia. "Maybe his parents need to be notified about this."

"I can't help it if my head hurts," Travis said.

The nurse was in his fifties, and wore what was left of his hair combed over his gleaming scalp. Although he looked exhausted, the skin around his eyes puffy and wrinkled, he was always patient.

He smiled at Delia. "What do you need?"

Seeing Travis and the two men standing there, Delia wanted to run away. She wasn't sure she could say the words with them all looking at her. She stared at the nurse, willing him into understanding.

He made a noise, a small "oh" of comprehension, and moved toward a cabinet in the back of the room. Both Travis and Mr. Folks watched as the man grabbed the box of pads and fished one out.

Delia leaned forward, her eyes lowered, resting on the plastic replica of the human body sitting on the nurse's desk. Someone had removed the figure's intestines, and they coiled around a bag of cough drops.

When Delia could bring herself to raise her eyes, the nurse handed Delia the pad in a brown paper bag. He handed it to her in the fluid way crack dealers in anti-drug PSAs palmed tiny baggies into their customers' hands. Travis was bright red, and Mr. Folks tapped his index finger against his forearm.

"Cold day, isn't it, Delia?" he said with forced casualness.

Delia put the pad on in the bathroom and then walked back to class. This one was thicker than the panty liner she had put on in the morning, and it felt unnatural, like she was wearing a diaper. Once she sat back down in class, she kept shifting in her chair in discomfort.

*   *   *

After her morning classes, Delia met Meg at the entrance to the cafeteria. The two girls grabbed plastic trays the faded green color of sick plants and got in the hot lunch line. The food in the cafeteria was often beige or pale orange–the breading of chicken nuggets, the unnatural tint of mac and cheese, the soggy French fries.

They each grabbed a slice of pizza and a cup of fries.

Once they were sitting down, Delia told her. "I got my period."

"Duh," Meg said. "I heard Travis talking about it in gym. He saw you in the nurse's office. Couldn't you have asked a girl in your class for a pad? Or you could have texted me."

"I didn't think about it," Delia said. "What did Travis say?"

"He told everyone to be extra nice to you because you were on the rag. It was really funny."

"Great," Delia said. She had eaten a few fries but there was a hollow ache below her stomach. She pushed the fries away from her and wiped the grease off her hands on a paper napkin. "I think I have cramps."

"When you go to the store tonight, get Midol," Meg said, blotting the grease off her pizza with a napkin. "Also, get tampons with a plastic applicator. They're easier to use. Then once you get the hang of it, switch to the ones with a cardboard applicator or no applicator. They're better for the environment."

Meg had started her period at the beginning of the school year and now considered herself an expert on all things related to the subject.

"I didn't think there'd be so much blood," Delia said.

"Ladies," a male voice said. It was Travis.

"Delinquent," Meg said in her haughtiest voice.

Travis clutched his chest as if he had been stabbed. Then he held out his phone to Delia.

"Read it," he said. Delia grabbed the phone. It was pulled up to a webpage about lions kept in captivity. Meg read over Delia's shoulder. The paragraph Travis had highlighted said that female lion caretakers who were menstruating couldn't be around the animals because the lion would smell the blood and attack. The lion in the photo was male, his mane wild and his teeth bared. Blood soaked his muzzle. Delia's lips curled. She handed the phone back to Travis.

"Watch out for lions," he said.

"Go the fuck away," Meg said, throwing a fry at him.

Laughing, he walked back to his table where a group of guys were whispering.

Delia's face was hot. She wanted to make it out of the cafeteria before she started to cry.

*   *   *

After composing herself in the bathroom, Delia walked back to her locker with the stream of students leaving the lunchroom. The walls were grey and the lockers were metal that had been painted a yellow-orange that reminded her of bile.

Delia thought about Travis' face as he showed her his phone. She remembered his expressions when they used to play in the backyard or alone in one of their rooms. She remembered how they used to play soap opera, taking off their cut offs and dingy sneakers and climbing naked into bed. They were only seven, but she remembered how good it felt with his warm skin against her warm skin, and how he smelled of sweat and soap and grass.

Sometimes, even now, she'd look at him in homeroom and remember the way he used to smell, the way he used to feel. They were just kids and it hadn't meant anything, but she wondered if he ever thought about it. She wondered if he remembered how she had felt, too.

One afternoon, a few weeks before Travis' parents announced their divorce, Delia's mother walked in the room as Travis was taking off his shorts. Delia was already naked sitting on the bed. She had been waiting for the moment when Travis would jump into the bed next to her, crush himself to her, and say, "Baby, you're beautiful," like the actors on General Hospital. Sometimes he would put his fingers inside of her—what Travis' older brother called second base—and it felt strange but exciting, like traveling someplace completely new. Delia's mother had paused in the doorway, her face all the more scary because it was so blank.

"Put your clothes on, both of you," Delia's mother had said. "And then, Travis, you get out of our house."

Delia remembered Travis' face then, the wounded eyes and trembling lip, as he pulled his shorts up his skinny legs and reached for his shirt. When Delia's father got home, Delia's mother made Delia tell him what had happened.

Her father set his car keys down on the counter, the lines in his forehead pronounced as he watched Delia's face. She could only get out the words, "Travis and I," before she began to sob and couldn't continue. She was so ashamed she dropped to the kitchen floor, her thin arms wrapped around her scabby knees, her head tucked against the warmth of her body. She tried not to listen to what her mother was telling her father. Words like, "perverted," and "disgusting." She tried to pretend she was one of the pill bugs that she and Travis used to poke until they curled into tiny, hard balls. Delia refused to move from her position on the kitchen floor until hours later, after her parents had already gone up in the den to watch TV. Once the kitchen was dark, Delia got up off the floor, her neck and arms sore, and went to bed. She and her parents never talked about the incident again.

*   *   *

Delia had five minutes before her next class. She thought about calling her mother, but she still didn't like the way the word "period" felt in her mouth. Besides, her mother was 2,000 miles away, and she would just remind Delia that she was a woman now with all the responsibilities that entailed. Travis was right. A girl's period made her vulnerable—whether to lion attacks or to a life-ruining unintended pregnancy.

As Delia entered C Hallway, she realized there was something stuck to one of the lockers. As she neared, two things became clear. The first: The locker belonged to her. The second: It was a maxi pad, its white wings also adhered to the locker, so it looked almost like a butterfly. Someone had colored the center of the pad with a red marker, and Delia was struck by how unrealistic the whole effort was, a boy's idea of what a used pad must look like, the same conception Delia would have had until this morning.

Delia pulled down the pad, but one of the maxi wings stayed stuck to her locker. She flung the pad to the ground. When she turned around, her face was red but not from embarrassment. The image of the lion from the webpage Travis had shown her was still in her mind. She stalked toward Travis and his friends. They were looking at her and smirking, but with each step she took, Travis' smile wavered. When he lived on her street, she saw that same slow fade of expression each night when his father's car pulled into the driveway.

"Do you think you're funny?" she asked him, once she was standing in front of him.

"I think I'm hilarious," he said.

When she grabbed for his hair, she wasn't consciously trying to start a fight with him. She had never physically fought with anyone. She just felt an urge, deep inside her, to pull at that gleaming crown of hair, to tug his white-blonde tresses until he yelped like an animal. He tried to push her away. "You're crazy," he said. But she moved her hands from his hair to his chest, taking him by surprise, and shoving him backward. His friends moved out of the way, their little clique disintegrating, and she pushed Travis against the school's trophy case. The glass of the case rattled as his skull knocked against it, and the wooden frame rocked forward and back once, gold trophies for wrestling and cheerleading shimmying.

"Let go of me," Travis said, trying to pry her hands from his chest, but he was smaller than she was. She kicked him in the shin, and he fell to one knee. Then she dropped to her knees, too, pushing back on his windpipe until he had fallen back against the dingy floor. Then they were scrabbling against each other, both of them clawing and rolling against the ground.

"Fight! Fight! Fight!" the students yelled. Delia sank her teeth into Travis' earlobe, biting until he screamed like a cat whose tail had been slammed in a door. She felt the sting of Travis' sweaty palm against her cheek, and then a firm hand tugged her arm, pulling her to her feet.

She turned around and saw it was Mr. Folks, his eyes wide behind his glasses. He stepped in front of Delia and stared down at Travis, who was still crumpled on the ground. "What do you think you're doing?" he asked Travis. "You think you're a big man, attacking a young girl?"

Mr. Folks looked at the crowd of students gathered around. "Get to class," he said, his arm slicing through the air. Then he turned to Delia. "Are you all right? Did he hurt you?"

Delia swallowed. No, she wanted to say. We hurt each other. But no sound came out of her mouth. She stared at Travis on the ground. He looked dazed. His face was red and his eyes were unfocused.

"Go to class, Delia," Mr. Folks said, his voice gentle. Then he pulled Travis up roughly by the arm and said, "You, follow me." She watched the two of them walk toward the principal's office, and the fullness she had felt inside during the fight began to deflate.

She didn't go back to class right away. Instead, she leaned against the row of lockers. She was certain she had just committed social suicide. This was the kind of thing a girl could never live down. She would always be the crazy period girl, rabid and unhinged.

But she didn't regret it. Fighting Travis, she had felt full in a way she couldn't understand. She knew violence was wrong. She had learned a whole anti-violence song set to the hand jive in fifth grade that the students performed before assemblies. But that didn't change how she had felt with her fingers in Travis' hair, her teeth against his earlobe.

*   *   *

A few minutes after fifth period, Delia was summoned to the principal's office by an announcement over the loudspeaker. When she arrived, the principal, Dr. Castle, was opening his door. Travis walked out of the man's office, crying. Delia pictured Travis' mother having to come pick him up after getting the phone call from the principal. She pictured Mrs. Shultz's tired, downcast eyes. She envisioned Mr. Shultz's gruff lecture to Travis once he found out. She remembered how she and Travis used to hide from Mr. Shultz as kids. Once, Travis had picked up a toy gun and told her he was going to shoot his father with it.

"You can't," she had told him. "We can't play together if you're in jail."

He had stared at her for a long time. "I won't then. For you."

"Delia," Dr. Castle said. "Please come in."

Travis didn't look at her. He wiped the snot from his nose with the arm of his black shirt, leaving a shiny film on his sleeve, as he passed by her to go and sit in one of the chairs in front of Dr. Castle's secretary's desk.

Dr. Castle's office had a window that looked upon the frozen soccer fields. He gestured for her to sit in a chair, and she watched a cardinal peck near the goal posts for food, a blot of vivid red on the white landscape.

She studied the diplomas on his wall and the photos of him with his wife and baby. Dr. Castle was younger than the previous principal, Mr. Brooks. It was hard for Delia to gauge adults' exact ages. Still, she knew he seemed more nervous than Mr. Brooks, less at ease around the students.

"Delia, you've never been sent to my office before," Dr. Castle said, sitting back down. "That says to me there had to be some special circumstances that pro-voked you into violence today."

"I got angry, so I shoved Travis," she said.

"What made you so angry?"

She shrugged.

He cleared his throat. "Was there something that happened to you today that..." he gestured with one hand, as if he was twirling a string in the air. "That Travis was teasing you about?"

She met Dr. Castle's eyes. She knew he knew. It amused her that he wouldn't say it.

She shook her head. "I don't know what you mean."

He cleared his throat again. "Mr. Folks mentioned this might have been a big day for you as a young woman. He thought Travis might have been teasing you about these...changes."

Dr. Castle's cheeks had turned pink. He disgusted her.

"You mean my period?" she said. For the first time that day, she liked the feel of the word in her mouth. She liked the way it made him cringe.

"Yes," he said. "Was that what Travis was teasing you about?"

"No," she said. "I just got angry, and I felt like hurting someone. I was the one who started it."

Dr. Castle stared at her. She stared back. Finally, he shook his head. "Then you owe Travis an apology. We take violence seriously in this school. You'll be suspended, and I'll be calling your parents."

"Parent," Delia said, enunciating the last consonant of the word. "My dad."

Dr. Castle waved his hand as if the distinction didn't matter. "Go wait outside until he arrives."

Delia opened the door. In the waiting room, Travis' head jerked up like a man awaiting a firing squad. "Mr. Shultz," Dr. Castle said. "You can go back to class after Delia apologizes to you."

"I'm sorry for fighting you," Delia said. She met his eyes, and she felt that fullness again, that pressure in her chest that made her feel like she might burst.

Travis eyed her warily. "It's okay," he said.

Dr. Castle nodded. "You can go now, Mr. Shultz."

Then he shut his office door. Travis still stood there in front of her.

"Why didn't you tell him what I did?" he asked.

Delia shrugged. She couldn't put it into words, although she knew it had something to do with how Mr. Folks and Dr. Castle had looked at her. Like they knew without question that she would always be the victim rather than the lion.

Travis stood there a moment longer. Finally, he turned and left.

Delia sat in one of the waiting room chairs. She felt that hollow ache in her lower abdomen again, and she leaned her head against the wall, prepared to wait a long time before someone came for her.

TOWNSHIP
STEPHANY WILKES

It came faster and farther down the dirt road than anything else ever did. Later, Brian would remember it as an approaching force before it became the sound of tires crunching gravel, spinning out on creviced drought ground. It was as if a storm cloud of freeway noise from the Detroit they'd left in February had sniffed them out and tracked them to the far north woods, from the Lower Peninsula to the Upper, across the frozen strait that stopped freighters and that only the wolves walked.

It first passed Mr. Jepsen's farm, with its llamas that spit at each other and the knee-deep furrows where he'd accidentally run over his seven-year-old daughter with a spring-tooth drag harrow. It rounded the first bend past Mrs. Culver's, now 98 and not on a single medication, never seen a doctor in her life. She made eight-year-old Brian and his older sister, Beth, balance pennies on the backs of their hands when they practiced piano at her house. They slipped off constantly and Mrs. Culver let them keep the ones they dropped.

Kicking up barn-high clouds and vortices of dust, the sound became visible as it headed for the second bend. Grit settled over the crab apple tree that Mrs. Froelich transformed into pies, meticulously removing worms with her pocket knife on the screened-in porch she'd built around an old pine tree. Mr. Delpier's tasty pigs, who would get drunk on fermented drop apples a few days before slaughter, were unfazed by the frantic wheels that shot stones against the dilapidated row of metal mailboxes beside their electric fence.

Brian knew it had lasted too long, far longer than it would have taken for one car going so fast. He was the first and only person to see it all, fresh out of the lake, the ends of his khaki life vest and camouflage bathing shorts dripping. He'd run up and over the hill, down the strawberry meadow's edge of sharp, parched grass and milkweed, and up to the boat house that bordered the low road. He needed an additional boat cushion so he and Tom would each have one while they ran the outboard around. Brian was so surprised by the fast approaching cars that he dove under the boat house door when it was only about waist high, skinning his knee before rolling to a crouching position, the late summer air close. A train of black Suburbans tore past, breaking low tree branches, interspersed with police cars, sirens and lights off.

Almost everyone on the lake had a Suburban or something like it but Brian had never seen a police car out here. Kids on the lake learned to drive real young, most by the time they were 12, because even if the police or ambulance was willing to come all the way out here they might not be able to find you. Brian liked this because, as Tom said, driving at 12 was a damned sight better than having to wait until you were sixteen. Tom was almost eleven.

The cars were going faster than anyone should be going out here. *Try that at night sometime*, Brian thought, *with no street lights and no moon. See how far you get.* He counted like he did between lightning and thunder when he wished a thunderstorm would stop: one one thousand, two one thousand. Brian hit thirty before he felt safe enough to bolt from the boat house, the cushion long forgotten, lifting his knees higher so as not to stub his toes on the logs that formed the stairs, shouting to his mother. As he approached, Brian could see Beth, his older sister, and Tom standing still in thigh-deep water, their fingertips seeming to float on it, while his mother, Linda, sat on the dock with her knees over the side of the chaise lounge. They were all turned toward the white fisherman's cottage out on the point, about eight houses from theirs around the gentle curve of the lake.

The black Suburbans and police cars had stopped there, marked by a dust cloud slow to dissipate in the heavy humidity. Brian looked at his mother in her blue sea shell bathing suit, the untied halter strings dangling long in front, horizontal lines across the front of her puckered thighs. Condensation slid from her beer can down her freckled wrist as dozens of silhouettes, some with shields and some with long guns drawn, fanned out around the white cottage.

Brian ran into the water, slowed as it got deeper, plowing through with his knees, unzipping his life jacket and tossing it onto the dock. No boat ride now.

"Out of the water!" Linda announced, standing up and walking toward shore, setting the dock bouncing.

"No! We want to watch!" Beth whined.

Tom said, "Ms. Tillander, I think we're safer in the water. It'll be harder for the bullets to hit us."

Was that even true? Brian wondered. *Did water slow bullets like water slowed him?*

"Then stay behind the dock. And keep your heads down!"

Brian's mother wrapped herself in a threadbare terrycloth tunic before sitting on top of the picnic table to watch the action. Tom, Beth and Brian floated toward the end of the dock until they passed under it, the deeper water closer to the white cottage on the point. Pencils of light shone through the slats onto their wet hair. Brian held on to one of the sawhorses upon which the dock rested, and which he and Beth had had to put in right after the thaw, wearing waders. He'd been surprised to learn that waders didn't keep you warm, just dry. The sawhorse was slippery with algae but he held on anyway, pushing down against it to float higher. He didn't want even the tiniest leeches on his toes from the muck.

The water level was low that year, which worried the adults, but now it afforded Brian a view. He could just see the white cottage and the black, helmeted men, big beetles with shields for wings. Some braced themselves against trees while others disappeared into foliage or hid behind police cars, peering over their roofs. One of the men had a megaphone but the sheriff said something to him and took it. Brian thought he hardly needed it: everything echoed perfectly around the lake. When he and his sister rowed out alone their mom could hear everything they said, especially if they were arguing. When she wanted them to come in she just walked to the end of the dock and said so.

"That's Larry Minor," Tom said. "Constitutional. He's what you pray you get as a sheriff in your county." Brian was pretty sure Tom was repeating something he'd heard from his dad.

Sheriff Minor's voice came over the megaphone. "Now, you got a DEA SWAT team out here, and I want you to know they'll be coming 'round that door. But nobody wants this to go ugly. There is no reason for this to go ugly. But we do gotta' talk to you."

"Was there even a car outside when they pulled up?" Beth asked. "Is anyone even there?"

"It's August. They could've gone home already," Tom said.

The megaphone continued. "Now, we gotta' talk to you. I am unarmed. I am going to walk up and knock on your front door. We can talk for a few minutes and I can tell you what's going on."

"See!" Tom said. "Constitutional guy!"

Sheriff Minor set the megaphone on the roof of the police car and, in his jeans and t-shirt, walked to the front door of the fisherman's cottage. He knocked, waited. Knocked again. He leaned to the right to see if he could see anything through the curtained window and turned back toward the police car.

"Don't think anyone's home," he said. He knocked again and gently tugged the screen door, which opened. "Think it may even be unlocked." He seemed relieved at this. Half-facing the lake he announced, more loudly than before, "In a few minutes a DEA SWAT team will begin a search of your home." He turned and walked back toward the police car.

"Aren't they supposed to say 'Come out with your hands up. You will not be fired upon?'" asked Brian.

"Maybe if Minor wasn't here, they would," said Tom. "But they probably can't even say it anymore because it's not true. They say you will not be fired upon and then they do, just like they 'didn't fire upon' Gordon Kahl."

"Who's that?" asked Brian.

"Posse Comitatus?" Brian shook his head and the water moved.

"Gordon Kahl was a WWII vet. They put him in prison for not paying taxes. U.S. Marshals tried to arrest him and there was a shootout and he got away. He hid on someone's property and a SWAT team fired thousands of bullets before setting these poor people's house on fire. And it was the sheriff who actually killed him, but it turned out sort of fair because the sheriff ended up dying from one of Gordon Kahl's bullets. That's why you pray you have a sheriff like Minor."

The SWAT team rearranged itself again. Five men approached the house from various directions while three more moved closer to the boundary with Tom's family's property, marked by its red A-frame with a front deck, about 50 yards to the left of the fisherman's cottage. Like most of the lots, Tom's family's was lake-front with acres of forest and farm behind it.

"They're on our property now!" Tom hissed, indignant. "I'd like to see my dad start picking them off!"

"Me too," Beth said, icily.

"If anyone could pick these guys off, it's your dad!" Brian said, confident. Tom grinned.

Tom's dad, Don Pullum, was a barrel of a man who'd been a Marine in Viet-nam before he came to his senses about the government. He could still pick up each of the kids as if they were toddlers and heave them, sailing, into the lake while they screamed with joy. He built them rope-log swings over the water and taught them to chop wood without cutting their legs or feet. He let them bow shoot into stacked bales of hay in the woods. Tom's family had a chest freezer full of salmon and venison that they got themselves and canned goods that glowed like jewels in their coat closet pantry: deep violet blackberries, amber peaches, emerald pickles. Brian's mom had used Tang to get Brian and Beth to drink well water but they drank it plain at the Pullum's.

"I wonder where your parents are," Beth said, anxious.

Brian knew how much Beth liked Tom's parents, both of whom had attended high school with Linda. When he and Beth had been dragged to tennis camp down at parks and rec, Beth had spent the entire ride fuming that Don and Winnie let them do useful things instead of waste all this time, and didn't talk to them like they were stupid, like the tennis coach would.

*   *   *

On the first Saturday in February, when they'd moved in to the musty old cabin that had sat empty for nearly two years, Winnie had appeared on snow shoes across the frozen lake, bearing a foil-wrapped loaf of cinnamon bread between her mittened hands. Once inside, she'd pulled a gallon bag of goop from the interior pocket of her green down coat. She'd taped a list of instructions to it with the title "Amish Friendship Bread." Though Beth hadn't even known what a bread starter was, as soon as she read the instructions she'd treated the bag of goop like a pet, raising Cain and frantically retrieving it when someone put it in the fridge, shrilly insisting it stay in a certain corner of the kitchen counter and noting on the calen-dar when to add flour, sugar and milk and even when to squeeze the bag.

To Brian's amazement, this had not been the end of it. Beth had proceeded to make photocopies of the instructions at the IGA and gave sandwich bags of goop to various neighbors (even though Brian thought they probably already had some from Winnie, he did not dare say so), to near strangers at church, and even to the teenage tennis coach. Beth attached a painstakingly typed note to each bag that read:

> "Hi! We are your new neighbors at the olive green cabin that was the Lloyd's. DO NOT USE ANY METAL SPOONS OR BOWLS FOR MIXING THE STARTER! Contact with metal will cause a chemical reaction and kill the yeast colony that is keeping the starter alive! Keep the starter at room temperature, NOT in the refrigerator. Cold temperatures will slow or stop its growth. When air starts to accumulate in the bag, open the top and let it out. Sincerely, Beth."

Brian's mom took this as a sign that Beth was "improving" but Brian wasn't sure she should. Adults often didn't like Beth because she was a good judge of character and refused to be swayed by their overly sweet attempts to win her over. Beth had had problems with teachers because of this. In first grade, Beth's teacher had asked her to stop talking before class had actually begun. Beth did—and maintained her silence for the rest of the school year, even when called upon to respond. In third grade, Beth received a B on her first assignment of the year and had not turned in any work since. Brian's family was perplexed because they all saw Beth do school work at home. One day after school, Beth's teacher and Linda lifted the top of Beth's desk. There, neatly stacked, was all of the completed work that Beth had not turned in. When Linda asked about this Beth only said, "I am not going to get Bs for A work."

Linda relayed this to Beth's teacher who said, "Well, it was A work but most students stop trying if you give them an A too early in the year." Linda assured the teacher that such games were not necessary: anything less than perfect drove Beth crazy, she who kept herself up until 11 p.m. crying while trying to perfect her cursive, who didn't understand why friends who came over to play didn't want to read books with her, who cried in frustration from clashing noises like talk radio and conversation at the same time.

Whenever someone asked why they'd moved, Brian would say "My mom is from here and wanted to move back." Linda would say "It just didn't pan out." Both responses had the same effect: people felt satisfied that their choices had won out over Linda's, who'd made the mistake of moving downstate on the false promise of decent wage jobs, and then marrying someone who had one of them. When Brian finally asked his mom what "didn't pan out" meant, she said "I think it came from panning for gold. People went out West for the Gold Rush and didn't find any, so when they came home they'd say 'It didn't pan out.' When you're panning for gold, you pick up part of the stream bed in a bowl and shake it underwater. The gold sinks to the bottom and the lighter materials, which are worthless, rise to the surface so you can sweep them away."

Linda Tillander was worn down by a decade's worth of pink slips that came without warning right after you'd finally gotten a new vacuum or screen door, or repaired the car or the gutters. She felt the shop owners must be able to see their employees' bank transactions in a crystal ball, that they waited for one of these indulgences to appear so they could reproach you for acting bigger than your britches. For Linda, pink slips were palm-sized punishment for being fool enough to do the things you were supposed to have done: buy a house, have some kids.

Linda had also lost patience with everything that followed the terrible pink harbingers: the bicycling in sleet to deliver bill payments by hand rather than spend money on gas or a stamp; drinking powdered milk instead of regular; living on pasta and pancakes under a president who claimed ketchup was a vegetable; foregoing dryer sheets and haircuts and never being able to buy strawberries. But strawberries were tough even when they were both working, alternating shifts so one of them could always be home with the kids.

Linda adored strawberries. She felt rich when she ate them. In Michigan they were bright red gold, present for just a few months, every bit as dazzling as the Northern Lights. Even though they were grown locally, their appearance was so brief as to make them the most decadent thing in the world.

Brian remembered riding in the grocery cart while Beth walked, the pace slowing along the wood-lipped, produce-piled tables. Linda would sample one red grape, one green, which was okay, she said. Everyone had a right to know if grapes were sour or sweet, ripe or not before they paid good money for them. Brian felt guilty, worried someone might find out they couldn't buy any of it anyway, no matter how sweet the sample. Grapes and maybe even cherries were one thing but sampling a strawberry, so substantial and dense and expensive, felt like stealing. But neither Brian nor Beth could bring themselves to ask about it and ruin the only strawberry their mother allowed herself. When it had come time for spring planting on the lake, strawberry seeds were the first thing Linda picked up at Erickson's Feed. She'd planted the entire sloped meadow with them and nothing else. "You'll see," she said. "I'll grow strawberries like the Dutch grow tulips."

Nothing Brian's dad did could make strawberries possible or stop the waves of lay offs from coming: his willingness to alternate between day and night shifts, to work swing shift, to work holiday overtime made no difference. In April, Brian's dad had been doing their taxes, the newsprint how-to booklets from the library beside his big-buttoned calculator. Brian doodled on the scrap scrolls the machine pushed over the edge of the kitchen table.

"I worked 15 months last year," Brian's dad said.

Brian's pencil paused. "A year only has 12 months, dad."

"Oh, I just mean hours. Like I worked three extra months last year."

The breaking point came just before Christmas, preceded by a pink slip after presents had already been purchased. Brian's mom had sent he and Beth out to play in the backyard snow with their favorite supplies: two Tupperware cups, two teaspoons, and brown sugar and baking vanilla. They filled the cups with snow, added the brown sugar and baking vanilla, and mashed it all together to make snow cones. They ate and wondered why the birds they could see didn't migrate for winter.

Beth closed her eyes, tilted her face upward and stuck out her tongue to catch snowflakes. Suddenly she said "Ow!"

"What?" Brian asked.

"It feels like a bee sting!" Beth said. "But there aren't any bees right now!"

Looking at her, Brian noticed that Beth's knit hat appeared to have pieces of Christmas tinsel on it. His eyes widened. "Beth, you have silver snow on you! It's snowing silver!" he cried.

Crimped, wrinkled staples stood in the snow like pins, as if the frozen drifts were magnets. Brian saw Linda at the kitchen window looking angry. He said, "We should probably be quiet," but his mom was already in the yard without coat or shoes on. She grabbed the plastic cups from their hands and threw them into the snow. Half dragging and half carrying Brian, she yelled at Beth to run inside. She threw both of them into the bathtub and started pulling off their clothes.

On the verge of tears, Beth asked "What's happening, mom?" Linda, turning on the water and breathing deeply, said "It's metal pieces blowing over from Zug Island. It's just...metal. We need to wash it off so it's bath time now."

Afterward, wrapped in matching robes Linda had sewn, they had gotten hot cocoa and popcorn made on the stove and been allowed to watch *Rikki-Tikki-Tavi* on PBS. Linda had dialed her parents up north, made he and Beth say hi, and then stretched the phone cord taut from the kitchen down the landing steps that led to the basement. Brian heard her say "Metal, mother! Metal. What if they ate it?!" and "No. No. I don't care. We are *done*. We are *moving*." And, less than two months later, they had, which was when Brian and Beth realized that "we" had not meant all of them.

Brian missed his dad, which adults dismissed by saying well, he wasn't around that much anyway. They were partially right: Brian's dad was a part of the household who was and wasn't there. But Brian had seen hard, verifiable and regularly occurring signs that confirmed his dad's existence. There was his Thermos soaking with dish soap on the counter as you passed the kitchen coming out of the bathroom at night. There were his work clothes in the basement dryer that his mom made him bring upstairs, clothes washed separately because they transferred steel remnants and metallic smells to everyone else's if you washed them together. Most mornings there were the sounds of shower water running, a whistling tea kettle, and a car warming up in the dark morning while Brian was half asleep. Brian's father had always been somewhat ephemeral but now he wasn't even that.

*   *   *

"I hope the summer people aren't home. And if they are, I hope they don't come out," Beth said.

"Then they'll just bust in and kill them," Tom said.

"I know they didn't do anything," Beth said, convinced.

"Oh yeah? How?" Tom challenged.

"Do you think they did?" Beth asked.

"No, but they're not here a lot. They're summer people, so who knows?"

Waves licked the bottom of the greasy aluminum fishing boat, generating lively, hollow taps. The insects whined on in their constant, surrounding summer buzz, snapping as if electrified. Brian had laughed when they'd gone back to Detroit to visit his other grandparents for Easter and they'd asked if he found the woods too quiet.

Spots of color appeared behind the sliding glass door on the Pullum's front deck. The door slid open a few inches and they could see Don in the opening, but he didn't stick his neck out.

"My dad!" Tom said, elated. He ducked out from beneath the dock and half swam, half walked to shore. Brian and Beth followed. The water was colder when you were out of the sun and not moving.

Tom kept his eye on his house while he wrapped himself in a Bugs Bunny towel. Brian's mom rapidly rubbed Brian's arms up and down along the outside of his towel.

"Your lips are blue!" touching them lightly with her index finger.

"Bomb Pops," Brian said.

"More than that." Linda smiled and wrapped Brian's towel tighter. "Do you know those neighbors?" she asked Tom.

"Not really. We don't see them a lot. Sometimes my parents check on things for them and they keep a set of keys with us after summer."

The sickening crack of an agent shouldering the cottage's maple door open reached them. Beth winced over the audible noises of the SWAT team rifling through the house.

"I about can't stand this," Linda said, reaching for the mini Coleman cooler. "To see them do that to that beautiful old cottage." Tom stood slightly behind Brian's mother, everyone oriented toward the white house on the point like a strange sort of human sundial. Linda popped a beer can from a plastic ring. *We could be watching a bonfire*, Brian thought.

Don's voice sounded over the water. "You still out and about, Minor?"

Larry Minor turned toward the A-frame and took a few steps. "Sure am, Don."

"Like to step out on my deck and come down and talk to you—unarmed, of course."

"'Course. I'll walk over that way myself."

Sheriff Minor placed himself at the bottom of the deck stairs, where Don met him. They shook hands.

"So much for the idea that you're the type to just start shooting," Larry said.

"We all know how that would turn out. What the hell's going on over there, though?" Don asked, pointing toward the white house. "Nice to not be shot dead while these guys figure it out."

"Don, there is...*acres* of marijuana back there. It's not just on their land but a lot of it is, and on yours, too."

"You think we go in for that hippie business, me and Winnie?"

"Aw, Don, I didn't say that. But I'm asking you: it's really not yours?"

"No. Eventually you all will figure that out, because some of it runs on through the back of the Girl Scout Camp, and some of it stretches so far that you can get to it by walking through that corn field that backs up to the county road."

"You call it in?" Larry asked.

"Think I'd rat to the law?"

"To save your hide and your land? Maybe. I sure as shit would."

Don shook his head back and forth but they could tell he was smiling. "Well, just don't tell anyone else, ruin my reputation."

Brian glanced at Tom and immediately down at Tom's toes moving dirt back and forth. "What the hell," Tom said, quietly.

A distant boom like an expensive firecracker grew and echoed, followed by smaller, far off pops. The kids glanced at each other and Linda raised her eyebrows at them.

"Sounds like your boys may have found their men. Glad I've got you between them and me," Don said.

"Don't suppose I could take your ATV out there?"

"Sure can." Don and Larry turned away from the lake and walked toward the Pullum's garage.

Linda asked, "Did you kids ever see anything playing out there? I know you get all the way back to the farm house sometimes."

They had seen something, and they all remembered it because it had been the same day as the tornado. They had been on their way to get their parents, Brian recalled, but other things happened. A few days later it didn't seem as important to tell them.

*　*　*

They had all three been back by the abandoned farm house, nearly a mile into the woods on the Pullum property, where they were not supposed to be. The rear of the farm house sat on a creek. Its east facing side looked out on a wind break of pines between it and someone else's corn field, with an overgrown two-track road that eventually reached the county highway. The rusted farm equipment raised threats of tetanus shots from Tom's mom but that was nothing compared to Winnie's longwinded exhortations about the old well shaft she suspected was there. Nearly one year after the fact, Winnie had photos of Baby Jessica on the fridge, strapped papoose-like to a board and wrapped like a mummy, dangling from ropes. Baby Jessica had been wedged in a Texas well shaft for 58 hours.

They'd felt wide ranging and restless on that unusually hot day in early June, the last day of school less than a week before. They'd wandered behind the farm house, with its dishes still sitting in the rotting, glass-doored sideboard, to the creek. On almost every visit they'd find a fledgling beaver dam and agonize over whether or not to destroy its handiwork. They always did because they worried about it flooding the old house or the corn field. But this time, they'd found a brand new hose in the creek instead. Brian remembered the combination of being elated to find something new and deeply afraid because someone else had been there. They'd reasoned that the corn field must need more water this year, with the water low, and removed their shoes to tramp barefoot up the creek and follow the hose to its source.

"Maybe someone bought this land?" Beth had asked, leading the pack.

"No way," Tom had said. "It's ours and we haven't sold any."

They'd stared so intently at the hose, tracking it through plants and fallen branches along the heavily shaded stream bed, that Beth had run into the man with the gun in his waist holster, whose huge black boots kept them from following the creek any farther. Beth screamed, startled, then laughed shrilly.

The man did not smile at her, nor did he look like Don did in hunting photos. Noticing details about the man had felt like solving a puzzle, the situation coming into focus piecemeal only when Brian stepped back on his heels and looked at all of it together. The man was wearing too many clothes, and dark clothes, for this heat. Brian had begun to notice his own breathing, a vein in his forehead. It wasn't hunting season of any kind. Brian knew Tom had to wait until September to go on his first hunt of the year, and the man's gun wasn't any kind he'd seen before. Brian looked at Tom and knew he knew these things, too. So the man was a poacher or...worse.

Beth, with her blonde braids, had been the first to speak, going right from screaming to using the dumb girl routine that Brian had seen get her out of things for years, blameless, ever the innocent.

"Hey!" She cried. The man looked almost as startled as Brian felt. "Are you going to get a deer today?"

The man stared at her for a second but seemed to relax a little. "Maybe. Maybe I will."

"I bet they come here to drink water! Have you seen any yet?"

"No, not today. But uh, it ain't safe for you to be in the woods when there's hunting."

"Yeah, we didn't know. Thanks!" Beth had already turned away from him.

Tom got it. "Let's go back to my house and play hunters. We can use my bow!"

"Good luck with your deer!" Beth said, thrusting her right arm into an awkward wave and bolting back down the creek.

And Brian had run like he'd never run, not for the President's Physical Fitness program, not for soccer try-outs. He ran with bare soles slick against slimy pebbles but didn't stay on them long enough to fall, desperately trying to keep up with his sister, the gazelle. She was already so tan that she looked like something out of *The Jungle Book*. Brian felt his pounding temples would crack his skull and he pushed down on the cramp in his side with his right arm, telling it to wait. His palms were clammy and his forearms pink. He didn't think about how he was running, he just ran.

They'd paused just enough to bend and pick up their shoes, and run on behind the farm house, putting it between themselves and the creek. They'd collapsed against its weathered walls of slivers and stared up at the sky. Brian could feel the pin-sized base of every hair on his head pulsing, lightly itching, and a beating behind his eyes. The circle of tree branches framing the sky seemed to pulse smaller, larger, smaller, larger. Then, as crisp and distinct as the first fall day with flurries, a chill breeze had blown across the ground, grazing the dirt, chilling their feet and legs and hands while their heads and arms sweltered. For several, long seconds the woods went absolutely still and silent. Tree branches did not move, the background insect hum had ended abruptly, and there was not a peep from a single bird. Wrong, Brian thought. *All wrong.*

"That's a storm," Tom said, puffing but with certainty, eyes on the sky, cheeks still red. He began to put his shoes on.

"And that man is still there!" Beth said, as if they could forget.

The very last thing Brian wanted was to run. He wished Don or Winnie would come through on the ATV, even if they'd get in trouble. But they had to go again. Brian knew they couldn't stay here, sheltering from a storm in a half-collapsed house, the armed man seeking shelter himself. They'd run the full mile back through the woods, feet heavier, trying not to trip on roots, tall green plants with downturned fronds scratching their arms, some waist high. They'd slowed to a stumbling sort of fast walk upon reaching the low road, and when they'd finally reached the lake they were met with a rainbow sky, a big stripe of bright blue losing out to pale gray and green behind it, like a sick sort of sunrise. They'd found their parents arrayed in lawn chairs.

"Isn't the sky amazing?" Linda said behind her big owl sunglasses, head tilted to the left, smiling at him.

"Watching storms come in across this water is something else," Winnie agreed.

What's wrong with them? Brian wondered. *They're so calm! How can they be so calm?*

The chop was forming whitecaps as Beth unhooked the padlock and threw open the cellar doors that fronted the lake. Beth, Brian and Tom pitched inner tubes and buckets and towels into its dark, half-dirt maw, telling their parents to move while their parents laughed at their panic. Linda, Winnie and Don didn't budge until the wind pelted beach sand that stung. Then they'd all stood at once as at the beginning of mass, holding on to lawn chairs to avoid losing them. That was the moment the funnel cloud appeared, still tiny in its distance, high above the tree tops but well on its own, gradually building motion, wisps of clouds wrapping inward and joining, the approaching sound of a runaway trunk, a faint but growing siren. Moments later, the rowboat lifted out of the water and hovered level, still tethered to the dock, until the boat and dock section ripped away and shot horizontally toward the Pullum's house.

Fighting the wind, Brian ran up to the cabin with his mom to move lamps to the floor and open the windows, surprisingly difficult in the mounting wind and shaking with fear. Linda grabbed the kerosene lamp and and long matches, yelling at Brian to grab the flashlights. Don was halfway up the stairs and yelled at them to leave the main door open and latch the screen door from the outside. In the cool, pitch dark cellar, Brian, Beth and Tom had sat together on the big, black rubber inner tube, held hands and, knees touching in its middle hole, prayed like they never had.

Brian remembered the hours and days after the tornado as a fun sort of time, even without power and water. They'd primarily eaten food that could be kept in coolers and it was fun to visit your neighbors and try to sort out the garage doors, life jackets and other paraphernalia that had been sucked up, cast out and floated in to shore.

*   *   *

"We saw a man with a rifle once," Brian said, evenly. No one expected him to know all the guns yet and his mother didn't, either, unlike Winnie. He didn't have to say what kind it had really been.

"And you didn't say anything?!" Linda half shrieked.

"Well, it's not *that* weird to see a man in the woods with a rifle," Brian said, making it sound like the most normal thing in the world. Tom glanced at him and seemed satisfied. Every so often, Brian wondered at the possibility that the man in the woods might have worked for Don, who didn't seem to have a normal job, but Brian always kept his mouth shut. Normal jobs didn't seem any better.

The news described it as the largest marijuana seizure in Michigan history, but since there weren't very many of those no was sure of exactly how large it was. The single local news channel, relieved for something to break up reports of tornado damage, repeatedly interviewed a deeply freckled, frizzy-haired woman described as a "local resident," whom none of them had ever seen, standing in front of a trailer though the lake had none. She claimed to have seen packages dropped into the water from low-flying airplanes and that the first lake resident who noticed would immediately retrieve it by boat. "The whole lake is on the take," she kept saying, and it morphed into a headline.

A small army of men would invade the woods for a day and a half, rooting out and binding the dank, stinking plants. They would not return, leaving the beaver to build its dams and the farm house beams to rot and sink, rot and sink. School would start and, with it, Linda's job and Brian having to wear snug shoes and a full set of clothes every day.

Just a few more years and he'd be able to drive, maybe even all the way downstate to surprise his dad. He'd learn in their Suburban, wide and burnt orange and brown with rust spots, an automatic with no seat belts in back. Linda promised Brian his first lesson would be in a cemetery, just like hers with his granddad, where he wouldn't have to worry about hurting anyone or being thrown off track by someone else, safely buffeted by the stone markers of so many ephemeral men.

CONTRIBUTORS

Ron A. Austin holds a MFA from the University of Missouri–St. Louis. His stories have been placed in *Black Warrior Review, Natural Bridge, December, Gulf Stream, Drafthorse,* and other journals. He has received Pushcart Prize nominations and teaches Creative Writing at the Pierre Laclede Honors College while completing his first collection of short stories: *Avery Colt Is A Snake, A Thief, A Liar.* He currently resides in his hometown of St. Louis with his wife, Jennie, and their dog, Carmen. He may be contacted at ronaaustin@gmail.com.

Dane Bahr is the editor of Dock Street Press. He lives in Seattle with his wife. He can be reached at danebahr@dockstreetpress.com.

Boyd Bauman grew up on a small ranch in northeast Kansas and has lived recently in Japan and Vietnam. He is now a writer and a teacher in the Kansas City area. His work has appeared in *Plainsongs, The Front Range Review, The South Dakota Review, Nomad's Choir, Mobius, The Rockhurst Review, Heartlands,* and *Barbaric Yawp,* among others. He's been honored by the Kansas Voices Poetry Contest and has appeared on the website 150 Kansas Poems.

Monica Berlin's recent solo work has appeared or is forthcoming in *Crazyhorse, Hayden's Ferry Review, The Cincinnati Review, TriQuarterly, Ninth Letter, Witness, DIAGRAM, Third Coast, RHINO,* and *Passages North,* among others. She is the project director for The Knox Writers' House digital archives of contemporary literature, and serves as the associate director for the Program in Creative Writing at Knox College, where she is an associate professor of English.

Eric Boyd is a line cook living in Pittsburgh. His work has been published by *The Missouri Review, Guernica, Akashic Books,* and *PEN,* among others; he has upcoming stories appearing in Akashic Books' *Prison Noir,* edited by Joyce Carol Oates, as well as *Make Mine Words,* a teaching manual from Trinity University Press, featuring work by Oates, Jamaica Kincaid, Tim O'Brien, and Denis Johnson. Boyd is a winner of the 2012 PEN Prison Writing award, a program which he now mentors for. His Tumblr page is featured on the poetry section of that website, highlighting his daily six word stories / poems, and longer works.

John Counts is a crime reporter at *The Ann Arbor News* and the Michigan editor for the *Great Lakes Review* literary journal, where he runs the regional online Narrative Map essay project. His fiction and nonfiction has appeared in the *Chicago Reader, A Detroit Anthology, Wayne Literary Review, Kneejerk,* and *Monkeybicycle.*

Kaitlin Dyer is a founding editor of *Harlot: A Revealing Look at the Arts of Persuasion.* Her work has appeared in *[PANK], Potomac Review, Hawaii Pacific Review,* and

The New Welsh Review. She loves dogs and hates when the rain seeps into shoes to make wet socks.

Cal Freeman was born and raised in Detroit. His poems have appeared in many journals including *Commonweal, The Journal, Nimrod, Drunken Boat, Ninth Letter,* and *The Paris-American*. He is the recipient of the Howard P. Walsh Award for Literature, The Ariel Poetry Prize, and the Devine Poetry Fellowship (judged by Terrence Hayes). Additionally, he has been nominated for Pushcart Prizes in both poetry and creative nonfiction. More recently an excerpt of his novel, *Tractors*, was published by the journal *Works in Progress*. He currently lives in Dearborn, Michigan, and teaches at Oakland University. He also serves as managing editor with Marick Press.

Gabe Herron was born in Omaha, Nebraska. He now lives outside a small town near Portland, Oregon. He's had a winning story in *Glimmer Train*'s Short Story Award for New Writers. His stories have also appeared online in *[PANK]* and *Hobart* (Web).

Michael Hill grew up in western Wisconsin and currently lives in Austin, Texas, where he wears a number of hats, including those of husband, dad, fisherman, librarian, guitar player, and dog owner. His poetry has been published by Dos Gatos Press and *Verse Wisconsin*.

Sarah Howard is an MFA student at Hamline University and has a BA from the University of Minnesota. Her work has appeared in *Thirty Two, MNArtists.org,* and *Twin Cities Runoff*. She lives in Minneapolis with her television.

Amorak Huey was born in Michigan, grew up in Alabama, and returned to Michigan as an adult. A longtime newspaper reporter and editor, he now teaches writing at Grand Valley State University. His chapbook *The Insomniac Circus* is forthcoming from Hyacinth Girl Press, and his poems appear in *The Best American Poetry 2012, The Southern Review, Rattle, The Collagist,* and many other journals. Follow him on Twitter: @amorak.

Michael Lauchlan's poems have appeared in many publications including *New England Review, Virginia Quarterly Review, The North American Review, English Journal, The Cortland Review,* and *Innisfree*. Lauchlan's collection, *Trumbull Ave.*, is forthcoming from WSU Press.

Mark Maire's poems have appeared most recently in the *Minnetonka Review, Slant: A Journal of Poetry,* and on Northern Community Radio. He lives in Duluth, Minnesota.

Beth Marzoni's poems have appeared or are forthcoming in *Cimarron Review, Grist, Hayden's Ferry Review, American Literary Review, New Ohio Review, Cream City Review, Fifth Wednesday Journal,* and *Crazyhorse,* among others. She is co-editor of *Pilot Light*, a journal of 21st century poetics and criticism, and is currently an assistant professor in English at Viterbo University.

David McGlynn's memoir, *A Door in the Ocean*, appeared in 2012 and was reviewed on NPR's *Fresh Air* with Terry Gross. His story collection, *The End of the Straight and Narrow*, won the 2008 Utah Book Award for fiction. His stories and essays have appeared in *Men's Health, Best American Sports Writing, The Yale Review, The Missouri Review, The Southwest Review*, and elsewhere. He teaches at Lawrence University in Wisconsin.

Rebecca McKanna is currently earning her MFA in creative writing from Purdue University. Her fiction has appeared in journals such as *New Delta Review* and *Carve Magazine*. A native Iowan, Rebecca now lives in Indiana with her pet hedgehog Beatrix.

E. Ce Miller loves points of ellipsis and doesn't think twenty-six letters are enough. She is a writer of essay, memoir and fiction, whose writing life has taken her to ten countries spread across four continents. In 2013 she graduated with distinction from the Masters of Arts in Writing & Publishing program at DePaul University in Chicago, Illinois; where she was previously awarded a Bachelors of Arts in Peace, Justice & Conflict Studies. Her words have been published in *Sixfold Journal*, a Chicago-based anthology titled *How Long Will I Cry? Voices of Youth Violence,* and *The Sun Magazine.* You can follow her on Twitter at @ECeMiller. She is a writer, activist, artist, fighter, lover.

Brian D. Morrison is an Assistant Professor of English at Ball State University. He has served as an editor at Slash Pine Press and an assistant editor at *Black Warrior Review.* He has also been an intern of *Mid-American Review.* His poetry has been seen previously at *Cave Wall, Copper Nickel, Verse Daily,* and other journals. His primary interest lies with monsters and how people represent human behavior through them.

Jessie Ann Foley is a Chicago writer and teacher, and her first novel, *The Carnival at Bray*, was the recipient of the Sheehan YA Book Prize, and is being published by Elephant Rock Books in October 2014. Her work has additionally appeared in *Salon, McSweeney's, The Madison Review, The Chicago Reader, Word Riot, Copperfield Review, Writer's Digest*, and many other publications.

Leslie Pietrzyk is the author of two novels, *Pears on a Willow Tree* and *A Year and a Day*. Her short fiction has appeared in *Gettysburg Review, River Styx, Shenandoah, Crab Orchard Review, The Sun*, and other journals. Her fellowships include awards by Virginia Center for Creative Arts, The Hambidge Center, Kimmel Harding Nelson Center for Arts, and the Bread Loaf and Sewanee Writers' Conferences. She grew up in Iowa City, Iowa, and now lives in Alexandria, Virginia.

Ellie Rogers is currently enrolled in the MFA Creative Writing program at Western Washington University. She is the Assistant Managing Editor of the *Bellingham Review*. Her poems have been published in *Floating Bridge Review* and *Crab Creek Review*. She resides in Bellingham, Washington, but still thinks of the Midwestern prairie as home.

Chuck Rybak lives in Wisconsin and is currently a Professor of English and Humanistic Studies at the University of Wisconsin—Green Bay. He is the author of two chapbooks and two full-length collections of poetry. His most recent full-length collection, */war*, was released in 2013 by Main Street Rag. Poems of his have appeared in *The Cincinnati Review; Pebble Lake Review; War, Literature & the Arts; The Ledge; Southern Poetry Review; Verse Wisconsin*; and other journals.

Samuel Sayler is a writer from Topeka, Kansas. He has written and edited for the *Washburn Review* and served as an editor for *Inscape*.

Meri Sheffler is a riding instructor at The University of Findlay—Findlay, Ohio. She also has a horse training business. Ms. Sheffler grew up in New York and has lived in the Midwest since she was 18, in both Ohio and Michigan. She is currently working towards a degree in the Master of Arts in Rhetoric and Writing at The University of Findlay.

Mark Patrick Spencer was born and raised in northern Kentucky. He now writes fiction and poetry in New Orleans. His work appears or is forthcoming in *[untitled] Publications, Punchnel's, The Rusty Nail, Neutrons Protons* and *Wisdom Crieth Without*. He has also sold his first feature length screenplay, *Six String*.

Ashley Swanson is currently completing her Masters of Fine Arts in Fiction from Minnesota State University Moorhead, and she is slated for graduation in May 2014. Along with her studies, Ashley also teaches English Composition at MSUM. Upon graduation, she and her husband are hoping to relocate back to their home state of Iowa.

Fritz Swanson is the director of Wolverine Press, the letterpress studio of the Helen Zell Writing Program at the University of Michigan. His work has appeared in *McSweeney's, The Believer, Print Magazine, Esopus* and the *Christian Science Monitor*.

Keith Taylor has published 14 books, chapbooks, co-edited volumes or translations. He teaches part time at the University of Michigan, where he also directs the Bear River Writers' Conference and is Associate Editor of *Michigan Quarterly Review*.

Jeff Vande Zande teaches English at Delta College and writes poetry, fiction, and screenplays. His books of fiction include *Emergency Stopping and Other Stories* (Bottom Dog Press), the novel *Into the Desperate Country* (March Street Press), the novel *Landscape with Fragmented Figures* (Bottom Dog Press), and *Threatened Species* *and Other Stories* (Whistling Shade Press). His poetry has also been collected into a book, and one of his poems was selected by Ted Kooser to appear in Kooser's syndicated newspaper column, "American Life in Poetry." His most recent book is a novel entitled *American Poet*, which won the Stuart and Vernice Gross Award for Excellence in Writing by a Michigan Author and a Michigan Notable Book Award from the Library of Michigan. He maintains a website at www.jeffvandezande.com.

Dennis Vanvick winters among the 8 million inhabitants of Bogota, Colombia, and summers amongst the flora and fauna of northwest Wisconsin. His work has appeared on the web and in print at *Rosebud Magazine, Boston Literary Magazine, The Humanist, Birmingham Arts Journal, Lowestoft Chronicle, Aethlon, Lifelines, Penduline Press*, and others.

Wendy Vardaman (wendyvardaman.com, @wendylvardaman) is the author of *Obstructed View* (Fireweed Press), co-editor of *Echolocations, Poets Map Madison*, co-editor/webmaster of *Verse Wisconsin* (versewisconsin.org), and co-founder/co-editor of Cowfeather Press (cowfeatherpress.org). She is one of Madison, Wisconsin's two Poets Laureate (2012-2015).

Jim Warner's poetry has appeared or is forthcoming in various journals including *The North American Review, [PANK] Magazine, Five Quarterly, The Minnesota Review*, and he is the author of two collections *Too Bad It's Poetry* and *Social Studies* (PaperKite Press). He is the Managing Editor of *Quiddity* housed at Benedictine University in Springfield, Illinois.

J. Weintraub has published a variety of fiction, essays, poetry, and translations in all sorts of literary reviews and periodicals, from *The Massachusetts Review* to *Modern Philology*, from *Gastronomica* to *Prairie Schooner*. Many of his pieces have been anthologized, and he is a recipient of Illinois Arts Council Awards for fiction and creative nonfiction. He's been an Around-the-Coyote poet, a Stone Song poet, and has had one-act plays produced by the Theatre-Studio in New York City, the Summer Place Theatre in Naperville, Illinois, and Theatre One in Middleboro, Massachussetts. He is currently a network playwright at Chicago Dramatists.

Stephany Wilkes is a Detroit native who spent much of her childhood in northern Michigan, to which she still returns (if not as frequently as she'd like). She holds a B.A. in English from the University of Detroit–Mercy and an M.S. and Ph.D. from the Illinois Institute of Technology. She writes, knits, shears sheep and fights for the free web in her day job at Mozilla, where she works on Firefox OS, an open source mobile operating system. Stephany lives in California–for now–where she feels deeply uncomfortable relying on snow pack for water. "Township" is dedicated to her brother, Nicholas, and to Sean in Mesick, Michigan.

About the Editorial Staff

Lauren Crawford recently graduated with a bachelor's degree in English Literature from the University of Michigan. She has a penchant for telling jokes poorly and a passion for writing in the margins. She loves science fiction novels, Suprematism, and survival horror video games, and has begun to run out of places to properly store her books. Currently, she is applying to graduate school, and hopes to become a professor one day.

Jon Michael Darga is a senior studying English and creative writing at the University of Michigan. Native to Ann Arbor, he is also an editor for U-M's *RC Review* literary magazine. He hopes to write and work in publishing when he grows up, while also delaying the growing up bit for as long as possible.

Cammie Finch loves tea and hula-hooping. She is a junior at the University of Michigan, studying Creative Writing and English. Her favorite ice-cream is vanilla drizzled with maple syrup, and her favorite poets are Pablo Neruda and Sylvia Plath. Her favorite book is always the one she is currently reading. Three of her favorite words include betwixt, akimbo, and kerfuffle. After graduation, Cammie hopes to spend a summer writing a novel on a Dutch houseboat, attend an Indian wedding, and increase the world's love for audiobooks, one expressive voice at a time.

J. Joseph Kane is a poet and fiction writer from Michigan. His work has appeared in *The Newer York, Clapboard House, Elimae, RHINO, Cricket Online Review, Psychic Meatloaf, Right Hand Pointing, The Splinter Generation*, and others. He grew up on Lake Huron and loves the smell of water.

Katie Marenghi is a senior studying creative writing and international studies at the University of Michigan. A true Ann Arbor native, Katie enjoys the classic Midwestern pastimes of smiling at strangers and complaining about snow, and hopes to be a poet when she grows up.

Kelly Nhan is a senior studying English and Women's Studies at the University of Michigan, and originally from Connecticut. She loves finding good coffee places, exploring cities, reading good poetry, and chatting about feminism. She is interested in going into book publishing, or eventually going to grad school to study postcolonial literature and feminist theory.

Christina Olson is the author of a book of poems, *Before I Came Home Naked*. Her poetry and nonfiction recently appeared in *The Normal School, Gastronomica,* and *RHINO*. She lives in Georgia and online at www.thedrevlow-olsonshow.com.

C.J. Opperthauser writes in his kitchen and blogs at http://thicketsandthings.tumblr.com.

Jeff Pfaller is a novelist and short story writer. His short fiction has appeared or is forthcoming in *Jupiter, North Chicago Review*, and *Fiction on the Web*. A Midwesterner through and through since the day he was born, Jeff has transplanted his wife, two children, dog, and cat from Michigan to Des Plaines, Illinois.

Robert James Russell is a two-time Pushcart Prize nominated author whose work has appeared in *Joyland, Great Lakes Review, Squalorly, Buffalo Almanack, Pithead Chapel*, and *The Collagist*, among others. His first novel, *Sea of Trees*, is available from Winter Goose Publishing. Find him online at robertjamesrussell.com.

Andrea Uptmor is a fiction writer living in Minnesota. Her work has appeared in *McSweeney's Internet Tendency, Hot Metal Bridge*, and the *Chicago Reader*, among others. Her new year's resolution is to blog more at http://www.andreauptmor.com.

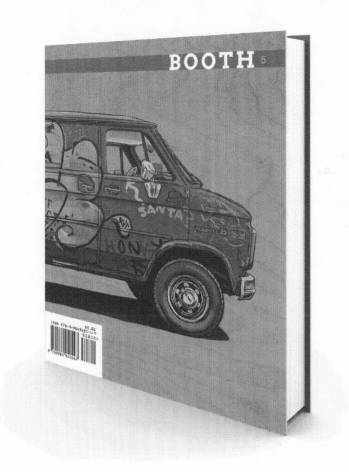

"The *Booth* editors seem to have a knack for attracting and selecting pieces that get right into my marrow, fill my bones full with breathing and want."
Vouched Books

"It is a beautiful journal to hold, with its quirky cover illustration and snappy design, and a moving journal to read. Just the thing to convert anyone into a literary magazine enthusiast."
The Review Review

"Its creative lightheartedness makes it a welcome addition to the crowded ranks of literary magazines, so many of which tend to dwell on the more depressing aspects of life. *Booth* provides a lot of bang. It's certainly worth adding to contemporary American literature collections."
Library Journal

booth.butler.edu

Made in the USA
Charleston, SC
17 August 2014